TRY WHISTLING THIS

Try Whistling This

WRITINGS ABOUT MUSIC

ANDREW FORD

Published by Black Inc.,
an imprint of Schwartz Media Pty Ltd
37–39 Langridge Street
Collingwood Vic 3066 Australia
email: enquiries@blackincbooks.com
http://www.blackincbooks.com

The National Library of Australia Cataloguing-in-Publication entry:

     Ford, Andrew, 1957-

     Try whistling this : writings on music / Andrew Ford.

     9781863955713 (pbk.)

     Includes bibliographical references and index.

     Music--History and criticism.

     780.9

Book design by Peter Long
Typeset by Duncan Blachford
Index by Andrew Ford

Printed in Australia by Griffin Press an Accredited ISO AS/ NZS 14001:2004 Environ-
mental Management System printer.

Contents

for Richard Gill

Introduction

What you are holding is, I suppose, a book of music criticism. Do you sense the reluctance with which I use the term? Can you detect my unease at labelling myself a critic? Would it help if I said that this is a book of critical writing? Probably not.

In the introduction to his own collection of essays, *How Beautiful It Is and How Easily It Can Be Broken*, the literary critic Daniel Mendelsohn suggests that the popular uses of 'critic' (as in 'Everyone's a critic!') and 'critical' ('Don't be so critical!') lie behind our society's poor opinion of the critic's trade. When it comes to music criticism, however, it gets worse: tensions escalate. We have all had the experience of attending a concert we have loved or hated and next day reading a review that points out we were wrong to have had that response. The critic was disappointed by things we never even noticed, and cringed at the very aspect of the performance that most impressed us; or the critic found profundity and eternal values in what we thought was trash. We are appalled at the travesty and write letters of complaint to the newspaper that printed the review. One famous example of this phenomenon, discussed in the following pages, was the open antagonism displayed to most of the Western world's classical music critics when they pointed out that, in terms of the classical tradition, David Helfgott's piano playing wasn't terribly good. Capacity audiences across America, Europe and Australia had loved Helfgott's recitals, so what did critics know?

With music it is personal and more so today than ever, for in the age of the iPod we own our music and identify with it. The playlist defines us, just as our clothes do. But there is a difference: the purpose of the 'songs' on our iPods is not to tell others who we are, but to tell ourselves. We buy the music (or steal it) and then carry it around with us as a tortoise carries its home. If someone suggests that 'our' music isn't as good as something else – something that isn't in our iPod, something, perhaps, we have never even heard of – we are quickly defensive. It is a cliché to say it, but when it comes to music, most of us know what we like and like what we know. And on Facebook, apparently, that is enough. Thumbs up.

But liking should never be enough, certainly not for a critic. Indeed, it is such a subjective matter that it is scarcely worth discussing. Why should your likes concern me? Why should my dislikes be of the least interest to you? If a music critic cannot get beyond this level of commentary – and the worst of them seldom do – they deserve all the opprobrium we can heap upon them.

The critic's job is to listen harder than anyone else and offer context, from which it becomes possible for the critic or reader to assess the worth of the music. It is not sufficient to announce that a work is good or bad, successful or unsuccessful; we have to be told the reasons and these come from context. The critic must therefore have a wide experience of all music, and especially today's music, because that is where the context is to be found – there is no point in reviewing a concert from a nineteenth-century perspective. It is not that we must agree with critics – on the contrary, we should be prepared to argue – but we ought to be able to trust them to be musical (and in classical music to be musically literate), to have their facts straight, to have background knowledge and to be able to make illuminating connections – all of which is context; they should also avoid clichés and try to be fair. The last bit is tricky, but what I mean is that they should, as far as possible, leave any agenda at the box office. All good criticism begins from the point of view of the music. The critic must ask what it is the composer and/or performer is aiming for, and then whether *on its own terms* the music has succeeded. It is also permissible to enquire whether the original aim was worthy (which involves context again), but this should not be the critic's starting point.

All that said, the truth is I am not a critic, or not really. Most days of the week I am a composer, but like nearly all composers I supplement my income with other work. Some of us perform, some teach, some work in arts administration, and some write and talk about music. Throughout history, much of the best writing about music has been by composers. I am thinking of Berlioz, Schumann, Debussy, Copland, Carter, Tippett, Virgil Thomson and Peggy Glanville-Hicks, among others. It reassures me to name them: if Schumann and Debussy did it, criticism cannot be a dishonourable pastime for a composer, however much other composers may disparage the business, and however much I do so myself when I cop a nasty review.

In fact, I have only written one concert review in my life (as an unpaid favour). My reviewing is more long-distance, dealing with books and recordings. Writing about concerts in newspapers might be the frontline of music criticism, but my 'long-distance' writing is nevertheless critical, even when it isn't passing judgement. And it attempts to provide context, avoid clichés and be fair.

So why do I resist the label 'critic'? I suppose it is *because* I am a composer, and because I would like these pages to be read with that in mind. It isn't that composing necessarily gives me special insights, more that it is my sole justification for writing about other people's music. Were I not in the same boat, I don't think I'd have the nerve. I claim the right to discuss and comment on and judge the creativity of others because I put my music out there for similar scrutiny. Of course, I don't say all music critics should themselves be composers – there are some very good ones who are not – but for me, and for my peace of mind, it is important that I know the work that goes into writing music, and the frustrations, and also know how it feels, in Stephen Sondheim's words, to 'make a hat / Where there never was a hat'.

The present collection consists of a few reviews, rather more essays, a couple of lectures and the scripts of my radio series *Music and Fashion*. As far as the essays and reviews are concerned, I am fortunate that my editors usually allow me to write about the things I want to write about, and to that extent I notice that some of the subjects in this book are the same as they were in my earlier collection, *Undue Noise*. Here again are Dylan and Cole Porter, Vaughan Williams, Tippett and Britten, Mozart, Shostakovich and Elliott Carter. And favourite themes are revisited – you might call them obsessions – such as the intersection of words and music, the necessity of modernism and its concomitant dangers, and the fundamental importance, in music and in life, of listening. In each case, I have returned to my original writing and re-edited it, changing as little as possible. Mostly I have been on the hunt for repetitions, though a few remain.

The principal rewriting happened in the radio scripts and this was unavoidable. *Music and Fashion* was a six-part radio series about why certain types of music – or even certain pieces – are fashionable at certain points in history, and what we might learn from this. The series had a very wide musical brief, a very informal tone (which I've tried to preserve), a lot of other people's voices (see the acknowledgements page) and a lot of actual music. Given that the voices and the music are gone, the scripts obviously had to be rejigged to stand alone on the page. The programs can still be listened to online.

I had thought to call this entire collection 'Music and Fashion', since one way or another the theme underpins quite a lot of the writing, but my publisher felt that a book with that title ought to have something to say on the subject of apparel, and that a brief digression into Elizabethan ladies' underwear wasn't sufficient. So instead I embraced the present title for its slightly combative air, its hint of musical fashions (because, more often than not, tunes that are whistled are in fashion), and its acknowledgement that, although this book is by a composer, it is not actual music. Of course, it is a moot point how whistleable my music is at the best of times, but I am myself a whistler and was once congratulated for it in the street by an elderly lady who stopped to tell me how unusual it was to hear anyone whistling these days.

Coming back to *Music and Fashion*, the origin of the radio series is perhaps germane to the general contents of this book. My first idea for the series was almost the opposite of where I ended up. I'd been reading John Ashbery's Charles Eliot Norton lectures, *Other Traditions*, in which he examines the work of six poets to whose writing he sometimes turns in order to get started on his own work. I was only familiar with the work of one of these poets, John Clare, and to my shame had never even heard of three of the others, but Ashbery argued persuasively for all of them and I found myself entranced. It occurred to me that a radio series examining the music of six obscure composers might be equally interesting.

The idea of fashion came in as a unifying feature. What if these six composers had all, at some point, been fashionable, and only now were obscure? It provided a nice twist. In the end, of course, I became so interested in the business of what dictates musical fashion itself that the whole project turned itself inside out. But that first idea, of bringing to listeners' attention the music of composers whose work – or even names – they might not know, is the basis for everything in this book.

Not many of the composers considered in these pages are really obscure. Some of them are very well-known indeed. But my aim in each case is to present them in the clearest possible light and to encourage the reader to listen to their work. I am not necessarily an enthusiast for all the music I discuss – and, in case you're wondering, I certainly don't 'like' it all – but I am an unfailing enthusiast for listening and for thinking about what we hear.

If that's criticism, then at least some of the time I must be a critic.

Andrew Ford
Robertson, NSW
January 2012

Music and Fashion

Dirty Dancing

It is hard to live in the twenty-first century, at least in the material-istic West, and not be conscious of fashion. Fashions dominate our perceptions of popular culture, and they come and go with bewil-dering suddenness, especially in music. Throughout history, our experience of music has been mediated, managed and manipulated by entrepreneurs and advertisers, by big business and the media, by politicians and popes. Musical fashions are usually shaped by the societies that inspire them, but sometimes, however briefly, it is the other way round: fashion shapes society. Fashion is often illusory – it is to do with the trappings of music more than the music itself – and style nearly always wins over content. Fashion tends to be shallow, but occasionally allows itself to believe it is seeking deep values. Although, by definition, fashions are up-to-the-minute, they have often embraced the past. And even the fashion for nostalgia, for history, is not as recent as you might think.

Much of the time, of course, history puts fashion in its place. What one generation thinks is 'the bee's knees' or 'groovy' or 'fab' will cause the next generation to smirk. There is nothing so ridicu-lous as yesterday's fashions. Most of us have items of clothing we would no longer be seen dead in – unless, that is, the clothes come back into fashion. Because fashions do return, especially if you leave them alone long enough. What was cool in the middle of the twentieth century can be cool again at the start of the twenty-first – as the word 'cool' itself proves.

7

One area of music where fashion has played a crucial role is music for dance. Dancing is as popular today as ever. In fact it seems to be going through a particularly popular phase right now. Modern dance steps, such as they are, seem to change very little, but the categories of music associated with today's dancing are constantly proliferating. At the beginning of 2012, I asked a colleague who knows about such things if he could tell me the names of the current types of dance music. He sent me a list comprising well over 200 categories, among which the following represent the tip of a very large iceberg: Breakbeat, Big Beat, Drum and Bass, Broken Beat, Euro Disco, Downtempo, Nu jazz, Crunk, Electro, Grime, IDM, Glitch, Laptronica, Dark Wave, Breakcore, Deep House, Psytrance, Progressive House/Trance and Garage.

I imagine that no one over thirty could possibly keep up with this, and I imagine that is half the point. Musical fashions need not be global in their impact; very often they are rather exclusive, designed to keep people out.

Perhaps it is because we can see them as well as hear them that dance crazes have always been tied to fashion. Or perhaps it is because they are so closely linked to fashions in dress. Whatever the reason, dance is nearly always fashion's victim. We have all seem film of people dancing as recently as the 1960s and 70s – even the 90s – and we've laughed. That is a pretty good way to tell if a particular style of dance was once the very height of fashion.

In Woody Allen's 1969 film, *Take the Money and Run*, a psychiatrist asks the bank robber Virgil Starkwell, played by Allen himself, if he thinks sex is dirty. Virgil replies that it is, if you're doing it right. The same might be said of dancing. *Dirty Dancing* was one of the worst movies of 1987 – or any other year – and since it brought the late Patrick Swayze to international prominence I suppose you might say it was doubly culpable. The film asked us to believe that in 1963, behind closed doors, young people routinely abandoned the twist, the shake and the mashed potato for sessions of vigorous mutual groin rubbing. As far I am aware, there is no historical evidence for this, and the film's famous dance sequences look almost as silly as its dialogue sounds. What *Dirty Dancing* exploits is what Methodists have been trying to warn us about since the eighteenth century: the idea that dancing is stylised sex. There is plenty of evidence for this.

The Bible does not actually condemn dancing. After all, in the Old Testament, David dances before God and he gets away with it. But it is true that dancing in the Bible is often a sign of impending trouble: the Israelites dance round the Golden Calf and before you know it virgins are being slaughtered; Salome dances for Herod, and John the Baptist loses his head. As often as not, you feel, religious objections to dance have been founded on these sorts of examples. The objections did not start with the Methodists, and among the more puritan of spirit the problem often seems to be the mere sight of people having fun with their bodies. As recently as 2001, Reverend Ian Paisley, leader of Northern Ireland's Free Presbyterian Church, announced that, of all things, line dancing was sinful.

'With its sexual gestures and touching,' Dr Paisley insisted, 'the country and western style of dancing ... clearly caters to the lust of the flesh.'

Until I read this, I had always believed that line dancing was for losers, but now suddenly I found myself wanting to sign up for lessons. But is that not always the way? Throughout history, killjoys and wowsers have consistently failed to grasp a very basic principle: if you try to ban something you will only succeed in making it fashionable. Every major dance craze has been helped along by stern, moralising, vociferous critics. The dirtier the dance, the sterner the moralising; and the sterner the moralising, the greater the craze.

Consider the volta. If we listen today to a recording of one of these Renaissance dance tunes, it will sound utterly innocuous. Certainly, you would never imagine that dancing to music like this might lead to 'an infinity of murders and abortions'. But that is what the sixteenth-century French lawyer and philosopher, Jean Bodin, predicted as the likely outcome.

Originating with the peasantry of Provence (or possibly Italy), by the late 1500s the volta had spread across much of western Europe, becoming, in the process, a favourite dance at court. Queen Elizabeth I danced it with the Earl of Leicester, and that well-known good-time girl, Catherine de' Medici, who travelled from Italy with her own dancing master, introduced the volta at Versailles. But in 1610, the year Louis XIII came to the throne, the dance was banned. This was presumably on the orders of the Queen Mother, the distinctly humourless Marie de' Medici. One imagines she considered it unsuitable for a nine-year-old king.

But what was it she objected to? Why did the volta create a frisson of scandal wherever it was danced? There are two parts to this. First, until the volta came along, dancing – at least court dancing – occurred in rows, just like Ian Paisley's despised boot scooting. In pavans and galliards, men and women danced alongside each other, not face to face; and while they might have touched hands with arms outstretched, that would have been the extent of the physical contact. The volta changed that. Not only did men and women turn to face each other during the dance, but at the climax the man grabbed the woman about the waist, brought his left knee up under her backside, and heaved her body, twisting, high into the air, catching it on the way down. As the laws of gravity brought her back to earth, an Elizabethan lady's skirts would have behaved very much in the manner of a parachute. Beneath her skirt, she would probably be wearing a bumroll to enlarge her hips and a hooped frame or 'farthingale' to give the skirts a sort of bell shape. This of course only enhanced the parachute effect. Elizabethan ladies also wore petticoats beneath their skirts, but not a lot else. So it isn't hard to see why the volta raised eyebrows.

Imagine you are one of Elizabeth's courtiers. The Queen's love life is already the talk of England, and her name, as today's tabloid newspapers would say, has been linked to that of Robert Dudley, Earl of Leicester. The Queen loves glamour and glamorous people. Why only the other week, she had a hissy fit, ordering from her sight everyone she deemed less than beautiful. It is whispered she has a passion for silk stockings. She loves a party and she loves to dance. And when she dances the volta with Robert Dudley, the Patrick Swayze of the English Renaissance, and he throws her up in the air, everyone gets to see – at the very least – the royal legs; everyone gets to see the silk stockings. It's quite a modern scene when you think about it. All that is missing are paparazzi.

It should not surprise us that the volta began as a dance for the lower classes. This is a pattern repeated throughout history. It is the same with most other musical fashions. If you think only of the last hundred years, we know – or we think we know – that jazz came out of the whore houses of New Orleans; rock 'n' roll grew from a union of the blues and country & western – the music of poor black Americans and poor white Americans; rap and hip hop began in the tenements and projects of the South Bronx and Harlem. It is impossible to be really precise about any of this, simply because the people who invented these musical styles usually were not the sort of people to write things down. But it is safe to say that the various forms of twentieth-century pop music had lowly origins, before being given a commercial makeover by the recording industry.

Since the Middle Ages, it has been the same with dance steps. Dances began with working people, with the peasants, the *folk*, and then were taken up by the aristocracy, often taught by a professional dancing master. Perhaps the upper classes found something exotic, daring, carnivalesque about rough-housing it on the dance floor. Whatever the attraction, time and again, the common country dances were ennobled in the courts of Europe. Nowhere did this happen more famously than with the waltz.

In the hundred years between the end of the volta craze and the advent of the waltz, plenty of other dances came along to capture the courtly imagination, and the vast majority had their roots in the soil of peasant life. The minuet was the dominant dance, but the saraband, the rigadoon, the bourée, the hornpipe and the jig also enjoyed periods of fashion. All of these were relatively chaste affairs. The waltz was another matter. To our eyes, I suppose, waltzing could scarcely seem more tame and sedate. But in the late eighteenth and early nineteenth centuries, it raised not a few people's blood pressure. As late as 1816, by which time it had gained acceptance on the continent, it provoked thundering disapproval from the *Times* when it was danced in London at the Prince Regent's ball:

> We remarked with pain that the indecent foreign dance called the Waltz was introduced (we believe for the first time) at the English court on Friday last … It is quite sufficient to cast one's eyes on the voluptuous intertwining of the limbs and close compressure on the bodies in their dance, to see that it is indeed far removed from the modest reserve which has hitherto been considered distinctive of English females. So long as this obscene display was confined to prostitutes and adulteresses, we did not think it deserving of notice; but now that it is attempted to be forced on the respectable classes of society by the civil examples of their superiors, we feel it a duty to warn every parent against exposing his daughter to so fatal a contagion.

With that sort of publicity, waltz fever could only escalate.

The word 'waltz' probably comes from the same original source as the word 'volta', both dances involving turning. But the direct predecessor of the waltz, in both its steps and music, was the Austrian ländler. Because it came from the peasantry, the ländler was typically danced on rough floors in heavy shoes, so it involved much picking up of the feet. But translated to a Viennese ballroom with dancers in elegant slippers, the whole thing became a little more streamlined. The ländler became the waltz.

Throughout the eighteenth century, the waltz had something of a double life, developing in tandem at European courts and in dance halls. It was relatively simple to learn, which helped it catch on, but another part of its attraction – in the dance halls, if not the courts – was that salacious reputation remarked upon by the *Times*. To us, this seems extraordinary. After all, it is the waltz that fathers dance with their newly wed daughters: how could it ever have been thought of as a form of 'dirty dancing'?

Like the volta, the waltz was danced face to face, whereas most dances in the eighteenth century had been side-by-side affairs, and so this immediately singled it out. Furthermore, it involved holding your partner and keeping her close. Within the 'closed hold', made fashionable by the waltz, you created a small, intimate space in which you had little option but to breathe the same air and stare into one another's eyes. In a society where ladies and gentlemen did not speak unless they had been introduced, and seldom found themselves alone unless they were married, the idea that a dance might require such intimacy could indeed be found shocking. Even the poet Byron, whose lifestyle was scarcely a model of propriety, suggests in 'The Waltz' (admittedly with some irony) that this dance left little for a couple to discover on their wedding night.

> *Hot from the hands promiscuously applied,*
> *Round the slight waist, or down the glowing side,*
> *Where were the rapture then to clasp the form*
> *From this lewd grasp and lawless contact warm?*
> *At once love's most endearing thought resign,*
> *To press the hand so press'd by none but thine;*
> *To gaze upon that eye which never met*
> *Another's ardent look without regret;*
> *Approach the lip which all, without restraint,*
> *Come near enough – if not to touch – to taint;*
> *If such thou lovest – love her then no more,*

Or give – like her – caresses to a score;
Her mind with these is gone, and with it go
The little left behind it to bestow.

So the waltz was salacious, and in some people's minds it came to represent the breakdown of an established hierarchy in society, the beginning of the waltz craze in Paris coinciding with the French Revolution, while the Viennese waltz was never more popular than during the last days of the Habsburg Empire. But why was the waltz ubiquitous?

It was partly a matter of its adaptability. The basic steps were easy enough to learn, but if you wanted to show off, there were plenty of flashy moves you could add. This was a dance you could personalise, and that was significant, because the waltz was a very personal dance. The corollary of the closed hold, after all, was exclusion: it kept others out. Here, then, was a perfect dancing model of the rising bourgeoisie and the exaltation of the private individual, which, in turn, made it a dangerous dance for kings and emperors. And yet, one of the most famous waltzes ever composed was written for an emperor. The *Kaiser-Walzer* – the *Emperor Waltz* – was composed in celebration of the fortieth anniversary of the accession of Austrian Emperor Franz Joseph.

It was Vienna, of course, that ultimately put its stamp on the dance, the waltzes of Joseph Lanner and Johann Strauss sweeping across Europe like dancers over the floor of a ballroom. Hector Berlioz, who in 1830 was inspired to include a delirious waltz scene in his *Symphonie fantastique*, heaped praises on Strauss in particular, speaking of his technical perfection, his fire, his intelligence and, above all, the rhythmic verve of his orchestra. And that was only Johann Strauss I. His son was *really* popular.

Strauss Senior, whose career coincided with what we might think of as the first waltz craze, composed music of a rather raw, urgent nature, absolutely in keeping with the fashion. The music of Johann

Strauss II was more refined and actually more conventional in its orchestration. But structurally it was far more ambitious. This development was probably inspired by Carl Maria von Weber's 'rondo brillant', *Invitation to the Dance*. As a solo piano piece, it would exert an influence on composers such as Chopin and Schumann, but in its orchestral versions – the first by Lanner, the second and more famous orchestration by none other than Berlioz – it prompted the younger Strauss to invest his waltzes with an almost narrative quality. The pieces gained elaborate introductions and featured episodes distinguished by changes of mood and tempo, until finally they came to resemble dramatic *scenas*. (Johann Strauss II, indeed, would end up taking his music into the theatre, composing waltz-filled operettas such as *Die Fledermaus*.)

But ambitious though his waltzes might have been, they were still intended for dancing, and it was partly as a conductor – really, as a dance band leader – that the younger Strauss gained much of his celebrity. He was, above all, an entertainer, as eager to please his audiences as he was to please his political masters. In 1848 he had been a revolutionary, but as his music became ever more fashionable and he was asked to conduct his waltzes at the royal palace, Strauss cheerfully acquiesced. In 1889, his last big success with a waltz was that *Kaiser-Walzer*. It was his Op 437.

The popularity of the waltz affected nearly everything in the nineteenth century. Inevitably it found its way into ballet music (Tchaikovsky's ballets are full of waltzes) and into the operas of Gounod and Verdi. Composers of instrumental music, too, were irresistibly drawn to the fashion, and most of them composed sets of waltzes, particularly for the piano. Johannes Brahms, who was no exception, once admitted that he wished he himself had composed the 'Blue Danube', and everywhere you look in his music – in the concertos and symphonies, even in *Ein deutsches Requiem* – is music you could waltz to.

But of all the composers influenced by the waltz, Frédéric Chopin must be singled out. Chopin had heard the waltzes of Lanner and

Johann Strauss I in Vienna, but his own piano waltzes were not meant for dancing, they were for listening and playing in the home. Chopin's waltzes are wistful, sometimes melancholic, always Romantic, and they conjure the nineteenth-century drawing room rather than the ballroom. Or if they do speak of the ballroom, it is of the memory of waltzing rather than the act itself.

So the waltz lived on. And so did the second Johann Strauss, who outlived Brahms, dying in 1899 – the same year Scott Joplin wrote 'The Maple Leaf Rag', one of the most perfect examples of the music that would inspire all of the next dance crazes.

Ragtime affected popular dancing like nothing else. Most significantly, although it is seldom remarked, it changed the metre of dance. Before the twentieth century, there had been dances in duple time – the pavan, for instance, had two beats to the bar – but these were exceptions to the rule. European dancing – from the galliard to the volta to the minuet to the waltz – was a triple-time phenomenon. This was not so in Africa. The basic pulse of African music is corporeal – it is the rhythm of the body, the rhythm of walking (left–right), the rhythm of breathing (in–out). African music nearly always has two principal beats and, presumably because early ragtime was mostly developed by African Americans, that music was also two-to-a-bar. Such was the influence ragtime exerted that you would be hard-pressed to think of any twentieth-century Western dance craze – or any twentieth-century form of popular music – that is not also in duple time.

By the first decades of the twentieth century, dance crazes were coming and going with great frequency as one fashion gave way to another. This was thanks to sound recordings and later radio, but also to the movies – even before they had sound. For example, in 1914, a New York actor called Harry Fox developed a little ragtime dance in his stage act that was nicknamed 'Fox's Trot', and before long half of New York was dancing the foxtrot. This led in two directions. Almost inevitably there was a series of dances with animal names, among them the turkey trot, the grizzly bear and the bunny hug. But the foxtrot itself was transformed, as before it the waltz had been, when it was simply speeded up. A fast foxtrot is a Charleston.

And on it went. Craze after craze. The jitterbug, the jive, the swing, the shag. All with local variants and all powered by dance bands that drew on jazz rhythms to furnish their repertoire. Many of these fashions began among African Americans in Harlem and worked their way south to the richer parts of Manhattan. One such craze began in Harlem's Savoy Ballroom in 1926. It was called the lindy hop after the aviator Charles Lindbergh who had just hopped across the Atlantic ocean in an aeroplane.

While New York had been busy producing this stream of fashionable dances, another dance had gone global. If jazz had begun in the brothels of New Orleans, the tango seems to have started in the brothels of Buenos Aires. But as with the origins of jazz, not much detail is really known, and things tend to get made up. For example, there is a particularly tall story that is still sometimes rolled out when people discuss the origins of tango. The gauchos – Argentinian cowboys out on the Savannah – spent their days riding horses and, over time, the animals' sweat caused the gauchos' chaps – their riding pants – to stiffen into the shape of the horse's body, so they were forced to walk with bow legs. Heading off to the nearest bordello in search of rest and recreation after a hard day in the saddle, but having failed first to take a shower – or change their riding pants – these macho men would dance with the ladies of the night. The prostitute was held in the crook of the gaucho's right arm, but forced by dint of his body odour – and doubtless his horse's body odour too – to keep her face as far away from him as possible. Hence the thrown-back head. Her right hand, meanwhile, was placed on the gaucho's left hip, near his wallet.

Quite apart from the cultural stereotyping, the explanation does all seem a bit neat. The truth is that no one knows how the tango began or where it came from. One theory has it that it came from Cuba as the 'danza habañera', which before that had come from Spain as the 'contradanza', which as the 'contre-dance' had previously come to Spain from France, where the term was in fact a corruption of the English 'country dance'. This would mean the tango could trace its origins back to Surrey. I am more inclined to believe the horse sweat story.

What we certainly do know is that the tango first became popular in Buenos Aires in the 1880s, really as a dance of the under classes in the suburban slums. Only after it had travelled to Europe around the turn of the century was it embraced by the whole of Argentine society. Some of the early tangos had words, and the French-born Carlos Gardel, in particular, developed the tango song, which was passionate and gloomy in more or less equal measure. Perhaps this is why it appealed so much to the Finns, because, strange as it may seem, the tango remains the unofficial national dance of Finland.

Early in the twentieth century the tango arrived in Finland from Germany where it had collected traces of the military march and so become a little more four-square than the Argentinian version. At the height of its popularity in the 1920s, the tango was a pan-European fashion, but long after that had receded it retained its popularity in Finland, where it continued to acquire local characteristics. It is popular there today, especially in vocal music, having become the Nordic equivalent of country & western, melodramatic and bleakly tragic. If nothing else, this explains why Finland has such a proud and enduring record of coming last in the Eurovision Song Contest.

Dance fashions come and go. Sometimes – like the tango in Finland – they remain, losing their faddishness and adapting to a more steady popularity. But sometimes fashions return. And of course this is what happened to the tango. By the middle of the twentieth-century, the tango, everywhere but Finland, had been relegated to the ballroom dancing circuit. It was taught at suburban dance classes along with the military two-step and the jazz waltz. Even in Argentina it was no longer fashionable. But suddenly, in the

1980s, it was back. Tango troops began appearing in theatres and at arts festivals; tango music was all the rage – particularly that composed by Ástor Piazzolla, the Chopin of the tango – and a lot of people felt suddenly compelled to take lessons.

There was no one reason for this. The return of the tango coincided with a growing interest in music from non-Western cultures. This was partly the response of an ageing audience to the banalities of pop. Looking for something better than boy bands and girl power, listeners who had grown up with 1960s pop now turned to Africa and South America for their music. Tango music was part of that and along with it came the dancing. But there was also something alluring about tango's reputation for licentiousness. The people who began attending tango lessons around the world might have argued about whether the dance was sexual or merely sensual, but for someone like Reverend Ian Paisley, worried about the salacious nature of line dancing, such a subtle distinction would hardly have counted for much.

So the Methodists were right. Dancing and sex, sex and dancing: there's a connection. But there is one thing about dirty dancing they failed to account for: the changing fashions. When you think about it, this is quite surprising. Because if dancing, at some level, is a form of stylised sex, why have dance fashions changed down the centuries, when sex seems to have remained broadly the same?

Heaven on Earth

Some religions disapprove of music. Others believe that it is all right in its place, just not their place. But mostly, throughout history, music has been a vital part of the way that people worship their gods. In particular, Christianity has produced some of the greatest music ever heard.

There are various sorts of religious music. First, there is unapologetic ecclesiastical hucksterism, advertising jingles for God. Another sort, usually rather more gentle, sets out to concentrate the believer's mind in contemplation. Some music attempts to represent the very doctrines that have inspired it. Some seeks to inspire us, to make us want to go out and do great deeds. And some seeks to create transcendence, a musical equivalent of the ultimate bliss on offer from the religion itself – a sort of heaven on earth. Christianity has embraced all these musical types. As theological priorities have shifted – as a particular branch of a particular church has become more or less evangelical or mystical or fundamentalist – so its soundtrack has shifted too.

One of the Anglican Church's best-known hymns emphasises the view of God as reliable and, above all, constant:

Swift to its close ebbs out life's little day;
Earth's joys grow dim; its glories pass away;
Change and decay in all around I see;
O thou who changest not, abide with me.

But whether or not you believe in an unchanging deity, religions themselves are made by human beings, and we, mostly, are susceptible to fashion. Down the centuries, religious dogma has influenced music, but equally musical fashions have affected religion.

*

There is a rather strange – and, I always think, slightly creepy – bit of music from the twelfth century that ought to have landed its composer in hot water. It's a Christian hymn, 'Nobilis humilis', addressed to Magnus the Martyr. Most of its significance is that it does not sound like other mediaeval hymns. It was composed in the Orkneys, that group of islands off the north coast of Scotland on the way to Scandinavia. At the time, the Orkneys belonged to the kings of Norway and they were governed by two earls, Magnus Erlendsson, the martyr in question, and his cousin Hakon. Magnus was that rare bird, a Viking pacifist, and Hakon found him quite annoying, partly because, understandably, Magnus was pretty popular with the average

Orcadian compared to his more violently disposed cousin. So Hakon had Magnus murdered on or about 16 April 1117, whereupon miracles began to occur. It took only two decades for a cathedral to be built in Magnus's honour in Kirkwall, the Orkneys' main town. Perhaps that's when the hymn was composed.

Magnus's story is certainly an odd one and the hymn that celebrates him would have seemed equally odd to most mediaeval ears. But composing odd religious music in the Middle Ages – going against the prevailing ecclesiastical fashion – could be bad for your health. Looked at in a certain light, it was tantamount to heresy, and if the church authorities in Rome got wind of it, you might be in trouble. So who was this brave or foolhardy composer? And why does the music sound so odd?

In the Middle Ages, Western music was reaching a watershed. Polyphony was breaking out. Very simply, this meant that when people sang songs in a group, they no longer all sang the same notes as each other. The word 'polyphony' just means 'many sounds' or 'many voices', and so polyphonic music is in several parts, though in the twelfth century there were usually just two or three voices at a time.

How did polyphony begin? We don't really know, but I would guess that it probably came down to human frailty. For centuries Christian hymns had been chanted in unison. Everyone sang the same notes. This is popularly called Gregorian chant after the sixth-century Pope, Gregory I. It is not a very accurate name. For one thing it has nothing to do with Gregory at all. This sort of chant was only standardised 300 years after his death. And for another, it is simply the most common form of Christian chant – there were plenty of other styles in the first thousand years of the church. So I'll call it by its generic name: plainsong, or plainchant. What all types of plainchant had in common was that they were sung in unison. At least they were meant to be.

Plainchant was not always sung by trained singers, any more than hymns are today. It was chanted, usually, by groups of monks or nuns. Some of them would have been good singers; others might not have been so vocally gifted; some would have had higher or lower voices than others. So the starting note for a particular chant would seldom have suited everyone in the room. Those singers with a strong sense of pitch might have tried hard to get the notes that were difficult to reach, but those with less good – or more original – ears might have given up reaching for the notes that were too high or too low and sung the tune at a different pitch, ideally to the same notes but an octave lower or higher. Sometimes, though, jumping an octave would make the chant too low or too high in the other direction and so – and this is where I'm guessing – the monk in question would settle for halfway, singing the plainsong where it felt more comfortable, a fifth higher or – which is basically the same thing – a fourth lower.

Why the interval of the fifth or fourth? Why not the third or sixth? It is what comes naturally. When nature vibrates, it makes a noise, and the noise will consist of overtones or harmonics. The simplest of these – the easiest to hear – are the octave and the fifth (or its inversion, the fourth). So these notes are the ones that blend best. If you like, they are the most consonant. Which is why monks and nuns ended up singing in parallel octaves, fifths and fourths. This style of singing was called *organum*.

We have no idea when the practice began. It was probably quite early – maybe the ninth century – and doubtless at first it was simply tolerated by the other monks or nuns: there's old sister Agnes singing a fourth too low again. At some point, however, composers must either have decided they really liked the effect, or they came to take it for granted that plainsong would occur in more than one part. Either way, chanting in fifths and fourths became standard.

But 'Nobilis humilis', the Hymn to St Magnus, doesn't use fifths and fourths. It uses thirds, and thirds were anything but standard in a twelfth-century church. The musical interval of the third comes in two forms, major and minor, and in the Middle

Ages both were considered 'imperfect'. They were not exactly banned from music, but you would look through a lot of manuscripts before you stumbled upon a piece in which the interval occurred anywhere at all prominent. You would seldom find a third on a strong beat, for instance, and never in a final cadence. But 'Nobilis humilis' not only uses thirds, it hardly uses any other intervals.

Well, Kirkwall is a long way from Rome. Whoever composed the Hymn to St Magnus probably didn't know what was happening in Edinburgh, let alone on the Continent. Doubtless what sounded imperfect to European ears, sounded very nice indeed – possibly even very natural – to the average Orcadian.

But on the Continent itself, they were already composing some extremely sophisticated stuff. At Notre Dame cathedral in Paris, at the end of the twelfth century, the history of Western music was taking one of its strangest, most vigorous and most beguiling turns. The brand of *organum* favoured by composers such as Pérotin – or to give him his Latin name, Perotinus – involved far more than two voices singing in parallel. In a piece such as *Viderunt omnes*, the voices move at different speeds and sometimes in different directions, while the bouncing triplet rhythms arrest us with their energy, even after more than 800 years. In their vividness, in their intricacy, in their dazzling air of celebration, these chants are the perfect aural equivalent of an illuminated manuscript. And just like a book of hours, with its gorgeous coloured inks and gold leaf, the *organum* of the Notre Dame composers is meant to impress us.

This music is also one of the earliest examples of what modern commentators like to call 'site specific art'. The *organum* was not just composed at Notre Dame, it was meant to be heard in the cavernous space of the cathedral itself, and, to that end, Pérotin ensured that the proportions of the music matched those of the architecture. In Pérotin's mind, they also matched the proportions of the cosmos. The cathedral was made to resonate with the sound of the music, but it was also filled with coloured light from that famous Notre Dame stained glass, so this great Gothic building regularly offered one of the first and best sound-and-light shows in Christendom. And when you think about it, this is not so far removed from a modern Pentecostal gathering in a giant entertainment centre. Except the music was better in the twelfth century.

There is one more side to Notre Dame, and it is entirely theological. To say that we are meant to be impressed by Pérotin's music in its cathedral setting is an understatement. Walk into Notre Dame – or any great Gothic cathedral – and you find yourself looking upwards. You have no choice in the matter. The lines of the building lead your eyes up those columns, the pointed arches direct your gaze, your head tilts slowly back and you stare at the vault – and to heaven beyond. A Gothic cathedral, like the light streaming down through the stained glass and the sheer grandeur of the music, doesn't just impress us, it dwarfs us. We are made to feel small, literally and metaphorically. We are all miserable sinners and there is no health in us.

What an astonishing difference on walking into a Renaissance building! Late fifteenth-century churches are all rounded arches and horizontal lines. We don't look up, we look about us. We see a building constructed on a human scale, and we see other people. And something has happened to the music too. Where in the mediaeval church the scripture was chanted in one, then two voices, growing ever more imposing and elaborate, yet always somehow implacable, by the late fifteenth century the elaboration in the music has transcended itself. Renaissance polyphony is musical democracy: four, five, six parts or more, each with an equal say, each contributing its own thread to the weft of the music. And there is depth too. Renaissance music – like Renaissance painting – has perspective. If we listen to the motets and Masses of the early Renaissance by Franco-Flemish composers such as Guillaume Dufay, Johannes Ockeghem and Josquin des Prez, what strikes us above all is a sense of balance.

So what's happening theologically? As ever, it seems, artistic trends keep pace with theological trends. Reformation is in the air. All that Gothic God-fearing is swept away on a tide of optimism. Reformation theologians had the human figure of Christ at the centre of things, just as the human form dominated Renaissance art. But which came first? The new attitude to God or the new attitude to art? Is the humanity at the heart of the humanist Renaissance a reflection of a version of Christianity with Christ as the focus? Or is it the other way round? It would not be the first time in history that a religion had tried to be fashionably relevant, and it would not be the last.

And on the subject of fashion, we must mention a musical conceit that began in the late Middle Ages but, like much else, had its full flowering in the Renaissance. This was the wholesale importing of popular songs into liturgical and other religious music. It might sound like an unseemly grab for more parishioners – the mediaeval equivalent of the bearded vicar with a guitar – but we must remember that the mediaeval church did not need to advertise itself; in fifteenth-century Europe there wasn't much alternative to being a Christian, at least not in public. Anyway, the use of popular songs is more interesting than that. It is partly about putting together related texts and so giving the religious words a kind of worldly perspective. There are, for example, motets that combine a hymn in praise of the Virgin Mary with a rather more down-to-earth popular song about the good-looker down the street. But there are also more spectacular structures where an entire sung Mass was based on a familiar tune. The most commonly used song was 'L'homme armé' – 'The Armed Man'. This anonymous song seems to have originated in the middle of the fifteenth century at the start of a crusade against the Turks following the Fall of Constantinople, the man of the song's title armed, one presumes, against the Infidel. The tune formed the basis for more than forty settings of the Mass, including versions by Dufay, Ockeghem and Josquin – Josquin, indeed, wrote two Masses on 'L'homme armé'.

Like many Continental fashions, the use of popular songs in church music took a while to catch on in England. But by the time John Taverner came to compose his *Western Wind* Mass, early in Henry VIII's reign, he was a master of the technique.

Western wind, when wilt thou blow,
The small rain down can rain.
Christ, if my love were in my arms
And I in my bed again!

There is no obvious connection between the words of the song and the Mass, but it is tempting to speculate that Taverner heard the song as an earthy metaphor for straying from the path of righteousness before returning to the safety of the 'bosom' of the church. Translated to its new context, what is so striking about this song is that the tune can be plainly heard. The standard Continental practice was to slow down the notes of the familiar song until the rhythm disappeared and the tune itself was barely recognisable. Next, the composer would take the tune and bury it in the tenor voice, right in the middle of the texture where it would be further disguised by the voices above and below it. But the Tudor composer Taverner retains the original rhythm and tempo of the tune and puts it at the very top where no one can miss it.

Martin Luther approved of popular music in church. But he wasn't so happy about a congregation that just sat and listened to a choir, however 'democratic' the polyphony might have been. Just as he was opposed to the idea of a congregation observing the back of a priest mumbling to God in Latin, so he thought that congregations should sing their own songs of praise.

That the singing of spiritual songs is a good thing and one pleasing to God is, I believe, not hidden from Any Christian ... Accordingly, as a good beginning and to encourage those who can do better, I and several others have brought together certain spiritual songs with a view to spreading abroad and setting in motion the holy Gospel … These, further, are set for four voices for no other reason than that I wished that the young might have something to rid them of their love ditties and wanton songs and might, instead of these, learn wholesome things and thus yield willingly, as becomes them, to the good; also, because I am not of the opinion that all the arts shall be crushed to earth and perish through the Gospel, as some bigoted persons pretend, but would willingly see them all, and especially music, as servants of Him who gave and created them.

At which point, one imagines, John Calvin's ears would have been burning. In seeking to abolish all instrumental music – and painting and sculpture – from church, and to restrict the singing of any words not found in the Bible (ideally, in the Psalms), Calvin's version of the Reformation took a very hard line – one that is still shared today by some Christian sects. But Luther's view of Christendom was celebratory, rather than punitive. He wanted fewer rules, not *more* of them.

Martin Luther's desire to reform the church was driven by his theological views, which were boldly at odds with Rome. According to Luther, religion was an individual matter. You made your own peace with God. You did not have to do good works, and you did not have to give money to the church. You did not even really need priests, because now you could read the Bible for yourself in your own language. All you had to do was have faith and the gates of heaven would swing open. Not surprisingly, these views were popular. And not surprisingly, Rome was horrified at what it saw as a fashion for sacrilege.

The Catholic Church's response was to hold absolutely firm on matters of doctrine, but to repackage everything. Imagine a modern political party suddenly on the outer after years in power. What does it do? How does it make itself attractive again to the voters? First it needs unity, everyone singing from the same hymn sheet, so to speak. So it needs discipline and if necessary headkickers to insist on the party line. The sixteenth-century church's equivalent of this was the Inquisition.

But political parties also need to seem up-to-date and cool, so they often try to woo voters with celebrity candidates: sporting heroes, actors, pop stars. The Catholic Church went looking for some spanking new saints and the roll-call of names canonised at the beginning of the seventeenth century is still impressive: St Francis Xavier, St Ignatius Loyola, St Charles Borromeo and St Teresa of Ávila are still high on the list of most popular Catholic saints.

But most importantly, the church in Rome had to sell its message, clearly and simply. And so at the Council of Trent, really a twenty-year-long party conference, the church had set out to convince the waverers, and part of this involved changing the nature of music. With polyphony, with all those voices singing different parts, the sense of the text got lost. So it was back to simple chant where you could actually hear the words.

Had it not been for one man, religious music might have become a very dull affair, but fortunately right in the heart of Rome lived and worked Giovanni Pierluigi da Palestrina, one of history's greatest composers of polyphonic music, and he was secretly appalled at the new restrictions on his art. He set out to show the church that it didn't need to be so hard-line.

The very idea of a *Missa brevis* – a short Mass – suggests a no-frills approach to the liturgy. But Palestrina composed his to demonstrate that polyphony still had its place in church music. After all, the Counter Reformation was not just about getting the message across as directly as possible, it was also about making the message memorable and attractive. So in Palestrina's *Missa brevis*, the doctrinal text is comparatively unadorned and easy to comprehend, but when the composer no longer has doctrine to convey, when the words of the

Mass themselves lapse into repetition – 'Sanctus, Sanctus, Sanctus' ('Holy, Holy, Holy') – out comes the polyphony again and the effect is all the more magical. This is frankly dramatic music. Not to put too fine a point on it, but this is Hollywood. We are not just being told words here, we're experiencing the full force of the sentiments behind them. This is more than illustration, more than illumination – it is action, emotion and special effects. This is the baroque!

If you visit the church of Santa Maria della Vittoria in the heart of Rome, you will first be overwhelmed by the glitz of the place. It is full of gold. But make your way into the Cornaro Chapel and you will find a remarkable figure in white marble by the great baroque sculptor Gianlorenzo Bernini. It is one of those new saints, St Teresa of Ávila. And she's in ecstasy. You can see her body writhing with religious pleasure, her eyes cast heavenwards, her flowing habit a turmoil of folds and billows. This is the Catholic Church giving Luther's Reformation both barrels. What a contrast with the bare, lime-washed walls of a Protestant church in northern Europe! And there is the music, too. In northern Europe, Lutheran hymns; in Italy, Monteverdi's *Vespers*. Really, the difference could not have been much greater.

We could continue this history of European church music. We could talk about Bach. We could talk about the great English hymn composers of the eighteenth and nineteenth centuries, or the Gothic revival, or the second Vatican council. But having reached the seventeenth century we are at a point where, theologically, Christendom is a series of almost unbridgeable chasms, and music – or in some cases the absence of music – is more than ever tied to doctrine. Let's look at one or two of the extremes.

The greatest musical extreme of all, of course, is silence. Calvin's insistence that the sound of instrumental music was little short of blasphemy (and at the very least, weak-minded) lives on, not only in various brands of Christianity, but in much of Islam. It is not hard to see why. Music, as the playwright Congreve noted, has powers to soothe the savage breast. It can soothe the mind, too. If we swap the church aisle for the supermarket aisle, there is all the evidence we need that music can numb our sensibilities and turn us into trolley-pushing automata. So when the Amish, for instance, disapprove of music, I take their point. Some Amish communities reject everything except the singing of simple melody lines, taking us back, of course, to the idea of chant. And the same goes for the Orthodox church, which discourages both harmony and counterpoint, and those branches of Islam that permit music. Think of the various forms of Sufi chant. And think of the chanting of a Jewish cantor. In each case, the music is there to reinforce the word.

Igor Stravinsky, who grew up in the Russian Orthodox Church, maintained that writing religious music was good for composers. 'We commit fewer musical sins in church,' he said. Another twentieth-century composer, the Frenchman Olivier Messiaen, regarded his commitment to musical modernism as an act of his Catholic faith. But Messiaen was unusual. More typically, composers faced with religious commissions have looked backwards, not forwards. Bach, in his B minor Mass, employs techniques used by Palestrina 150 years earlier. Mozart, in his C minor Mass, looks back to the oratorios of Handel. And at the start of the twenty-first century, both Arvo Pärt and John Tavener – apparently a distant descendant of the Tudor composer, John Taverner – cheerfully drew on archaic forms and sounds to furnish their religious music. Well, maybe not cheerfully. But still, both composers must have been gladdened by their bulging royalty cheques. Tavener even made it into the pop charts.

Today most of Christendom has little interest in notated music, be it modernist, postmodernist, forward-thinking or backward-looking. Since Ray Charles, Sam Cooke and Aretha Franklin took African-American gospel music, left out the word 'God' and turned it into hard-hitting commercial soul, the traffic between pop music and the church has travelled in two directions. If it was all right for

Ray Charles to turn 'This Little Light of Mine' into 'This Little Girl of Mine', then surely it was all right for churches to stake a claim in pop music. After all, they had been doing something similar since the Middle Ages.

But what sort of pop music? There is Christian country & western, Christian heavy metal, Christian rap and hip hop, even Christian blues – the Devil's music reclaimed: it all exists. And what one church embraces, the next will heartily disapprove of. Pope Benedict XVI is on record as calling rock music 'a vehicle of anti-religion'. When it comes to the vehemence of opinions about music and religion, nothing has changed since the seventeenth century. Nothing except the music.

In most major Western cities, on any given Sunday, you still can probably track down a Palestrina Mass, a Lutheran chorale, a hymn by Charles Wesley or Isaac Watts and, if you are lucky, some plainchant or maybe even an organ piece by Messiaen. But it will be far easier to find something that resembles a white-bread form of American gospel/soul that is broadly indistinguishable from the music of the pop charts. The churches that play this music resemble popular entertainment centres and tend to be filled by the crowds they draw. The attitude to music is simple. First, music itself is morally neutral – there isn't one sort that is inherently holier than another. And second, as many a successful entrepreneur has reasoned, you have to give the people what they want.

Some of the music played and sung at these churches – and recorded, and marketed by them – is surprisingly vague. Sometimes God isn't even mentioned and the words might just as well be those of a secular love song. There is no clear message in the songs, no hint of doctrine. As you listen to that Whitney Houstonesque voice singing 'You're My One Desire', you might apply the words to God. But there's nothing to stop you thinking about the attractive girl sitting in front of you. And if songs like this are ambiguous, there are others that send no message at all. In some modern Pentecostal churches, the idea of glossolalia – of speaking in tongues – has found a musical counterpart.

This is about as far from plainchant as you can get. Music in the mediaeval church was a way of presenting scripture and liturgy as clearly and memorably as possible. In the beginning, after all, was the Word. A lot of modern Christian music seems far more concerned with establishing mood. But in terms of musical fashions, the question remains the same as ever: is music responding to religion, or is religion adapting to musical fashion?

Showtime

Alfred Hitchcock was one of the most popular directors in film's short history. Not only were his movies popular, but he became popular himself. He was the first director whose name was known to a wide public, the first whose name appeared regularly above the titles of his films (Alfred Hitchcock's *Rear Window*, Alfred Hitchcock's *Psycho*), and he was the first to give himself a small walk-on part in every feature. Finally, he even landed his own TV show. If you had told him the films he was making were art, he would have been very surprised – at least until the late 1950s, when people (especially French people) told him this quite often. Hitchcock set out to make popular entertainment for mass audiences. He set out to make money, too. And he succeeded. But the status of his films has changed. We've come to think of them as works of art. At the same time, they have become rather fashionable.

There is no clear-cut distinction between art and entertainment. We think we know the difference, but a case like Hitchcock's proves that it is not a straightforward matter. Art is often believed to be an improving form of entertainment, one that might do you some good; whereas regular entertainment is escapism – meaningless, time-wasting fun. Art is what entertainment aspires to. Art has the reputation for being 'better' than entertainment. So a Hitchcock film is 'better', say, than a Wes Craven horror flick. At least for the time being. Because that's the thing: Hitchcock's films, evidently, haven't changed, though audiences might have done. Perhaps art is in the eye – or the ear – of the beholder.

When it comes to differences between entertainment and art and how one can change into the other, the case of George Frideric Handel is particularly instructive. In the early twenty-first century, one of the most fashionable choices an opera company can make is to put on a work by Handel. Ideally, down in the orchestra pit, there will be a collection of instruments more or less authentic to Handel's day – a mixture of originals and copies of originals – so that the sound of the music, as far as we can gauge it, will be what the composer himself would have heard. And the singers will have been working on their more-or-less-authentic ornamentation.

Handel's operas with titles such as *Radamisto*, *Admeto* and *Alcina* might not be the household names that *Don Giovanni* and *Carmen* and *Madama Butterfly* are, but they are becoming increasingly fashionable in the repertoire. And there are forty-six of them, so it is safe to predict that the fashion will subside long before we come to know the complete works. The Handel fashion has been coming slowly to the boil for half a century, since the operas began to be revived and recorded in the 1960s. The revival was necessary, because in the nineteenth century they had been totally ignored, an almost inevitable response to their rampant fashionability the century before. During Handel's lifetime it was often all the composer could do to keep up with the public's demand for new operas.

Handel was not just a composer; he was, from the very start, an entrepreneur, a wheeler-dealer, an operator. He was born Georg Friedrich Händel in northern Germany in 1685. This was just four weeks before the birth of Johann Sebastian Bach and about 100 kilometres away. They never met.

At seventeen, Handel got his first job as the organist in Halle, his home town, but that didn't last. The following year he went to Hamburg, which was the only place in Germany for an aspiring opera composer. There, his first opera *Almira* was quite a success and it prompted his move south to Italy. This, after all, was where they had invented opera. This was where Handel could learn the ropes as a composer and businessman. Three years later his opera *Agrippina* was the talk of Venice. The composer was just twenty-four.

The next year Handel was back in Germany as court composer to the Elector of Hanover, Georg Ludwig (remember that name). But Handel's sights were set on London. So only weeks into his new job, and with his new boss's permission, he took leave from Hanover and headed for the British capital, where songs from his Italian hit *Agrippina* were already being translated into English. Handel played the harpsichord for Queen Anne, who was not terribly musical but was impressed anyway, and he scored a major success with his new opera *Rinaldo*, which had its London premiere at the Haymarket Theatre on his twenty-sixth birthday.

Rinaldo starred the great castrato Nicolini, and the occasion is recounted in John Mainwaring's biography of Handel, published anonymously the year after the composer's death. (This was the first book-length biography of any musician and it gives us some idea of Handel's fame.)

> *Rinaldo*'s success was very great, and Handel's engagements at Hanover the subject of much concern with the lovers of Music. For when he could return to England, or whether he could at all, was yet very uncertain. His Playing was thought as extraordinary as his Music. One of the principal performers here used to speak of it with astonishment, as far transcending that of any person he had ever known, and as quite peculiar to himself. Another, who had affected to disbelieve the reports of Handel's abilities before he came, was heard to say, from a too great confidence in his own, 'Let him come! We'll *Handle* him, I warrant ye!' (There would be no excuse for recording so poor a pun, if any words could be found, capable of conveying the speaker with

equal force and clearness.) But the moment he heard Handel on the organ, this great man in his own eye shrunk to nothing.

London's music lovers need not have worried they had seen the last of the composer. So fashionable had Handel and his music become and so eager was he to exploit this, that he determined to extricate himself from Hanover with all haste. He had still barely unpacked his bags in Germany, but, the following year, he again requested permission of the Elector to go to London, promising to return to Hanover 'within a reasonable time'. Once again permission was granted. But Handel had no intention of returning. Instead he settled into a posh house in Piccadilly, put Hanover and Georg Ludwig out of his mind, and got on with being London's most fashionable composer. He even Anglicised his name to George Frideric Handel, adding an e to his first name and dropping the umlaut from his surname, in the process inviting more of those dreadful puns.

It is sometimes said a foreigner seeking to fit into English society must acquire the ability to feel and appreciate that most English of conditions – embarrassment. Well Handel was about to take a crash course in this, because what happened next was very embarrassing indeed. Less than two years after the composer had walked out on his German job, Queen Anne died without an heir, and Georg Ludwig, Elector of Hanover, became George I of England. For a while the composer managed to keep a low profile, but his music couldn't. On the King's first weekend in the job, His Majesty attended a service in the Chapel Royal at St James's Palace, only to find himself having to listen to a *Te Deum* by that well-known Englishman, Mr Handel.

Handel's fashionability saved him. The King really had little choice but to overlook his earlier desertion. And Handel's skill at schmoozing didn't hurt his chances either. From time to time during his illustrious career, he was as much in need of a handout as any other composer in history, and he was always skilful when it came to buttering up his patrons. There are varying reports of how the

Water Music came to be composed and first performed at a royal party on the river Thames, but, according to John Mainwaring's biography, it was a sort of trick played on the King to get the composer back into his good books. If so, it certainly worked.

Handel was now the toast of London, and increasingly of Britain. The *Water Music* was his calling card. The suites were arranged and rearranged – for wind bands large and small, for string ensembles, for flute, for solo harpsichord – and they were played everywhere, in pleasure gardens and pubs and in private houses all over the British Isles. The *Water Music* was a hit and so was its composer, as Mainwaring's biography makes plain:

> Alexander Pope one day asked his friend Dr Arbuthnot, of whose knowledge in Music he had a high idea, What was his real opinion in regard to Handel as a Master of that Science? The Doctor immediately replied, 'Conceive the highest you can of his abilities, and they are much beyond any thing that you can conceive.'

Handel was indeed a great composer and this alone would account for the popularity of his music, which obviously continues today. But in order to be fashionable, you need something more than greatness. In fact you don't really need greatness at all. Handel's shrewd business instincts counted for plenty, and this included his ability to adapt to his surroundings. He was a musical chameleon. In the *Water Music*, for instance, he deliberately set out to compose music in an English style – he was, after all, now an English composer – and a lot of people commented on his success in this regard. But London audiences still required Italian opera, so he gave them this too, over and over again.

Handel's role as an impresario went beyond composing and conducting. He raised substantial funds for a Royal Academy of Music – really, what we would call an opera company. And he ran everything, including managing his temperamental Italian stars. Famous singers were half the attraction for the public – as they are in opera houses today – and each had his or her own claque of supporters, leading to great jealousies among the company members. One night, with the royal family present in the theatre, these rivalries culminated in an on-stage hair-pulling incident between the two leading ladies.

When Handel's first academy fell apart, he formed a second. Mounting opera was an expensive business then as now, and even so successful an entrepreneur as Handel came close to bankruptcy more than once. But he maintained his relationship with the monarchy, successfully ingratiating himself with George's son, George II, and he wrote music for all important royal occasions. So fashionable was Handel's name that audiences congregated to hear even the rehearsals of his music. There is a report of a particularly important one in an issue of the *Norwich Gazette* from October 1727:

> Yesterday there was a rehearsal of the Coronation Anthem in Westminster-Abbey, set to Musick by the famous Mr Hendall: There being 40 voices, and about 160 Violins, Trumpets, Hautboys, Kettle-Drums, Bass's proportionable; besides an Organ which was erected behind the Altar: And both the Musick and the Performers were the Admiration of all the Audience.

Zadok the Priest was one of four anthems Handel composed for the coronation of George II and Queen Caroline, and at least one of these anthems has been sung at every subsequent English coronation. That is the enduring legacy of the composer; that is his continuing popularity. But what of the eighteenth-century fashion for Handel's music? Like all fashions, it faded.

Handel's greatest successes were very great indeed. But he had just as many failures. What, in the end, is so impressive about this composer, from the entrepreneurial point of view, was his ability to adapt to the changing fashions of the day. When Handel's second academy hit financial problems he rapidly transformed himself into a composer of religious oratorios such as *Israel in Egypt*, *Saul* and *Messiah*. It was another of his chameleon acts, and this time a relatively subtle one. After all, these new oratorios were really just operas in concert form, with English words and religious subjects: they had precisely the same musical structures as the operas and most of them even had their first performances in theatres. Not all of them were immediately successful, but, unlike the operas, a handful of the oratorios have never lost their popularity. The nineteenth century saw the rise of the large amateur chorus, and in English-speaking countries all over the world it became nearly obligatory for choirs to sing Handel's *Messiah* each year. For some reason, the piece became associated with Christmas, although of the two hours of words and music in *Messiah*, only five or six minutes actually deal with the Christmas story. By the start of the twentieth century, Handel's *Messiah* had undergone a transformation not so much into art, as into sacred artefact, its performance a religious ritual.

Today, most of the music heard in concert halls and opera houses is what the paying punter would call art. Handel's operas would certainly be considered that. But for Handel, art was what you hung on your wall. Like Alfred Hitchcock, Handel considered himself a commercial entertainer. He was a showman with a showman's temperament. He enjoyed the spotlight. If, like Hitchcock, he had been offered his own TV show, he would have jumped at the chance – anything to sell the music. So is art, perhaps, made in the mind of the audience?

A century on from Handel – and back in the home of opera – Giuseppe Verdi was anything but a natural showman. He actually seems to have been quite shy and rather modest, certainly a reluctant public figure. But his operas were big business. Most of Verdi's operas, at some level, were also political tracts. Nineteenth-century Italy – or what today we call Italy – was seething with nationalistic aspiration. The Risorgimento – the movement to unite the disparate states that made up the peninsular – was in full cry and Verdi's operas seemed to reflect this. In *Nabucco*, Hebrew slaves in Babylon sang about freedom in the chorus 'Va', pensiero':

> *Oh, my country so beautiful and lost!*
> *Oh, remembrance so dear and so fatal!*

Whether or not Verdi intended it, Italian audiences heard their own song and identified with it. 'Viva Verdi!' they shouted – and they didn't just mean the composer. As chance would have it, the letters in Verdi's name formed an acronym for 'Vittorio Emanuele Re d'Italia' – 'Victor Emmanuel, King of Italy', the figurehead of the unification movement. Talk about being in the right place at the right time.

So while an eighteenth-century audience in London had been celebrating its own good taste in clamouring for Italian operas by a German composer, in mid-nineteenth century Italy something altogether more urgent was occurring. Verdi's operas really mattered. Oddly enough, they still matter to Italians today, not just to the wealthy or the educated, but to everyone. Visit an opera house in Rome or Florence or Milan, and you might well feel you are at the circus, particularly if your previous experience of opera has been in an English-speaking country. Audiences cheer and boo with a passion reserved for sporting events in Australia. You could be forgiven for thinking that, in Italy, opera still has to make the transition to art from popular entertainment. I tend to feel that is a good thing.

But what of Richard Wagner, Verdi's great contemporary and, in some senses, his polar opposite? Here is fashion with knobs on. To this day, there are people who travel the globe attending performances of his operas, particularly the cycle of four that constitute *Der Ring des Nibelungen* (The Ring of the Nibelung). Their Mecca is Bayreuth, the Bavarian town where Wagner built his festival theatre and first staged the *Ring* and *Parsifal*. Touring the world's great opera houses is an expensive business, and the social aspect of *Ring*-trotting is not to be underestimated. But many of those who devote large chunks of their lives and earnings to making the pilgrimages are true aficionados of Wagner's works, and this high level of devotion is nothing new. In the late nineteenth century, special trains ran from Paris to the Bayreuth Festival.

In building a theatre tailored to the requirements of his own works, Wagner was doing more than creating a shrine to himself, let alone a tourist attraction. The wood-lined auditorium with its double proscenium arch and buried orchestra pit was designed with the specific requirements of the operas in mind. The effect of the double arch was to distance the audience from the action in order to emphasise the mythical qualities of the stories – Brechtian 'alienation' before the fact – while the pit offered a glowing, blended orchestral sonority that magically filled the theatre. The aim was to put the works in the best possible light, and on that subject it is worth noting that Wagner was the first to insist that his audiences be plunged into darkness, the better to attend to his creations on the stage.

Is this, then, the moment at which opera moves from the realm of popular entertainment to art? Not necessarily. After all, modern cinemas and theatres aim to make some of the trashiest entertainment as vivid and thrilling as possible via new technology. Presenting entertainment seriously doesn't make it art. But taking it seriously possibly does, and here we are back with perception and with the audience.

Until 200 years ago – the time of Haydn, Mozart and Beethoven – people listened to new music; audiences wanted novelty, and that is what composers gave them. And concerts – smaller, far more exclusive affairs than today, with no paying public at the box office – were as much about entertainment as about art.

In 1806, Beethoven's violin concerto was given its first performance by one Franz Clement, a former child prodigy, every bit the showman. We think of this concerto as one of Beethoven's most profound and sublime creations. But at the premiere, immediately after Beethoven's first movement, the soloist seized the opportunity to play a party piece of his own composition. And 'party piece' is the accurate term, for he played his entire solo on just one string of the violin while holding the instrument upside down. After all, the audience was there to be entertained, and, at forty-five minutes, old Beethoven's piece was possibly a touch over-long. A bit of light relief, that's what was needed. When the applause had died down Herr Clement got back to the slow movement of the Beethoven.

But even in 1806, there were already people who were starting to believe that great music should not simply be a matter of novelty or fashion. If Beethoven's violin concerto was great in 1806, why would it not still be great in 1807 or 1907 or 2007? It was the nineteenth century that invented the concept of classical music. Along with this new enthusiasm came the public concert hall and the music critic. The nineteenth century also gave us musicologists – experts, if you like, in the conservation of the music of the past – and as the century went on, they dug back further into history.

Not many people would argue that the conservation of great music was a bad idea, but by the late nineteenth century and especially in the twentieth, the definition of classical music – perhaps I should say of *classic* music – had broadened. If a piece was by Handel, then it must be great, no matter that Handel himself had thrown it off in a matter of hours for a particular occasion and never given it a second thought. If it was by Mozart, then it ought to be edited, published and performed in our concert halls, no matter that Mozart hadn't even expected this music to be listened to. Little *divertimenti* that Mozart wrote for social gatherings, fully aware they would form the background to small talk, are today played to audiences of two thousand who sit in darkened auditoriums giving the music their undivided attention. Is the joke on us? Not all music, even by Mozart, is for the ages. Sometimes a piece belongs to its moment in history and would do well to remain there.

In a way, the operas of Handel and Verdi, Mozart and Puccini, also belong to their moments in history; they also served functions, one of which was to make their composers some money. But today we think of opera as something rather elevated; and we hear greatness in the best and the worst of these composers' works. There again, just because the composers themselves didn't intend profundity doesn't mean it isn't there. The pursuit of the dollar doesn't rule out eternal values on the side.

What is very hard for a modern audience is to feel the same thrill at a Handel opera that this composer's London audience would have felt at its premiere 300 years ago. How can even a modern Italian audience approach a work such as Verdi's *Nabucco* in precisely the same spirit as an audience at the time of the Risorgimento? Well, it can't. Yet when it comes to popular theatre, audiences' expectations have hardly changed at all. They wanted spectacle in the eighteenth century, they still want it in the twenty-first, and it is something that the modern musical has been rather good at delivering, from *Sweeney Todd* to *Les Misérables* and *The Phantom of the Opera*.

Will these works of popular entertainment become art? I think Sondheim's pieces already are. The songs are so well-made, with such dramatic poise in their words and music, that I cannot believe they will not be regarded as classics. On the other hand, Andrew Lloyd Webber's great showbiz talent is not for writing tunes, which are nearly always rhythmically inert and harmonically obvious, and occasionally too close to Puccini for comfort, but for having ideas and seeing them through. To work out that the world needs a musical about Jesus in the late 1960s, a musical about Eva Perón in the late 70s, and a musical based on T.S. Eliot's poems about cats in the 1980s is, without doubt, an impressive skill. Perhaps some of these ideas came from other people, but Lloyd Webber recognised them for the gold mines they were. It's the knack that Lloyd Webber most obviously shares with Handel and Mozart and Verdi and Wagner: how to have a hit. Will Lloyd Webber's musicals one day be considered art? I doubt it, but only time will tell and I won't be around to find out.

Ultimately, it is not the composer – or the painter or the playwright or the film director – who decides if the fruit of their labours is art. It might not even be their public that makes this decision. With the operas of Handel and Verdi, and with the films of Alfred Hitchcock, it has been posterity that has decided there is more to their work than disposable entertainment. Time doesn't make art; but art often takes time.

Fame

If you listen to recordings of Alessandro Moreschi's singing, you will hear a slice of musical history. And I do mean slice. Now more than a century old, these recordings were made at the Vatican in 1904, and the singer in question was a 46-year-old castrated man.

Moreschi is the last known castrato, and the only one, it seems, ever to have been recorded. I must say that I find it quite touching, hearing him sing Gounod's *Ave Maria*, though I'm not absolutely sure why. The piece is dreadfully saccharine, and Moreschi himself isn't that good. He sang in the Sistine Chapel choir, but his isn't really a solo voice. And yet there's something about the way he swoops from note to note, something about the grown-up vibrato allied to the childlike tone of the voice itself, that is oddly compelling.

Right up until the start of the twentieth century, boys were castrated to preserve their high voices. That eight-year-old son of yours who sings so nicely: a couple of snips and he could sing that way his whole life. Don't dismiss the idea out of hand; it might be a future source of financial security for the family ...

There were soprano and alto voices among the castrati – essentially boys' voices in men's bodies, with men's stamina and lung capacity. Moderately talented singers could sing in a choir, like Moreschi, while in the eighteenth century, at least, the really good ones were assured of work in the opera house. For composers such as

Handel – and for his audiences – the castrato was the epitome of heroism. Handel wrote dozens of roles for the castrato voice, including those of the great warrior/commanders Xerxes, Tamburlaine and Julius Caesar. The singers who took on these macho roles were extraordinarily popular with audiences, especially women, and they became exceedingly wealthy. They had the kind of fame that today you'd associate with an Oscar-winning Hollywood actor or a Brazilian soccer star.

The most famous castrato of his time or any other was Carlo Broschi, otherwise known as Farinelli. His reputation preceded him across Europe, and when he finally made his London debut in the 1730s, not in a Handel opera, but for a rival company, the audience shouted 'One God, one Farinelli!' Within the decade there was another new opera, this time not starring Farinelli but about him. It was a comic opera by the German-born composer J.F. Lampe. A century later, there was a second Farinelli opera, this time in French, by Daniel Auber. And there were novels and plays about the singer and finally, in 1994, a feature film.

Farinelli's younger contemporary, the musicologist and diarist Charles Burney, wrote approvingly of the singer:

> Of almost all other great singers, we hear of their intoxication by praise and prosperity, and of their caprice, insolence, and absurdities, at some time or other; but of Farinelli, superior to them all in talents, fame, and fortune, the records of folly among the spoilt children of Apollo furnish not one disgraceful anecdote.

The history of music is full of famous performers, fashionable in their day for singing higher or lower, or playing faster or louder than anyone else. And they keep on coming. We can sometimes be a bit sniffy about them – when we are not in the queue for their autographs – but although, like all fashions, superstars come and go, a few of them have left their mark and we still remember their names, even though we don't really know what they sounded like.

It is a testament to the scale of Farinelli's fame that his reputation remains intact when the closest we can come to the sound of his voice is that recording of the frankly disappointing Alessandro Moreschi. Farinelli is still sometimes referred to as the greatest singer ever, but obviously there is no way to prove this.

It is the same with the soprano Jenny Lind. The so-called Swedish nightingale was phenomenally popular in the middle of the nineteenth century. Her legendary tour of the United States was managed by the circus entrepreneur P.T. Barnum. But, frustratingly for us, her career ended before sound recording began.

With Nellie Melba, fortunately, we can get some idea of the singer's talents. Melba made quite a few recordings. The majority were done when the technology was still primitive, while the handful of electrical recordings, which are generally much clearer, took place when Dame Nellie herself was past her prime. Still, between them you get some measure of the quality of her voice. And anyway, you don't have both a dessert and a kind of toast named after you unless you're extremely famous; and you don't become that famous without real talent, unless it's for rampant eccentricity, striking good looks or very bad behaviour – none of which Melba exhibited.

But on the subject of bad behaviour as a component of fame we come to the towering nineteenth-century figures of Niccolò Paganini and Franz Liszt. Once again we can only read about Paganini's virtuosity on the violin and Liszt's apparently astounding pianism, but we do at least have the works they composed for themselves to play, and these tell us quite a bit about just how good they must have been as performers. And as with Farinelli, Lind and Melba, their fame has endured even if the fashion has ended.

Today, indeed, we think of Liszt primarily as a composer, rather than a virtuoso of the piano, and this change of focus is not limited to the Hungarian. As recently as the start of the twentieth century,

Gustav Mahler was regarded as a great conductor who composed on the side.

The most extreme example of this sort of change in reputation is surely Johann Sebastian Bach. In his lifetime he was the greatest organist in Europe. Organists were expected to compose music, so there was nothing particularly unusual about this sideline of his, but, divorced from his abilities at the keyboard, Bach's fame as a composer was modest enough. It is sometimes said that Bach's music was forgotten after his death. This is not quite true. The organ and harpsichord works were certainly played, and not least because they were so admired by other composers. Mozart arranged five of the fugues from the *Well-Tempered Clavier* and the young Beethoven made his name in Vienna as a pianist playing selections from the same work. What is true is that after Bach's death the piece that many consider his greatest achievement, the *St Matthew Passion*, was not heard again for almost a century.

It was Felix Mendelssohn who revived it on 11 March 1829 at the Singakademie in Berlin. In the audience were Paganini, the poet Heine, the philosopher Friedrich Hegel, and the King of Prussia. In the role of Christ at this performance was a singer and actor, Eduard Devrient, who wrote the following, not entirely modest, report of the occasion:

Whoever heard the three to four hundred highly trained amateur voices ... will understand that with perfect leadership, perfection was achieved.

Stümer sang the Evangelist with the most agreeable precision, entirely true to his role of Narrator ... The ladies, too, achieved the full effect with their moving numbers.

So far as I was concerned, I knew that the impression of the entire work depended largely on that created by the presentation of the part of Jesus ... It meant for me the greatest task a singer could be given ... Carried along by the performance as a whole,

I could thus sing with my whole soul, and I felt that the thrills of devotion that ran through me at the most impressive passages were also felt by the hearers, who listened in deadly silence. Never have I felt a holier solemnity vested in a congregation than in the performers and audience that evening. Our concert made an extraordinary sensation in the educated circles of Berlin. The resuscitation of the popular effect created by a half-forgotten genius was felt to be of epochal import. The worshippers of Bach ... must not forget that this new cult of Bach dates from the 11th of March, 1829, and that it was Felix Mendelssohn who gave new vitality to the greatest and most profound of composers.

It was indeed. For the resuscitation of the *St Matthew Passion* we can thank not only Mendelssohn's good taste, but also – more particularly and immediately – his fame. The brilliant, dashing Mendelssohn was a twenty-year-old wunderkind, and if he said everyone should listen to Bach, everyone did. The nineteenth century's appetite for this sort of superstar was insatiable. They were the equivalent of rock stars, and some of them – again, I suppose I'm thinking of Paganini and Liszt – actually conducted themselves like rock stars. Even when they weren't behaving badly, rumours of bad behaviour maintained their notoriety. Freakish ability in a musical performer has often led the public to speculate about deals with the Devil. Paganini was not the first to be suspected of having forged some sort of diabolical pact, and the great blues guitarist Robert Johnson wasn't the last. Liszt's reputation as a womaniser was such that you find yourself wondering how he fitted the concerts in, let alone had time to compose a few hundred hours of music.

It was not only the private lives of Paganini and Liszt that bring to mind rock music. In the 1950s, artists such as Little Richard, Chuck Berry, Jerry Lee Lewis and Elvis Presley did not just create a musical genre, they also helped establish a new way of listening. The transistor radio, the jukebox and the 45 rpm single – the means of production, or reproduction – came to define pop music as much as pop music defined them. In just the same way, the names of Paganini and Liszt became synonymous with the public recital. They might not have invented it, but they made it extremely fashionable among the new middle classes. Right across Europe, the nineteenth-century bourgeoisie flocked first to salon concerts and then to public concert halls. Soon, it seemed, the whole of the new middle class from artisans and shopkeepers to members of wealthy business families wanted a share of this new kind of entertainment. Not everybody approved. Writing in the magazine *Musical World* in 1845, one critic complained bitterly about cheap concert tickets in London.

> The art must not be degraded ... To play the finest music to an audience which has been admitted at a shilling apiece is what I can never give my consent to. I am a liberal but I have good sense to guide me.

Well, it must be admitted that there was a vulgar side to concert going, as arguably there still is. There is a gladiatorial aspect to the public recital. One man or woman up there on stage, pitted against Beethoven's *Hammerklavier* or Bartók's Sonata for Solo Violin or whatever it might be. It is probably inevitable that those performers who seem to demonstrate great virtuosity or great spiritual insight or, for that matter, great personal charisma, should attract the largest followings. So when a performer comes along who, for whatever reason, achieves virtuosity or insight or, indeed, charisma against the odds, we like them even more. Into this category falls the child prodigy. Mendelssohn's brilliant career was launched in childhood, as Mozart's was before him. Since both died in their thirties, it's good they didn't waste any time getting started.

Ambitious parents are often behind a prodigy, and William Crotch's mother was pretty pushy. Today we think of Crotch – if we think of him at all – as a very minor English composer, a younger contemporary of Beethoven. But he began his career as an infant phenomenon, advertised by his mum.

> Mrs Crotch is arrived in town with her son, the Musical Child, who will perform on the organ every day as usual, from one o'clock to three, at Mrs Hart's milliner, Piccadilly.

Mrs Crotch's advertisement appeared in 1779. Her son, the Musical Child, who gave a two-hour performance every afternoon, was four. As an adult, William Crotch recalled his time as a prodigy.

> I look back on this part of my life with pain and humiliation ... I was becoming a spoilt child and in danger of becoming what too many of my musical brethren have become under similar circumstances and unfortunately remained through life.

Organs in hat shops might be a thing of the past, but it seems we never tire of clever children. The pianist Geoffrey Tozer was one. In 1962, aged eight, he played with the Melbourne Symphony Orchestra, and at fifteen appeared in London's Royal Albert Hall with the BBC Symphony Orchestra conducted by Colin Davis. In 2004, he told me what it had been like as a prodigy.

> I wanted to be taken very seriously. I had no thought of being just a momentary figure of fashion, and most other children I have spoken to seem to exhibit the same feeling. They would like to be taken as musicians rather than just flashes in the pan. But the prodigy, by definition, is quintessentially fashionable. Because once the first wrinkle appears you are no longer interesting. And behind you is coming this army of 10-year-olds, 5-year-olds and 12-year-olds. You only have to look at those hordes and hordes of violinists that all came from the Orient in the 1980s and 1990s. Every year there was a different one – whatever happened to the

first one, and the second one, and the third and fifth, and the ninth and thirteenth? Where are they now? They have all grown up. That, to me, is the essence of fashion and the most horrible aspect of fashion in music. Because the worst thing about being a child performer is, where do you go from there? It's driven by what you'd have to say [is] the greed of managers or the big promoting desires of recording companies who make stars. And I find that quite objectionable because – going back to those Oriental violinists, all of whom were girls – they must have realised that they [were being] exploited. And they must [have thought], 'Well, I'd better record my Tchaikovsky and Mendelssohn concertos now because I'll never be asked to do it next year, because next year there will be another one coming up'.

Most child prodigies do not continue to have careers as adults. But a few of them do go on, including Geoffrey Tozer himself, though in some ways, perhaps, Tozer never fully grew up. His greatest struggles, indeed, came at the end of his life, when he found himself neglected by orchestras and promoters and took to drinking heavily, the drinking undoubtedly contributing to the neglect. He died in 2009, aged 54.

Child prodigies will come and go like the passing fashions they are, and there will always be more coming along. Our liking for novelty itself seems hard to satisfy – how long can someone remain 'novel'? – so we are always on the lookout for something new, and the other sort of star performer that has mass appeal, especially in our news-hungry world, is the one with a story to tell. Beating the odds is always the best sort of story, overcoming adversity and attaining fame and success.

In the 1990s, Italian tenors were all the rage in the wake of the marketing phenomenon that was the Three Tenors. Then along came a tenor with a really good story. Andrea Bocelli is blind. From the start, some people insisted that he couldn't really sing, and that there was nothing to him but his blindness. But Bocelli had a lovely natural voice and some genuine vocal personality. He sang Neapolitan songs with feeling and communicated them superbly, though this didn't make him an opera singer, even if his record company recorded him in operatic roles. But though he didn't lack talent, there were hundreds of tenors as good as Bocelli and one was forced to ask whether he would have become famous outside his home province of Pisa if he could see. Was his disability more important for his fans than his voice?

It certainly was for one woman. In 1999, an Australian newspaper asked the CEO of one of the country's biggest charitable organisations some friendly questions, including this one: 'What are you listening to?' It turned out that in her CD player, our charity boss had the latest offering from Andrea Bocelli. And what exactly was the attraction?

> Andrea has the most beautiful voice and I have a great deal of respect for her, as she shows you can achieve your potential despite a disadvantage – Andrea is deaf.

Blind tenor, deaf soprano: the exact details do not matter. You don't even have to listen to the CD. The singer's story – even if it is entirely the wrong story – fuels the fashion. It is not a musical fashion at all, but a fashion for the idea of music as a way of overcoming adversity. It's a branch of faith healing.

Sometimes in these situations the story takes over completely. When the film *Shine* appeared in 1996, based on the life of pianist David Helfgott, the real Helfgott undertook a world tour, such was the understandable interest in him and his singular life. In case you don't know, Helfgott's promising career as a concert pianist had been derailed by severe bouts of mental illness, but, eventually, with the help of his strong-minded wife, he had overcome enough of his problems to make a sort of tentative comeback. There were occasional concerts, but nothing more, and this rather brave tale inspired Scott Hicks's commercially successful film. It won an Academy Award for its star, Geoffrey Rush. But even before that the real Helfgott had begun turning up in the great concert halls of the world and selling them out. He sold out the concert hall of the Sydney Opera House four nights in a row. No other pianist on earth could have done that. But were people coming for the music?

The critics certainly were, and they were not impressed. Across North America and Europe, Helfgott's concerts drew audiences anxious to see Helfgott and critics whose job it was to listen to him and comment. What the critics found, time and again, was evidence of 'chaotic' thinking, to use the description of Anna Picard from the *Independent on Sunday*: in Beethoven's *Waldstein* sonata, which was the big piece on the program, there was no line, no long-range strategy that might provide the music with a coherent journey. In the *New York Times*, Anthony Tommasini wrote that Helfgott's *Waldstein* was 'sketchy' and 'monodynamic'. Tim Page in the *Washington Post* wrote: 'We have reached the point where a disturbed man who can barely play the piano is suddenly the hottest person in classical music.' Richard Dyer in the *Boston Globe* ended his review with the oft-quoted line, 'The sad fact is that David Helfgott should not have been in Symphony Hall last night, and neither should the rest of us.'

I don't think there's much point in comparing Bocelli and Helfgott. Their talents are completely different. But I do think there are some strong points of contact in the nature of their popular success. Thanks to the film and the Oscars, Helfgott briefly was the best-known concert pianist alive, as Page wrote, 'the hottest person in classical music'. If you had seen the film, why wouldn't you want to see the man who inspired it? Whatever else he might have been he was certainly, at one level, very inspiring.

Early in 1997 I was in New York for a few days and I found myself in the classical music department of a large CD store next to

Lincoln Center. The sales assistant, noticing from my accent that I wasn't a local, asked where I was from, and when I told her I lived in Australia, she immediately wanted to talk about David Helfgott. He was shortly to play in New York. What did I think? Before I had time to answer, she told me she had tickets for his concert, and she was taking her mother, who herself had a mental illness. She felt sure her mother would find the whole experience very moving, and I feel sure she was right. Helfgott's *music* – his actual playing of Rakhmaninov's third piano concerto or the *Waldstein* sonata – might well have been 'chaotic', but for his audience that was beside the point. They were not there to hear Rakhmaninov or Beethoven, but to see Helfgott. I imagine it was partly a matter of curiosity and partly a genuine delight in witnessing a man who was triumphing over a terrible illness and, apparently, enjoying himself into the bargain. I also imagine that many of those in his audiences were at a classical concert for the first time and, having seen Helfgott with their own eyes, were satisfied and felt no need to go back to the concert hall. But then that's fame for you. And that's fashion.

*

In pop music, fame, fashion and musical worth sometimes coincide, but not always. Careers are invented, personalities are invented, even people are invented. The members of the 1960s pop group the Monkees were not real musicians, but actors playing at being a pop group – actually, playing at being the Beatles. And they did it quite successfully, at least as far as their largely prepubescent TV audience was concerned. (I should know. I was one of them.) At the height of the Monkees' fame, this fabricated group, in which originally only one member could play an instrument, toured the United States with Jimi Hendrix, perhaps the most gifted rock guitarist who ever lived. Hendrix was the support act.

The pop industry depends on fame – that's axiomatic – and it depends on the changing of fashions. On the face of it, these fashions are driven by music, but that's only true up to a point. The story behind the music is just as important. Jimi Hendrix should be famous on the strength of his guitar playing alone, but at least some of his fame rests on the tragic story of a young man with prodigious talent, his career cut short by his death at twenty-seven. When Roger Daltrey of the Who sang 'Hope I die before I get old', he was, in a way, articulating not only the rather extreme dream of his generation, but also the motto of the pop star. There comes a point in every pop star's life where death, viewed cynically, is a smart career move. They might not have chosen to die – and we might still be sad they're gone – but there's no doubt at all that from Janis Joplin to Elvis Presley, from John Lennon to Kurt Cobain, shuffling off this mortal coil did wonders for their record sales.

Before her death in 1996, Eva Cassidy sang at clubs in and around Washington DC. She also once performed with her brother in Iceland. She sang backing vocals on a few records – nothing important – and she recorded some tracks of her own, but always singing other people's songs. She was not famous at all. And then she died of cancer. Someone thought it would be a nice idea to release a CD of her best recordings. It *was* a nice idea. But after a while there was a demand – a huge demand – for Eva Cassidy's records. By the first few years of the twenty-first century, they were selling by the truckload. It is hard to explain.

Were the hundreds of thousands of people who bought Cassidy's records were being had? This was hardly a case of commercial exploitation by a multinational record company. On the contrary it was, initially at least, all a matter of word of mouth, a genuine grass-roots movement. It was the kind of thing that multinational record companies routinely seize on and *try* to exploit, but here there wasn't that much that could be exploited because the poor woman was dead.

There was nothing very special about Eva Cassidy's singing. She sang mostly well-known songs – often quite famous numbers such as 'Imagine' and 'Bridge Over Troubled Water' – and she didn't do anything particularly new with them. She didn't reinterpret the material, she just sang it, simply and directly – artlessly, you might say. Was that part of the attraction? Given that her CDs began to appear at a time when Celine Dion was attempting the world record for adding unnecessary notes to songs, Eva Cassidy's very simplicity might have been thought refreshing. Perhaps in the face of terrorist horrors and political doublespeak at the start of the twenty-first century, the artless singing of well-known songs was somehow reassuring to people. Perhaps. But nothing except Eva Cassidy's story – which amounted to the fact that she was dead – could explain the extent of the *fashion* for her records.

So is fame always exploitative? Probably. If it's not the artist or the artist's memory that's being exploited, then it's us – the audience. And deep down we know it. Which, at one level, I suppose, makes it all right. The truth is that at least some of the time we are most of us willing victims. A few minutes on the internet, a moment's browsing of the covers of the women's magazines at the supermarket checkout, a glance at the tabloid headlines – which actor's having which pop star's baby – you'd have to be terribly stupid to believe any of it mattered. But you'd also have to be fairly dull not to find yourself, at least occasionally, reading on just a little longer than you know is sensible. Other people's fame might be escapism, but like great art – of which it is the merest of trappings – it helps put our own lives into perspective.

The Colour of Money

As you have perhaps heard, classical music is dead, at least as far the record industry is concerned. The famous labels – EMI with its logo of an obedient dog listening intently to 'his master's voice', Deutsche Grammophon with the distinctive yellow cartouche on every album cover, Decca, RCA Victor – names associated with classical music for a hundred years: they are all making fewer and fewer records. And why? Because, apparently, no one much would buy them. It seems the fat lady might have sung her last. Well, I don't blame the fat lady. I blame the Three Tenors.

In 1990 there was an outdoor concert in the ancient Baths of Caracella in Rome. Luciano Pavarotti and Placido Domingo were already well-known to opera lovers; less well-known, José Carreras was perhaps best remembered from a documentary film in which he spat the dummy during a recording of *West Side Story*. The general public, too, would likely have heard of Pavarotti, and possibly Domingo, but probably wouldn't have known Carreras from a bar of soap. Well that was all about to change.

The Three Tenors concert from Rome was later televised and a recording released. It doubtless helped that it all coincided with the soccer world cup, and that Pavarotti singing 'Nessun dorma' was used at the end of every telecast. Even so, I doubt anyone really expected the subsequent recording to sell six-and-a-half million copies in its first year. I remember visiting friends who had never previously shown an interest in operatic voices – or any music at all outside mainstream pop – but who now owned a copy of *The Three Tenors*.

Predictably, there were critics who objected to the recording. They pointed out that the repertoire was irredeemably low-brow, which wasn't quite true, and that some of the singing was out of tune, which was undeniable, and they argued that this was no way to introduce the masses to opera – as though that had ever been the intention. But there were also plenty of people on hand to argue exactly the opposite. It seemed an operatic golden age was fast approaching. It would start, they said, with the Tenors, and then bit by bit the millions of neophytes who had fallen in love with opera through the arias on the CD would want to experience the real thing. Opera-house box offices would be stormed by fans desperate for tickets; record shops would never be able to satisfy the demand for box sets of Verdi and Puccini.

As we now know, they were wrong. The Three Tenors were a showbiz phenomenon and, for a time, very fashionable. I imagine there really were some people who discovered a new love of opera through their exposure to 'Nessun dorma', but mostly what happened next was what always happens next with fashion. After the massive success of the first CD, there was a second CD. It sold a lot of copies too, but not as many as the first. Then there was a third CD which sold less well again. The sales, I should point out, were still very large compared to the sales of most CDs of classical music, but by now the record companies and record buyers were already casting around for a new fashion.

If that were truly the end of this story, it might form an amusing footnote to the history of late-twentieth century capitalism. But there's more. Amazingly, record company executives the world over seem to have misunderstood what was really happening with the Three Tenors phenomenon. They heard the cash registers, they saw the colour of the money and they decided that classical music was on the up and up. They thought that other classical recordings should do as well. It seems not to have occurred to them that the reason *The Three Tenors* sold like no classical recording in history was because it wasn't really classical ... Now, everything was compared to the success of *The Three Tenors*. When new classical recordings failed to sell in anything like the same numbers, they were deemed to have failed. The result was that, very quickly, the big multinational companies – the record labels of Toscanini and Karajan and Bernstein – lost interest in recording classical music.

It wasn't, of course, the fault of the tenors themselves. They knew as well as anyone that they were just providing classy entertainment that would be fashionable for a while. And neither was the collapse of classical recording simply a knee-jerk response to those slow sales – that was more like the circumstantial evidence needed by the accountants to prove that classical music doesn't pay. And accountants, increasingly, were making the decisions.

Another important facet of the decline of the classical recording industry was the CD itself. And fashion played its part here, too.

I don't think anyone in the record industry predicted that the invention of the CD would be quite the commercial success it was – particularly among classical music fans. But, when you think about it, this was the perfect medium for classical music, not least because of the length of much of the repertoire. Where, with the old vinyl LPs, you had to stand up, walk across the room and turn over your Brahms symphony between movements, now you didn't. You could fit an entire act of an opera on to a single CD – no more awkward fade outs or sudden silences mid-scene. Some people might have complained about a certain soulless quality to the digital sound, but, right around the world, music lovers with large collections of classical vinyl began trading it in and stocking up on CD replacements. The record companies responded by re-recording the standard repertoire – over and over again. Collectors could choose between twenty, thirty, fifty – sometimes even more – different versions of their favourite classical pieces. This boom continued right through the 1980s and into the 1990s. It was a sort of golden age. Then it stopped.

*

Studio recordings of operas are about the most expensive recording projects you can undertake, and in 2005 EMI announced that its new box set of Wagner's *Tristan und Isolde*, conducted by Antonio Pappano and starring Placido Domingo as Tristan, would be the last time the company recorded an entire opera in the studio. It would be live recordings only from now on.

Perhaps the most famous studio recording of Wagner's *Tristan und Isolde* was conducted by Wilhelm Furtwängler in 1953 – also, as it happens, for EMI – and many Wagnerians would argue that it remains the greatest version of the opera ever recorded. That recording did not make its money back in the first year, or even, probably, the first decade, but in half a century it has never been absent from the catalogue, and by now has surely generated for EMI a considerable profit. That is how the business used to work. Great classical recordings made profits over time; other recordings might at least hope to break even. They were long-term investments and you just needed to be patient. It is a bit like classical music itself. One reason that a recording of *Tristan und Isolde* will never sell like a pop single is that it requires time to appreciate it – probably a lifetime. The piece lasts four hours and is richly detailed. A successful pop single might last four minutes, and will be full of repetition; you're meant to get it immediately. The pop charts aren't interested in things that take time.

So the really big shift that has overcome the classical recording business is that it has run out of patience. It is no longer prepared to wait a decade or more for its profits. You see why the Three Tenors phenomenon – bucketloads of instant money from a seemingly classical record – helped seal the fate of classical recording.

I am painting a very black picture here of a business that – whatever its motivation and wherever its morals – has done more good than harm. Certainly, over the century and a bit of its existence, the recording industry has made available to the world an unprecedented amount of music, and an unprecedented range. But making music available is one thing, marketing it is another. And in order to shift large quantities, you need fashion.

Fashions can be relatively small and exclusive, or they can start small and then grow. Indeed, the most important achievements of the recording industry have come from an ability to spot small, local fashions, take them over, tame them, groom them, and turn them into global fashions. In doing this they have often transformed the very music that inspired the fashion. But that's progress.

The music business is first and foremost a business and always was. As soon as musicians realised they had something to sell – as soon as they became professionals – they began adapting their talents to whatever they perceived to be market forces. An Italian tenor notices that the longer he holds his top C, the more the audience likes it – so he practises holding it for as long as possible. I suppose one has to concede that this is fair enough, if musically not terribly interesting. But what happens when it is not the musician who is calling the shots?

I suppose you might say that busking is the most basic form of the music business, the bottom rung on the ladder of musical capitalism. Many of the earliest blues recordings are of blind musicians – Blind Blake, Blind Lemon Jefferson, Blind Willie Johnson, Reverend Gary Davis, Blind Willie McTell, Sonny Terry – who were forced literally into the marketplace as a means of survival. This is busking to save your life, and about as real as you can get.

The blues seems to have come to life sometime around 1900 in the Mississippi delta. It was a folk music, with stock expressions – words, phrases and musical riffs – recurring from song to song over a simple harmonic template of (at most) three chords. The simplicity of the form gave it its currency, while the distinction of individual performers – notably singers, guitarists and harmonica players – gave it its power. The blues was a music ripe for exploitation, and that began immediately. Before most of the world ever heard the likes of Blind Lemon Jefferson, they had heard Bessie Smith.

'St Louis Blues' is probably the most famous blues ever. But it is not what it seems. The song isn't the work of a poor share-cropper, let alone the product of an oral tradition, though it certainly draws on an oral tradition. It was written by W.C. Handy, a formally trained composer and bandsman, who had heard the blues, liked it and noted its potential. Bessie Smith's famous 1925 recording with Louis Armstrong on cornet was so successful that a two-reel film was shot, providing a story to set up the song. To modern eyes, of course, it looks like an extended video clip. It is a magnificent performance – there is no doubt about it – and the song isn't bad either, but it definitely isn't busking. Bessie Smith might have started out as a street singer, but by 1925 she was a professional vaudevillian. In this recording, then, the blues has already stopped being folk music. It is commercial.

Partly because of the success of 'St Louis Blues' and other Bessie Smith records, some fans now became interested in the folk tradition itself, and so folklorists, musicologists and record producers began making field recordings in the southern United States. You might say the rural blues provided a kind of template for most twentieth-century pop – for jazz, for r&b, for soul and for rock 'n' roll. The blues is international now, packaged to appeal – and sell – to an international audience; but from time to time it becomes fashionable again, and regretting the passing of the great blues originals is always part of the fashion.

So this is how commercial music works. First there is the search for something authentic. Once found, the music is harnessed, then packaged. If it is successful – I mean in commercial terms – the act is quickly cloned, with increasingly less success. This pattern has been repeated over and over. And of course eventually the clones kill the original model. It doesn't matter whether it is 1950s rock 'n' rollers or 1960s pop groups from Liverpool or willowy girl singer/songwriters with acoustic guitars and long, straight hair or glamrock bands covered in glitter or despairing grunge acts from Seattle: eventually there are so many of them, the standards ever dropping, that one ceases to care. Next fashion, please.

Thanks to recordings and radio and television, commercial music of one sort or another has dominated the last hundred years. As musical fashions have changed, so have the means of delivery: 100 years from the wax cylinder to the iPod is an astonishing rate of change. In the process, fashions for new technology have jeopard-ised the future of certain sorts of music, and classical music is a case in point. But technological advance has by no means always been the enemy of classical music. In the middle of the twentieth century, radio introduced the classics to a very broad cross-section of the pop-ulation. It was largely a matter of fashion. Before, during and after World War II, radio dominated people's lives. Families would sit together and listen to the radio – there was usually only one per house – and classical music was a significant part of the programming. Not just orchestral concerts and recitals, but also musical education came over the airwaves.

This was the era of the popular classic. It sounds a bit like an oxymoron today, but there were a lot of pieces of music – symphonies, concertos, sonatas, arias and even complete operas – that had this status. Their popularity was widespread, and by and large well-earned. The first piano concerto of Tchaikovsky and the second concerto of Rakhmaninov, the Mendelssohn and Bruch violin concertos, Beethoven's *Moonlight* sonata, Sibelius's *Valse triste* and *The Swan of Tuonela*: these are all not only good pieces but, in their individual ways, very striking. And they are still popular today. Unlike fashion, which by definition must end, popularity often lasts. But those pieces aren't *as* popular as they once were, and that is a matter of passing fashion – the fashion for listening to radio. In the 1930s, 40s and early 50s, popular classics existed alongside the pop music of the day – the dance bands and the crooners. And they went on co-existing until the invention of rock 'n' roll and the portable transistor radio, at which point teenagers disappeared into their own musical subculture, their dollars increasingly influencing the priorities of radio stations and record companies.

While for many classical music enthusiasts the recording is always flawed and secondary to the experience of the concert hall, it has occasionally been of great importance for a particular composer or even a particular piece. There are instances of recordings that actually changed classical music. If, today, the concept of 'popular classics' can seem a little quaint, it nevertheless suits *The Four Seasons*, and that is largely thanks to recordings.

The composer Antonio Vivaldi died in Vienna in 1741. During his lifetime, he had been successful, popular, even at times fashionable, but his luck ran out and he ended his days in poverty. Vivaldi's *music* remained out of luck for the next 200 years, but then something extraordinary occurred. The first recording of *The Four Seasons* was made in Italy during World War II. At the time, it was virtually unknown and even Vivaldi's name would have been familiar only to musicologists. His music simply wasn't played. A second recording of the *Seasons* followed in America in the late 1940s, but still the piece was just a recherché curiosity. Then in 1955, an Italian chamber orchestra called I Musici made its first record, playing *The Four Seasons*, and the piece caught on. It became so fashionable, so quickly, that four years later I Musici were forced to re-record the work in the newly available stereo. Today, as everyone knows, you can hardly get in an elevator or be kept on telephone hold without running across the piece. The word 'ubiquitous' might have been coined for it. The last time I looked there were 120 different recordings of *The Four Seasons*. That's not bad for a piece of 300-year-old music which sixty years ago no one had heard of.

I have never known anyone to argue that *The Four Seasons* is a bad piece. Surely popular taste has it right again. But I do feel I could live very happily without hearing it for the next ten years. With music, familiarity can breed if not contempt, then certainly something like dulled responses. But as I write those words there is a little voice nagging away at the back of my mind. It is the French philosopher, Pierre Bourdieu.

Bourdieu argued that there is something called 'cultural capital'. Put simply, it's a kind of intellectual advantage – the advantage, for instance, that an educated person has over an uneducated person. It doesn't have to be a real advantage, but it has to be perceivable. One form of this is when you know about something that very few other people know about. And it might be an enthusiasm for a piece of music, well outside the mainstream, that you share with a few other like-minded enthusiasts. It's a bit snobby, but it's harmless enough, and we've probably all done it. We've put some music on for our friends and said, 'I bet you can't guess what this is'.

This is how fashions usually start – as a minority enthusiasm. And often it is that very exclusivity that appeals to others. The trouble is that it doesn't remain exclusive. Word spreads about this obscure baroque piece called *The Four Seasons*, by this obscure baroque composer called Vivaldi. After a few years the whole world owns a recording. Now this is good, isn't it? It's good to share your enthusiasms. But what about your cultural capital? It's gone.

*

Since the bottom fell out of the big end of the classical recording business, smaller labels have taken up the slack. But there is not much point in their re-recording *The Four Seasons*. The world doesn't need that 121st version. Instead, the independent record companies rummage around in the murkier corners of the repertoire, digging out music that might well fit the bill of cultural capital, and then they sit back and hope that the world will find it suddenly can't do without this rediscovered opera or sonata.

But there's a danger in becoming fashionable, for what is fashionable today will be unfashionable tomorrow. At the very least you need a contingency plan, as a cautionary tale from Poland makes very clear.

The first performance of Henryk Górecki's third symphony took place in 1977. There was a recording made shortly after, and then a bit later there was a second recording. At the time no one took much notice, but the piece slowly built what we might call a cult following. I remember being told about it by a painter friend. He was bowled over by this hour-long symphony that he had heard on the radio. And the reason I remember the conversation so well is because I couldn't believe that I didn't know the piece. I expect my friend felt *his* cultural capital was pretty well stocked. Up until 1992, anyone who knew Górecki's third symphony might have felt the same.

But that year there came another recording, and for some reason it caught on. Fifteen years after the symphony was composed, this third recording sold more than a million copies. It was the first time a recording of music by a living classical composer had seven-figure sales. In the United Kingdom, the symphony even ended up in the pop charts, helped by a four-minute radio edit of a particularly poignant bit. Górecki's third was hugely fashionable. It was the CD you had to have.

Even if you don't know what happened next, you can probably guess. Nothing happened next. At least not from Górecki. As the world – and especially his publisher and his record label – held its breath in anticipation of Górecki's fourth or ... well ... anything of substance, the composer seems to have frozen. In the thirteen years following the success of that recording, Górecki produced hardly any new music – a few little pieces, something for violin and piano, a song or two. But that was it. Finally, in 2005, Górecki delivered to the Kronos Quartet, his third string quartet, which they had commissioned from him back in 1992. The composer insisted that it had been finished for a decade but that he hadn't wanted to part with it. He didn't know why.

I think I know. Listening to the recording of the third quartet is a terribly dispiriting experience. There is a hollow quality about it. The music seems to lack a soul. Surely this can't be from the same composer as the first two quartets or that third symphony! I'm guessing that the pressure of fashion finished Górecki off creatively. The premiere of the fourth symphony was finally announced for April 2010, to be given by the London Philharmonic Orchestra. But the score never arrived, the composer's ill health given as the reason, and by the end of the year he was dead.

I'm told that from the royalties of his third symphony, Górecki bought himself a very nice car. I certainly hope that's true.

Stardust Memories

Everyone has moments in life when they feel suddenly old. One day, without warning, you will be passing a couple of police officers in the street and it will occur to you they are really just children. And it is a commonplace that all men have the experience, sooner or later, of peering into a shaving mirror and seeing their fathers peering back. According to the poet Don Paterson, there is also the quintessential moment of reckoning for most men, 'so much more terrible we rarely speak of it', when you spot yourself naked in a full-length mirror and recognise your mother.

It has not quite come to that yet, but the other day I had a similar moment of reckoning, and it was when I noticed a compilation of early rock 'n' roll tunes – on a *nostalgia* label. They included the voice that in 1955 struck something close to terror into the hearts of respectable, middle-aged middle America. This was Elvis Presley, and, together with the Commies, he represented a twin threat to normal civilised life.

I'm not quite old enough to remember this Elvis – by the time I was paying attention he was already singing ballads – but I do remember the early Rolling Stones records, and the apparently burning question: Would you let your daughter marry a Rolling Stone? At the time I didn't have a daughter – I was six – so the question was academic, but I understood the point well enough: this music, and the musicians who made it, were dark and dangerous and very possibly in league with the Devil. So to find early rock music – real rock music, rock 'n' roll – classed as nostalgia is ... Well, it's like one of those moments in front of the mirror.

Nostalgia is always renewing itself, and yet the tendency to look back fondly has been around a long time. So how does a fashion for nostalgia take root? Why do we need the 'good old days'?

There is more than one sort of nostalgia. There is, for instance, personal nostalgia. This is when you get a whiff of a certain type of industrial floor polish and are instantly transported back to your primary school, or when you hear a song on the radio and it reminds you of a particular summer holiday or an early girlfriend. I don't think there's anything terribly mysterious about this sort of nostalgia.

But there is also what we might call societal nostalgia. This is far less specific and much more interesting. It is a general longing for the

past, real or imagined by a generation, say, or by the entire population of a country. In fact, I would argue that with this sort of nostalgia, some aspects of it must always be imagined. And idealised.

In some respects, the Renaissance was an exercise in long-range
nostalgia, all those artists in fifteenth-century Florence looking to
Ancient Greece for models of form and balance and civilisation and
humanity. But what did Raphael and Michelangelo and Piero della
Francesca really know of Athens in the sixth century BC? Learning
Greek was itself rather fashionable among the Florentine intelligentsia, so some artists were able to read Plato in the original, but what
seems to have inspired the early flowering of Renaissance art is something like a yearning for an ideal world that had existed 2000 years
earlier, a world that apparently prized human dignity. Well, Plato
might have prized it, but you do not have to read much of him to
understand that the world that *produced* Plato had a different view
and was far from ideal.

Just over a century after the dawning of the European Renaissance, we find another, very different, example of nostalgia. In early
Jacobean England, the cult of Good Queen Bess was flourishing.
Elizabeth I had only been dead a few years – and in truth the cult
had really begun when she was still alive – but men and women in
the early seventeenth century looked back on her reign as a Golden
Age. What was odd about this was the fact that Elizabeth had pre-
sided over something quite close to a police state, and there were
plenty of people still alive who ought to have remembered this.
Nostalgia nearly always requires selective memory.

In our own time there has been a common tendency to look back
on the 1960s as a sort of halcyon paradise of optimism, peace and
love. Like the Jacobeans' elevation of Elizabethan England, this
began no sooner than the 1960s were over; and it was equally selective. To view this decade in a roseate glow, you have to forget the fact
that the Cuban missile crisis came close to blowing the world to
bits; you have to forget the Vietnam war, and the assassinations of

some of the more prominent advocates of freedom: John and Robert Kennedy, Malcolm X and Martin Luther King Jr. You should also forget the mad Orwellian double speak of China's Cultural Revolution, the continuing suppression of basic freedoms in Soviet Russia, the USSR's invasion of Czechoslovakia, and the widespread ugliness of entrenched racism, not just in South Africa and Rhodesia and the southern United States, where innocent blacks were routinely lynched, but also in Harold Wilson's Britain and Robert Menzies' Australia, the latter which was only slowly dismantling its White Australia policy.

It is also worth remembering that the 1960s themselves were steeped in nostalgia. I am looking now at the cover of the Beatles' 1967 album, *Sgt Pepper's Lonely Hearts Club Band*. John Lennon wears little round spectacles such as his own grandfather might have worn – suddenly, these were fashionable; all four Beatles are sporting droopy moustaches that mirror those of quite a few of the historical figures featured in the collage behind them; and the fab four are wearing the military uniforms of some imaginary imperial army band, complete with braid, epaulettes and, in Ringo's case, a sergeant's stripes. One tends to forget that, along with everything else, the 1960s delighted in retro fashion.

I don't think we had the word 'retro' in the 1960s – not in the sense we have it today – and I am sure the denizens of Swinging London wouldn't have thought they were being nostalgic. Far from it. But it was in the 1960s that what we call retro fashions took hold. Antique shops were springing up everywhere, trying to satisfy the demand for Victorian thimbles and buttons and belt buckles and chamber pots. Laura Ashley had been sitting at her kitchen table cutting out those heritage pattern dresses since the 1950s, but it was in the 60s that they really caught on. So did real heritage dresses. By the late 1960s, tiring of miniskirts, girls were raiding op shops for their mothers' and grandmothers' cast-offs; their boyfriends, when they weren't sporting ruffles on the front and cuffs of their shirts, were cutting the collars off altogether so that – yet again – they would look more like their grandfathers; in an age of sexual revolution and unheard-of permissiveness, the trappings of chivalry returned. Young men referred to their girlfriends as their 'ladies', while treating them – and we tend to forget this – ever more like chattels. Harpsichords appeared in pop songs, as did string quartets and flutes. Strangest of all, perhaps, self-styled progressive rock bands sang songs about kings and queens and jesters, wizards and witches.

The 1960s was such a time of social and political flux that you cannot help wondering whether the fashion for nostalgia was in some way a reaction against the clamour for change. Oddly, in many cases it was the people who were lobbying hardest for social progress – hippies, students, the radical intelligentsia – who were most attracted to the retro fashions and other outward and visible signs of nostalgia.

And now, as we all know, the 1960s, that era of revolutionary ideals and a conviction that the times were indeed a-changing, is itself the subject of waves of nostalgia among baby boomers. So much so, at the beginning of the twenty-first century, that many right-wing commentators and politicians felt obliged, more than thirty years after the event, to take up cudgels against the decade for both its politics and permissiveness.

Regarding permissiveness: well, I suppose the 1960s were more permissive than the 1860s, but only in terms of what people admitted to. The Victorians had a healthy enough appetite for sex *and* drugs. You might say the 1960s were simply less hypocritical. But what, after all, did the decade achieve politically? As the 1970s dawned, Nixon was in the White House, Britain voted out its Labour government, Australia was entering its twenty-first successive year of conservative rule, South Africa still had apartheid, the Vietnam war was still being fought, and most of the student protesters had gone back to their studies (though not before a few of them had been shot dead). The 1960s was a time of left-wing ideals, not achievement.

Well, we still have the music. But when we listen today to those one-hit wonders, Thunderclap Newman singing 'Something in the Air', I suspect we feel more warm and fuzzy than wild and fanatical. That is certainly a hallmark of nostalgia, musical or otherwise: no matter how bad the times we are remembering, it somehow makes us feel good to remember them.

Take jazz. In one form or another, jazz has been around now for a hundred years. From time to time, it has been quite fashionable – though in different ways. Originally, New Orleans jazz was fashionable in New Orleans. In the 1920s, it spread to New York and Chicago and, via recordings, to other parts of the world. It was never exactly the pop music of the day. Not, at least, until it was transformed into big band swing in the 1930s and 40s. You do find people who maintain that swing bands had nothing to do with proper jazz, but if Benny Goodman wasn't jazz, I don't know what he was. This was fashionable; this was popular.

The next major jazz development was fashionable without being popular. Bebop left a lot of people behind – the people who wanted to dance to tunes they knew. Bebop was for listening to, ideally in dark glasses and a beret, and with a friend called Daddio. Now I don't mean to disparage bebop – it is perhaps my favourite style of jazz – but its fashionability, as so often is the case, had less to do with the music itself than with the smoky ambience of hepness and pretension that clung to it.

I wonder if something similar is going on among the fans of Diana Krall and Norah Jones, Kurt Elling and Michael Bublé. These four performers are actually very different from each other, but so far as their popular images are concerned they represent something cool and sophisticated. Because despite its humble beginnings, jazz is now firmly associated with glamour. Whether or not we like jazz itself, most of us like the *idea* of jazz. It is partly about a craving for sophistication, partly about wanting to feel grown up, partly about not wanting to confront the present – including the music of the present – and partly to do with the belief that the old songs are the best songs.

None of this is actually new. Not even in jazz. When Frank Sinatra began to acquire real superstardom in the early 1950s after he signed with Capitol records, he did it simultaneously with the birth pangs of that scary rock 'n' roll, and he did it singing old songs. We forget this, but of the tracks on those great Capitol recordings – *Swing Easy!, Songs for Young Lovers, In the Wee Small Hours* – most were songs by the likes of George Gershwin and Cole Porter and already more than twenty years old. This was quite deliberate.

Even Sinatra's new songs were often modelled on old songs. 'Young at Heart', one of his biggest hits, was composed by Johnny Richards, but based on a tune called 'Moonbeam' that Richards had written back in the 1930s. And what are the lyrics of 'Young at Heart' about, if not a wistful longing for lost youth? It's nostalgia. So the next time you're sitting in that retro café enjoying Sinatra's inimitable version of 'A Foggy Day (In London Town)' or 'They Can't Take That Away from Me' or 'I Get a Kick Out of You', it's worth asking if perhaps the sophisticated inner glow you are experiencing is actually nostalgia for nostalgia.

There is another side to the niche fashion for jazz nostalgia, and it has nothing to do with wanting to feel sophisticated, but with the desire for authenticity. In 2000, when Ken Burns made his nineteen-hour film documentary about jazz, he went to great lengths to show the seamy side of growing up poor and black in the southern United States, with jazz as your only escape. But the glorious soundtrack, the black-and-white photography and Keith David's narration – sultry and distinguished – all conspired to make it seem oddly glamorous, even the slums. I do not think this was Burns's fault and certainly not his intention, but it is a distortion the home of jazz is happy to go along with. Visit New Orleans as a tourist today and you will probably find yourself at Preservation Hall. Inside, it has the appearance of a small barn, old and dimly lit, and there is dirt on the floor – at least, that's how I remember it. The Preservation Hall Jazz Band comes on and plays the traditional jazz of the early twentieth century. Some of the players look old enough to have known Buddy Bolden. What could be more authentic? Well as it turns out, almost anything. The building itself is genuinely old – built in the early 1800s – but the idea of Preservation Hall dates from the 1960s. Far from preserving something, the place is a re-creation, selling the idea of authenticity to tourists.

We like to feel that things are authentic. Perhaps it's something to do with living at a time when public life seems to be a series of lies and half-truths from largely characterless men and women. We feel we need more; we look for something better. We move to the country and take up slow cooking. I am not criticising these actions – in the last decade I've done them both – but I do think the search for something like reality in an increasingly artificial world can lead to self-delusion.

And so to the fashion for 'world music', where nostalgia certainly plays its part. As far as the term itself is concerned, it is the product of a marketing department. Things need labels, but this is quite a canny label. At its most romantic, and probably its most meaningless, it is about the interconnectedness of all things. I don't know why people find this an attractive idea – it seems a bit scary to me – but it is a fashionable notion and the label 'world music' confirms it. Apparently it doesn't matter if you come from Senegal or Saskatchewan, Gothenburg or Johannesburg, whether you play the oud or the ukelele or the autoharp. The important point is everyone is doing the same thing. Well, perhaps. But I am not sure where that gets us. Unless it is back to the fashion for authenticity.

The very term 'world music' primes us to hear something that is in some way authentic. Now some of it obviously is; most of it obviously isn't – it is a commercial confection of more or less authentic sounds. But why do we want this so badly? I think it is another branch of nostalgia. Authentic music is made for its own sake – or for tradition's sake, which is possibly the same thing. Most of what ends up in the 'world music' section of the CD store or on iTunes is made for profit. There is nothing wrong with that, of course, unless you are claiming a purer motive. We want to believe things are pure, that they are not sullied by commerce, and that – in a way – is nostalgic. It's nostalgia for simpler times when people just sat around in huts and made up tunes. Did these times ever really exist? Who knows? But the closer we feel to them, the more closely in touch we feel with some sort of primal musical instinct, perhaps with the creative act itself. We feel we're there.

It's this wanting to be *there* that I think is behind performances of baroque music on historically appropriate instruments, which in the 1970s and 80s was a particularly virulent fashion. There were two sides to it. As well as the use of period instruments, there was baroque music itself. It is worth asking why music that is somewhere between 250 and 400 years old should have appealed so strongly to twentieth-century audiences and still appeal today. Was it the sleekness of the music? Was it the unchanging pulse? Was it indeed the fact of its age – was it better because it was older? Did it, as the music critic Anna Picard suggested, satisfy a desire for time travelling? If Picard was right, it certainly explained the original-instrument craze. Now we could convince ourselves that we were hearing just what Bach heard.

In the late twentieth century, period-instrument groups were also beginning to stake their claims in the core classical repertoire of Haydn, Mozart and Beethoven. Audiences and players alike felt they were coming closer to an authentic musical experience by hearing the music played on wooden flutes, violins strung with cat gut and trumpets without valves. Much of it was exhilarating, but all of it was speculation. And for every performance where the cleaner instrumental sound revealed something previously hidden, there was another where posturing obliterated the musical content, where style cancelled out substance.

In the United Kingdom, there is a commercial radio station called Classic FM which sells the idea of classical music as a cross between a fashion accessory and a form of auditory prozac. Classical music is nice; classical music won't put you to any trouble. On the contrary, it will take away the stress and make you feel better. Classical music marketers – orchestras and record companies, radio stations and magazines – increasingly want us to believe that this music might be the soundtrack of our lives. The fashionable soundtrack, what's more.

During the first part of 2005, British market researchers set out to discover who was listening to classical music and when. The research was being undertaken by a government-supported savings and investment organisation, financial backers of the Classical BRIT Awards, which were also backed by the commercial station Classic FM. So obviously they were all hoping that the survey would show that lots of people listened to classical music. And what do you know? That is what they found. Old people, young people, Scottish people, dentists, taxi drivers: they were listening in huge numbers.

In the 16 to 24 age range, 17 per cent of those polled said they listened to classical music while studying or reading. In the 25 to 34 bracket, 15 per cent were taking a bath. Twenty-nine per cent of 35 to 44-year-olds drove their cars while listening to classical music and so did 43 per cent of 55 to 64-year-olds, while 26 per cent of 45 to 54-year-olds did the cleaning. And the over-65s? Well, 30 per cent of them cooked while they listened, and I dare say there were never any lumps in the gravy. You notice that in this survey you can't just be listening, you must always be doing something that classical music can help you do better.

My favourite finding among all this market research is the fact that 26 per cent of men prefer to drive while listening to classical music, and not just any old classical music but 'the dulcet tones of Beethoven'. That's a quote from the press release. 'The dulcet tones of Beethoven'. Like the *Hammerklavier* sonata? The *Grosse Fuge*? The

fifth symphony? The clamour and chaos that starts the last movement of the ninth symphony?

Don't let anyone try to tell you classical music is nice. It is not.
If you fall for this marketing line, you will be endlessly disappointed, not to say affronted, by all manner of rude, violent, terrifying sounds that are just as much a part of what we call classical
music as the slow movement of Mozart's clarinet concerto. But
marketers are everywhere, and they are very powerful. It is the job of
a successful marketer to sniff out fashions before they become fashionable. If they can't succeed at this, the next best thing is to attempt
to convince us they've succeeded with a little discreet re-branding.
Black is the new white, white is the new black, classical music is the
new recreational drug of choice. This is almost the opposite of what
Beethoven was telling us in the finale of his ninth symphony, though
that piece has been sold as many things in the nearly two centuries
of its existence.

Beethoven's setting of the poet Friedrich Schiller's 'Ode to Joy' –
his plea for brotherly love – has been a pop song at least twice, it has
been used to sell cars, and in Anthony Burgess's novel and Stanley
Kubrick's film *A Clockwork Orange* it inspired the anti-hero Alex to
'ultraviolence'. But it was also sung and played in some of the Nazi
death camps; it was made into the national anthem of Rhodesia;
now it is the anthem of the European Union. I think any great work
of art is capable of many interpretations, but these unconsciously
ironic uses seem more like distortions.

In the case of Beethoven's ninth, once you separate the choral
finale from the three movements of perhaps rather greater music that
precede it, you are already on the way to distorting the piece. Without the first forty minutes of purely orchestral music to balance it,
Beethoven's finale can sound – or be made to sound – self-important
and gloating. Just the thing for Nazis. And consider the words: those
brothers that Schiller writes about, maybe they're Aryan brothers,
maybe they're white Rhodesians, maybe Schiller was thinking of a

band of Brussels bureaucrats. It's simple enough to re-imagine the piece to fit your needs. You ignore the bulk of the content, ignore the inconvenient associations, and concentrate instead on selling your own message based on a partial interpretation of the surface of the music. It is another example of re-branding. Well, after all, government is as transitory as fashion.

So in the end, is this how fashion works? Fashion is all about the surface of things. The shortness of a skirt, the length of a haircut, the tightness of a pair of jeans, the new black, the new white. Beneath the surface of a piece of music there may be nothing at all or great profundity, but since fashion only looks at the surface, it will never be the actual content of a piece of music that makes it fashionable. Great music can be fashionable and fashionable music can be great, but ultimately these concepts are unrelated.

I know people who will not listen to classical music because they think it would make them seem boring. In fact it is their refusal to listen that makes them boring. I know people who think jazz is just so 'yesterday'. There are those who believe traditional folk music is totally uncool. Well it is, actually, which is why it is worth investigating. And there are certainly people who will tell you all commercial music is bad. The truth is that the world is full of bad music. There is far more bad music than great music. But there is no such thing as a bad *type* of music. That is just fashion talking.

In the end, when music and fashion collide, my advice is this: Never believe the fashion. Always believe the music.

Adapted from the six-part series, *Music and Fashion*, originally broadcast on ABC Radio National between 17 July and 21 August 2005.

Modernism Down the Years

To hear some people talk, you would think that modernist music was a twentieth-century invention. But there were modernists in music, as in all the other arts, from at least the twelfth century. It is just that during the last hundred years modernism became an article of faith and, briefly, an orthodoxy.

Modernism is about making art anew, and not just in the obvious sense of being original (there is no point in being an artist at all if you have nothing original to say or, at least, a new slant on something familiar). Modernism is also about saying it in an original way, about finding a new grammar, a new syntax, a new vocabulary. It is about wiping at least part of the slate clean and starting again, and there will always be artists who want to do that.

In the history of Western music, composers of a modernist bent have loomed largest, simply because they have pointed music in a new direction and others have followed. That is not to suggest that those of a more conservative mien have failed to leave their mark. Some of the greatest music ever written has been by conservative composers or composers going through a conservative patch – for example, Bach, Brahms, Elgar, Fauré and the later Richard Strauss – to name only a handful whose music I listen to quite a lot. These composers did not really change anything. Bach might have written the best fugues in history, but he didn't invent the form; and fugue writing was actually considered an old-fashioned occupation by the second half of his career. As for equal-temperament tuning, which Bach also didn't invent but endorsed with the forty-eight preludes and fugues of his *Well-Tempered Clavier*: there have been people ever since who have believed this development only held music back.

To be a proper modernist, like Pérotin and Machaut, Monteverdi and Beethoven, Berlioz and Wagner, Debussy and Stravinsky and Webern, you have to alter the consistency of music. You also have to do it deliberately, although you do not necessarily have to understand the significance of what you're doing. Anton Webern, for example, doubtless believed that it was the serial organisation of pitches that gave his work its importance, and that is what a lot of other composers believed in the years after World War II. In fact, the fragmentation of melodic lines and bold use of instrumental colour turned out to be considerably more influential than the rather primitive maths that lay behind Webern's tone rows. Webern, indeed, was no mathematician. As his first biographer Friedrich Wildgans pointed out, maths was one of the schoolboy Anton's least favourite subjects.

Mathematics, though, has frequently been the modernist composer's inspiration. Many of the very striking compositions of Guillaume de Machaut, and other fourteenth- and fifteenth-century composers such as Dunstable and Dufay, used mathematical procedures to assist in the organisation of the pitches and durations of notes. As with serial composers in the middle of the twentieth century, musicians in the Middle Ages used simple maths – or at any rate, numerical calculation – to put some distance between their egos and their music. When, for example, Machaut composed his three-voice *rondeau*, 'Ma fin est mon commencement' ('My End Is My Beginning'), he arranged the pitches in such a way that the two upper voices have exactly the same melodic lines, laid on top of each other, but back to front. Voice One ends where Voice Two began and vice versa (hence the title, obviously). The lowest voice has an independent part, but it is a palindrome, so it also ends where it started. This produces a piece of music dazzling in its cleverness and possessed of a most satisfying sense of internal balance. But unless you know what to listen out for, you can't actually hear these qualities. What Boethius called 'arithmetic impartiality' distances the composer from musical wilfulness and helps his composition towards a sort of divine accountability. But that's really just on paper.

A similar desire motivated Dufay to construct his great isorhythmic motet, *Nuper rosarum flores,* in 1436. Scholars have yet to agree on whether the work's elaborate proportions reflect those of Brunelleschi's recently completed Florence Cathedral, the dedication of which Dufay's motet celebrated, or the measurements for Solomon's temple as given in the Old Testament – or indeed both, Brunelleschi himself having derived his numbers from those biblical dimensions. It scarcely matters. What is so striking in this music, as the Gothic Age shows some early signs of turning into the Renaissance, is that the music sounds (and, yes, this time you can *hear* it) both substantial and weightless. Like Brunelleschi's dome, it is solid and yet somehow seems to float.

Post-World War II serialists were mostly not very interested in divinity, but drawing on Webern's example they aimed in their music for a kind of objective justification that equated with the wishes of composers half a millennium before. And yet in the case of Olivier Messiaen, a generation older than the others, it was a precise and devout faith that led him to base some of his music on numbers. Religious and artistic conviction blur in the work of this composer. For Messiaen, giving up on spiky modernism for the calmer and more obviously 'spiritual' waters of an Arvo Pärt would have been like abandoning the Catholic Church for a dolphin poster and a copy of *I'm OK–You're OK.*

For Messiaen's young pupils, such as Pierre Boulez, Karlheinz Stockhausen and Iannis Xenakis, and for others of their generation who frequented the new music summer courses at Darmstadt in Germany – among them, Luigi Nono and Bruno Maderna – maths (of one sort or another) offered a way of dealing with certain intractable problems associated with creativity. For example, sentimentality

– something from which Messiaen never quite struggled free – is completely absent from the work of these younger composers; so, in any obvious and audible sense, are tunes, at least until the 1970s. Maths kept all that at bay, as the rigorous organisation of every musical parameter (so-called 'integral serialism') ensured a brave new world of musical relativity.

But, as I've suggested, it wasn't the maths *per se* that made this music modern or difficult or, let's face it, unpopular; plenty of non-modernist composers, Bach among them, had used maths. No, it was the fragmentation of the melodic line to the point at which no melody could be discerned, and it was the rhythmic dislocation that meant you couldn't hear or even feel the beat. This is the period that gives modernism its reputation as a twentieth-century phenomenon, because it is the period at which modernism was at its most extreme, the very nature of music being called into question. In 1952, the year that Boulez composed his most highly systematised piece, his only piece of integral serialism – the first part of the first book of *Structures* for two pianos – his American colleague, John Cage, moved as far as it was possible to go in the opposite direction, composing four minutes and thirty-three seconds of 'silence', the inverted commas around the word in deference to Cage's perfectly reasonable assertion that genuine silence is impossible, particularly in a concert hall full of people.

Nearly all of the most radical modernist experiments in music occurred during the ten years from 1949, even if it was the following decade that felt the ramifications of such an extreme attitude, the tentacles of modernism finally reaching into music's officialdom. This was the moment at which modernist music became orthodox, one might even say institutionalised, and there is a particularly strong element of paradox here. For the best modernist composers – *being* modernist composers – were never likely to be happy as part of the status quo. Consciously or not, as pressure increased on more conservative musicians to conform to modernism's hallmarks (somewhere along the spectrum from Boulez's serialism to Cage's conceptualism), most of the original modernists were becoming considerably less hard-line. Hangers on, many of them inside universities and music schools, might have failed to notice, but modernism's big moment had been and gone. In 1973, when Maderna died, Boulez felt free to compose a heartfelt orchestral work to his memory. *Rituel* is outwardly cool, but like Stravinsky's *Symphonies of Wind Instruments*, composed in memory of Debussy, it is deeply moving. Not only did Boulez draw on liturgical practice for the work's binary structure of 'versets and responses' (Messiaen must have been terribly proud!), he also included, and quite without irony, a musical quotation from Stravinsky's piece. If this was still modernism, it was with a very human – indeed a grieving – face.

Besides mathematics, the source of renewal most frequently explored by composers throughout history has been popular music. Again, the tendency can be found in the late Middle Ages and in the Renaissance, when composers included popular songs in their liturgical works, particularly in so-called 'parody' Masses such as Dufay's Mass on the song 'Se la face ay pale' and Morales's *Missa Mille regretz*, or the fifty-odd parody Masses composed by Palestrina until the Council of Trent told him to stop it.

The rationale for basing liturgical music on secular songs (which is what the Council objected to) had been as much theological as musical. There is generally a subtextual significance in the choice of song, as often as not love songs like 'Se la face ay pale' providing a veiled allusion to the Virgin Mary, whose cult persisted into the Renaissance. But later composers imported vernacular music to alter the sound and even the nature of their works. Haydn's gypsy rondos, Mozart's Turkish percussion, Schubert's Hungarian dances; 'folk' melodies in Liszt, military bands in Mahler, Indonesian gamelan in Debussy, early jazz in Ravel: these are all examples of composers pushing at the boundaries of musical style by drawing in 'exotic' influences. With Stravinsky and Bartók, push came to shove. Earlier composers had used the melodies of folksong, but Stravinsky and Bartók liked the noise it made. Between the two of them, they roughed up classical music until it allowed folkloric rhythms, gestures, vocal styles and occasionally even instruments into the concert hall. The source music might have been ancient, but it contributed greatly to the cause of modernism. It revitalised classical music.

It could be that the most significant figure of the second half of the twentieth century turns out to have been György Ligeti, who successfully and with great naturalness drew inspiration from both abstract calculation and vernacular musics. Born in 1925, Ligeti had three bites at the modernist cherry. First, in his native Hungary during the 1950s, he fell under the spell of Bartók. By this point, Bartók's music was scarcely at the cutting edge. The composer had died in exile in 1945, and his later works, such as the Concerto for Orchestra, had fully synthesised the earlier folk influence. But if Ligeti's initial interest in modernism came via aping the later, tamer style of his hero, in the 1960s he invented an entirely new musical style.

I choose my words carefully here: there really was no precursor of what became known as 'micropolyphony'. By now himself in exile, Ligeti began to create massive orchestral scores. The pieces were quite short, but typically every instrument in the orchestra had its own individual part. In such a work, all the violins might have lines that resemble each other but are not exactly the same. When they all play together, then, the individual details become lost in a gorgeous smudge of sound. There are several works in this much imitated style, with *Lontano* (1967) being perhaps the greatest and most beautiful. And it is significant that words such as 'gorgeous' and 'beautiful' can be used without fear of contradiction. There may be modernist calculation behind the composer's choices, but there is abundant sensuality in the end result.

To have composed such music would automatically qualify Ligeti for a significant place in the pantheon, but in the early 1980s he invented another new style. Once again the music was boldly original, although this time it was possible at least to spot some of the influences. In no particular order, these were Ligeti's reading of the literature on chaos theory, the music of sub-Saharan Africa, and the wildly intricate and jazzy player-piano studies of Conlon Nancarrow, an American long-based in Mexico City. In Ligeti's Piano Concerto (1985–88) and in the solo-piano *Études* that came before and after it, the composer created what in 1952 had been unthinkable. This music was certainly new. And it was complex, rhythmically as complex as anything in Boulez's *Structures*. But it was also full of familiar things: motor rhythms piled on top of each other, tunes and fragments of tunes, simple melodic cells that resembled bits of folksongs but that proliferated like fractals.

So is Ligeti's Piano Concerto modernist? In the broadest sense, yes. Ligeti is a modernist in the same way that Machaut and Monteverdi, Beethoven and Stravinsky were modernists: like those composers, he is an instinctive innovator, imagining types of music that nobody had previously imagined. This is really the only modernism that has ever mattered, and it is the sort of modernism that will never go away. In the context of the hard-line, dogmatic modernism of the 1950s avant-garde, of course, Ligeti's concerto doesn't fit at all. For one thing, and despite its complexity, it has become rather popular. In contrast, the post-war avant-garde had no hits. But then why would a work from the mid 1980s fit a 1950s definition of modernism? That decade of serial austerity was modernism's classical period, and Ligeti served his apprenticeship there (he even wrote a painstaking analysis of Boulez's *Structures 1a*). I think one might argue that this apprenticeship made possible his late pieces. But an artist that can find equal inspiration in fractals and pygmy music (not to mention the work of Lewis Carroll) is by nature no hardliner. Anyway, by the end of the twentieth century, the hardliners were elsewhere.

It is easy enough to see why modernism is generally considered to have been a phenomenon of the last hundred years. It was the twentieth century's shibboleth, part of its obsession with progress;

and if you weren't for it, you were against it. But the trouble with simple-minded dogmatism of this sort is its tendency to turn art into politics, and to make those not aligned with the new orthodoxy think of themselves (in just as simple-minded a fashion) as cultural freedom fighters.

For a short time, from the late 1950s until the mid 1970s, modernist orthodoxy belatedly took a grip of most of the Western world's musical institutions from publishing houses to university departments, and from public broadcasters to concert promoters. Composers who refused to toe the modernist line – and this usually meant adopting some sort of twelve-tone system – were often marginalised. Many composers found themselves writing serial music against their better judgement, modernists in spite of themselves. Paradoxically, these figures inflicted the greatest damage on the institutions they sought to appease and on modernism itself. Their hearts not really in it, they dutifully worked on their pitch charts and matrices and between them came up with thousands of very bad, if very correct, pieces. Audiences, who are often rather quick at spotting fakes, felt insulted. Their response was to give up on all new music, rejecting the good with the bad, and we continue to live with some of that legacy.

It is possible to view modernism as the aesthetic equivalent of Marxism. It's by no means an exact analogy, but it holds water surprisingly well. The dogma, the party lines, the endless internecine squabbling, the ostracising of backsliders: it's all there if you think about it. (We'll overlook the fact that anyone caught writing a twelve-tone row in the Soviet Union would have been packed off to Siberia.) The analogy certainly extends to the triumphalism that greeted public recanting by former aparachiks. While events such as the premiere of John Adams's postmodernist opera, *Nixon in China*, can begin to seem like the toppling of the Berlin Wall.

Unfortunately the resemblance doesn't stop there. Where once, briefly, our concert life was ruled by the likeness of the Central

Committee of the Communist Party, these days the neoliberals are in charge, measuring art against opinion polls and the market. Let us hope their tenure is equally transitory.

Australian Financial Review, 2003

Beethoven, the Moderniser

'Beethoven confuses the tragic with the comic, the agreeable with the repulsive, heroism with howlings and the holiest with harlequinades.' Thus the nineteen-year-old Franz Schubert wrote in his diary, not altogether happily.

Ludwig van Beethoven was Schubert's hero. The young man adored his music and, in common with most other nineteenth-century composers, seems sometimes to have found the older composer's example overwhelming. But equally he was not alone in feeling confusion over the apparent contradictions in Beethoven's work. Because Schubert was right: Beethoven's music does oscillate between extremes of mood, style and emotion. And when Schubert made this diary entry in 1816, Beethoven's most extreme music still lay ahead of him. His final decade yielded such advanced masterpieces as the *Missa solemnis*, the ninth symphony, the two late sets of bagatelles and the *Diabelli* Variations, as well as the last five piano sonatas and the last five string quartets – works that left even Beethoven's publisher scratching his head.

Had he read Schubert's remarks, Beethoven would not have been surprised. He had heard all of it before. His old friend, the cellist Bernhard Romberg, had been so outraged by the first four bars of the *Scherzo* in the String Quartet Op 59, No 1 – a cello solo on one note – that he had flung his music to the floor and stamped on it. But Beethoven knew how to deal with whingers. When the violinist Felix Radicati went so far as to tell the composer that his Three String Quartets Op 59 were 'not music', he is said to have received the lofty retort, 'Oh, they are not for you, but for a later age.'

This, of course, is the modern artist's stock reply: I am ahead of my times and therefore misunderstood; one day everyone will appreciate me and then I shall be vindicated. One cannot imagine that sort of rationalisation from the lips of Bach or Haydn or even Mozart. In many ways, Beethoven was the first modern composer – he feels like our contemporary – and not just because of his aggressively independent stance as a freelance artist. Music and the public perception of music underwent some fundamental changes in his lifetime and, as the Beethoven scholar Lewis Lockwood makes plain, these changes were exemplified by the composer's own astonishing musical output.

Lockwood's book *Inside Beethoven's Quartets* focuses on just three of the composer's sixteen string quartets – and only on their first movements – but the author, in conversation with members of the Juilliard Quartet, successfully demonstrates how radical this music was and, by extension, how Beethoven changed not only the nature of what we listen to, but also the way in which we listen.

It might have happened anyway – arguably this composer was in the right place at the right time – but it was Beethoven who made music serious. This is not to suggest that earlier music was merely a form of light entertainment. Patently, Bach's two great Passions, Haydn's Masses and Mozart's Requiem were extremely serious. But those pieces were music at the service of religious faith; purely instrumental music – secular music – was only slowly emerging as something more than entertainment, and while the process might have begun with Haydn and Mozart, it was Beethoven who took things so much further and nowhere more so than in his string quartets.

Because of the example of Beethoven's late quartets – a veritable touchstone of musical seriousness – we tend to believe that the string quartet is the medium to which composers turn when they wish to vouchsafe their most personal musical ideas. But as Lockwood demonstrates, Beethoven himself sensed from the start that, for him at least, the quartet would be a genre of particular significance. His first quartets, the set of six which form his Op 18, were written surprisingly late. When he embarked on them, Beethoven was nearly thirty (Mozart, remember, had died at thirty-five) and he had already composed two piano concertos, two cello sonatas, three violin sonatas, four piano trios, five string trios and his first ten piano sonatas.

So why did he wait so long to write a string quartet? Lockwood thinks that it is for the same reason that he delayed writing a symphony. These were the two genres that Haydn had pioneered, and Lockwood finds it significant that in his quartet writing Beethoven tended to avoid certain keys favoured by Haydn and Mozart – there are, for example, no Beethoven quartets in D minor – as though to do so might invite comparison. Beethoven worked hard on Op 18 – there are nearly three hours of music under this single opus number – and Lockwood notes that at least two of the quartets, possibly all six, underwent thorough rewrites. The influence of both Haydn and Mozart can be readily discerned. Lockwood points out the Mozart models for both Op 18, No 5 and Op 18, No 6, but he goes on to stress that Beethoven 'is never more himself than when he is working directly against a Mozartian template, as he sketches the larger shapes of movements and develops musical ideas that reformulate contemporary approaches to the genre'.

Soon enough, Beethoven would be working against his own templates as he took the quartet far away from its classical origins, but his knowledge and appreciation of these older composers might itself be considered a factor in his turning into a modernist. It is no exaggeration to say that the early nineteenth century invented the idea of 'classical music' (the *Oxford English Dictionary* gives 1836 as the first recorded usage of the expression), and with this awareness of music's past and of an emerging canon of great works came the notion of musical progress, of composers pushing form, style and technique into new areas, all of which Beethoven did. Moreover, it is clear that for Beethoven this was a matter of ideology. As he explained to the Archduke Rudolf, he believed in 'freedom and progress' – musically as well as politically. The result was that Beethoven kept coming up with music the like of which had never been heard before.

Compared to Haydn and Mozart (or Bach and Handel), here was a new sort of composer. For one thing, he was an intellectual, a freethinker. We know, of course, of his political ideals from *Fidelio* – an opera about free speech – and from his setting of Schiller's 'Ode to Joy'. Lockwood finds him copying into his diary quotations not only from Homer and other ancient writers, but also from moderns such as Immanuel Kant. More surprisingly, there are translated passages from the *Bhagavad-Gita*. This is all a long way from Haydn, and even from the Mozart of *The Magic Flute*.

But this is also where Beethoven's deafness comes in. He first began to notice the symptoms as a young man in 1796 or 1797 and, as Lockwood notes, by 1801 it 'had precipitated a severe personal crisis'. We know this because of letters he wrote and also because of the so-called 'Heiligenstadt Testament', written late the following year, although only discovered – and only *meant* to be discovered – among the composer's papers after his death. Addressed to Beethoven's brothers, the testament is part will, part confession, part maudlin introspection, part venting of spleen, part self-pitying melodrama. Indeed, in its mood swings and changes of tone, it dimly resembles Schubert's description of Beethoven's music. However one reads the testament, it was undoubtedly the loss of the composer's hearing that brought it on, and it seems likely that this also led to his increasing absorption in books, his encroaching deafness inclining him ever more to introspection and contemplation.

Because Beethoven's affliction has become the stuff of legend there has been a tendency on the part of modern musicologists to gloss over it. In the quest to say something original about the composer and his music, biographical details are associated in some quarters with a want of academic rigour. But we cannot simply dismiss this information because it doesn't fit the latest critical theory. Hearing loss would change anyone's outlook on life, a composer's more than most. In Beethoven's case, it also damaged his reputation as a performer and so his earning capacity. In 1814, Louis Spohr attended a performance of Beethoven's *Archduke* trio, the composer at the piano, and recorded that all his *forte* playing was so violent that it made the instrument's strings rattle, and yet he played the quiet passages so delicately that half the notes didn't even sound. In other words, he could no longer hear what he was doing. Soon Beethoven was to all intents and purposes clinically deaf.

But as Lockwood points out, while throughout his life Beethoven railed at the world and his position in it, he seems always to have been able to focus on a new composition, and that is what he did now. Out of his deafness came a deep inner music, and indeed much of what we know about the composer's last compositions is on account of his deafness, because he was forced to communicate with friends and colleagues via 'conversation books', seventy of which survive from the composer's final decade. Naturally, these are one-sided – Beethoven was speaking his half of the conversation – but the written portions are revealing and one learns to read between the lines, gaining a picture of a stubborn man going his own way, and nowhere more so than in the late string quartets.

The Op 18 quartets had been presented as a set of six, but the late quartets, despite their individual opus numbers, seem truly unified, almost chapters from the same book. In the composer's sketches themes from different quartets rub shoulders and it is clear that Beethoven considered the late quartets to be one large project. Lockwood points out (he is not the first to do so) thematic links between the pieces, and this is nowhere more evident than in the opening themes of Op 131 in C sharp minor and Op 132 in A minor. There is a further link to the subject of the so-called *Grosse Fuge* which originally formed the imposing finale to Op 130. What these themes share, besides their rather terse, stark nature, is a high level of chromaticism. That is to say the harmony slithers about, often refusing to spell out specific keys.

Yet while the harmonic ambiguity of these pieces might still be the first musical quality to strike an audience, the second quality will probably be the very opposite. Time and again in the late quartets, a barely tonal movement is followed by music that is radiant in its diatonic simplicity. A peasant dance leads us into music of slow, singing mysticism. A quite spiritual meditation, drawn out over ten or fifteen minutes, abruptly gives way to a minute and a half of thrusting vulgarity. This is the sort of thing that Schubert noted about Beethoven's earlier music, but in the late quartets the contrasts are without precedent. There would be nothing like them again until Gustav Mahler composed his symphonies, the best part of a century later.

Another striking feature of Beethoven's late quartets (something else they share with Mahler's symphonies) is the expanding number of movements. The late quartets were not composed in the order of their opus numbers, and if they are considered in their order of completion, an interesting pattern emerges: Op 127 consists of the standard four movements; Op 132 has five; Op 130 has six; Op 131 has seven. Beethoven's final string quartet, Op 135, was also his last completed work. It reverts not only to the traditional four movement structure, but also to the key of F major in which Beethoven had written his very first essay in the genre, Op 18, No 1. At its heart is a songful outpouring, intensely moving. But either side of this is some of the lightest, wittiest music Beethoven ever composed. This from a composer on his death bed.

This quartet calls to mind T.S. Eliot's words from the final stanza of 'Little Gidding', the last of his *Four Quartets*, the suite of poems itself inspired by the late quartets of Beethoven.

We shall not cease from exploration
And the end of all our exploring
Will be to arrive where we started
And know the place for the first time.

Very few of Beethoven's contemporaries seem to have been able to follow what he was doing by the end, but Schubert, at least, learned to accommodate his hero's contradictions. The quartet in C sharp minor Op 131 (Beethoven's own favourite) was not performed in public in Beethoven's lifetime or, in Vienna at least, for several more years. But in 1828, the year after the composer's death, a private performance was given for Schubert, now thirty-one years old and himself dying. One of those present reported that as Schubert listened to the music he was beside himself with excitement.

Australian Financial Review, 2008

Mahler's Secret Operas

Gustav Mahler was a part-time composer, best known in his own day as a great conductor, particularly in the opera house. Nearly a century after his death, the part-time nature of his creative work is very hard to credit. Mahler's symphonies seem like the work of a driven man: how could composition possibly have been just a summer holiday activity? The music is so obviously unified by some grand obsession that it seems beyond belief that he was able to put it from his mind for most of the year. What becomes easier to accept, the more one gets to know this music, is that Mahler's symphonies are the work of an opera conductor. Although he composed no operas himself, these symphonies are really operas without the action. Secret operas.

The pictorialism we expect in the theatre is everywhere in Mahler's music. If it isn't a passing marching band or a peasant dance, it's distant cowbells and alpenhorns. And this is more than a musical postcard from Austria, with stock *Sound of Music* scene-painting, because these sharply drawn musical characters behave dramatically: they creep around in the shadows, they step into the spotlight, they disguise themselves, they fight, they make speeches.

At the beginning of Mahler's third symphony, which is arguably the most typical of his symphonies, eight horns play a four-square fanfare. It has an undeniable nobility and, given its meter, might announce the start of a triumphal march. In fact, within a few bars, it has collapsed into a trudging funeral procession. So what is that about? And why, five movements later, does the weary funereal tread return to create such a horrifying contrast to the joyful voices of children singing about angels? Why are horn calls played off-stage, coming to us as though from some distant elf-land? Clearly this music is not abstract art; this is music about something. Fanfares, funeral marches and children's voices all imply meaning, even if Mahler never reveals precisely what that meaning is. In earlier dramatic symphonies – Berlioz's *Roméo et Juliette*, Liszt's *Faust Symphony* – the titles alone alert us to the story. In contrast, Mahler's Symphony No 3 in D minor, though as apparently dramatic as the other two, is semantically inscrutable.

At 100 minutes, the third symphony is Mahler's longest composition. The conductor Edward Downes pointed out that the first movement alone lasts longer than Beethoven's fifth symphony. Mahler called it his 'monster'. More famously, he claimed that the symphony contained 'the whole world'. It certainly contains the whole of Mahler's world. Fanfares and folk tunes, marches and peasant dances: these are found musical objects, real music from Mahler's real world. The presence of found objects in concert music was not without precedent, but the scale of that presence was new, and so was the manner of its use.

In the final movement of Mozart's violin concerto in A, a courtly minuet is rudely interrupted by a bit of wild Turkish dance music. Kitsch? Something more? A socio-political jibe? The music is clearly in quotation marks, like the tin-pot march that invades the final movement of Beethoven's ninth symphony, mocking the 'Ode to Joy'. It is meant to jar, to confound our expectations, to affront our senses, and it still succeeds. But in Mahler's symphonies the folk dances and military marches are not importations and they have no need of musical inverted commas. They form the composer's musical world; they are the raw materials from which his symphonies are woven.

In fact there is one quotation – one foreign body – in Mahler's third symphony, and it comes right at the start. The fanfare sounded by Mahler's eight horns is a version of the theme from the finale of Brahms's first symphony, a theme that (as was often pointed out to

Brahms, and as he was the first to admit) bore an uncanny resemblance to the 'Ode to Joy' itself. Mahler would not have been deaf to this connection. He had conducted both Beethoven's ninth symphony and Brahms's first. The Beethoven–Brahms–Mahler connection is intended and more or less explicit. The world that Mahler's third symphony embraced was one in which imperial ambition and ideological certainty were faltering, giving way to fears for the future. Perhaps that is one reason the music speaks so directly to Western audiences at the start of the twenty-first century. In Mahler's world, the Austro-Hungarian empire was in terminal decline, but perhaps more important for the mood of this particular symphony was the concurrent decline of the heroic Romantic artist. In contrast to the boundless faith in nature that characterised early German Romanticism, artists in the final decade of the nineteenth century were knee-deep in *Weltschmerz*. At the beginning of his D minor symphony, then, Mahler looks back to Schiller and Beethoven's utopian ode (Beethoven's ninth is also in D minor), filtered through the late Romantic experience of Brahms.

In 1895, Mahler's summer retreat to Steinbach on the Attersee resulted in the composition of five movements of the third symphony. The first and longest movement was written the following summer, the whole symphony being finished by early August 1896. Mahler was generally uncomfortable with the idea of program music. He had provided verbal elucidations of his first two symphonies at the request of his publisher, but was later inclined to disown them. In the case of the third symphony, however, he produced titles for his movements in advance of composing the music. Some of these were changed as he worked on the symphony, and later in his life he disallowed the use of all descriptive titles in association with his work. Even so, Mahler never actually repudiated the titles he gave the movements of his third symphony and while they might not illuminate musical meaning in the obviously programmatic manner of those symphonies by Berlioz and Liszt, they remain helpful.

The first movement had a series of titles, all of them suggesting the very force of nature, in one case making explicit reference to the god Pan. The later movements are entitled 'What the Flowers of the Meadow Tell Me', 'What the Animals of the Forest Tell Me', 'What Mankind Tells Me', 'What the Angels Tell Me' and 'What Love Tells Me'. The Mahler scholar Henry-Louis de la Grange has pointed out the evolutionary ascent from flowers to animals to humankind to the angels, but surely of greater significance is the fact that, in the course of this symphony, early-Romantic innocence gives way to late-Romantic soul searching. The blithe minuet of the 'flowers of the meadow' and the *Scherzo* abundant with birdsong for the 'animals of the forest' are followed by a mezzo-soprano voice singing words from Nietzsche's *Thus Spake Zarathustra*, words that warn mankind against self-pity and self-satisfaction, pointing instead to the grief and joy in the world.

Just as significant are the purely musical clues – the musical 'characters' and the 'secret opera' they enact. The 'animals of the forest' do not frolic and gambol to the very end of the *Scherzo*; they produce a shriek of terror suggesting the presence of humankind and its destructive ways. Indeed nearly everywhere in this symphony are painful interjections, from the sharp trumpet sighs that punctuate the first movement, to the extraordinary oboe *glissandi* of the Nietzsche setting. Oboes can't really produce *glissandi* (a smooth slide from one note to another) and the players' attempts to execute them – usually alarmingly vocal in tone – create the most apt accompaniment to what the actual voice is singing about. These intimate stabs of pain find their more public counterpart in the following movement as the dragging funeral march returns amid the children's choir's angel song with its 'bimm bamm' bells.

And then comes the final movement, where the pain is taken away. Just as we have had no stage action for the dramas of the first five movements, no explanation of the music beyond cryptic titles and philosophical words, there is no rationale – save a purely musical rationale – for the outpouring of lyricism in the last movement. 'What Love Tells Me': which love is this meant to be? Is it Mahler's for his wife, for his children? Is it God's for mankind? Mankind's for God? For nature? We don't need to know the answer, any more than we needed to know whose funeral march we were listening to. In the finale, we hear, quite simply, one of the greatest love scenes in music – one that can rank alongside Berlioz's 'Love Scene' in *Roméo et Juliette* – but if there are star-crossed lovers here, we're not told their names.

Mahler's musical objects might be outwardly realistic, and his treatment of them operatic, but ultimately his symphonies are as pure as Brahms's or Bruckner's. And 'What Love Tells Me' is about the 'pure good' of music.

Australian Financial Review, 2003

Mozart and Shostakovich:
Can we ignore the gossip?

In an interview in 1981, the year before he died, the Canadian pianist Glenn Gould maintained that Beethoven 'is one composer whose reputation is based entirely on gossip'. Gould enjoyed tossing these little grenades into his writings and conversations, but even for him this seems, at first, an extreme remark.

And yet it is really only extreme because of one word. Take away 'entirely' and the claim is hard to dispute. The stories recounting Beethoven's rages; the familiar grim countenance in the portraits of him; Fate knocking on the front door of his fifth symphony; his encroaching deafness; his writing of the 'Heiligenstadt Testament'; his having to be turned around to witness the applause after conducting the ninth symphony: such snatches of biography provide us with a story on which to hang our interpretations of his music. Without them, it seems, we wouldn't know what to think.

Most of history's famous artists owe some of their reputations to gossip. This year we celebrate the anniversaries of two composers whose well-known and partly fictionalised life stories are responsible for much of the continuing fuss surrounding their birthdays.

When Wolfgang Amadeus Mozart turned 250 in January, a few commentators took the opportunity to belittle his achievements. It was perhaps inevitable, certainly understandable. Given the scale of the celebrations in his honour, it was surely at least worth asking the question: was Mozart really that good? In his internet column, that arch-controversialist Norman Lebrecht went so far as to come up with a short list of the genuine masterpieces among the composer's

626 works catalogued by Ludwig Ritter von Köchel. It contained the last six symphonies, the two piano concertos in minor keys ('and maybe a couple more'), the operas with librettos by Da Ponte (*The Marriage of Figaro*, *Don Giovanni* and *Così fan tutte*) and *The Magic Flute*, the clarinet quintet and concerto and, perhaps rather surprisingly, *Eine kleine Nachtmusik* and the flute concertos. That, it seemed, was 'just about all the Mozart that is worth hearing'. So no *Idomeneo*, then. No *Sinfonia concertante*; no string quartets or quintets; no late piano sonatas; no Requiem. And, significantly, no special reasons given, either for why these particular seventeen works are worthwhile or for the casual junking of the other 609. All Lebrecht will say to justify his view is that Mozart failed to alter the direction of musical evolution and must therefore be of small historical importance.

We certainly did not need to wait for the centenary of the birth of Dmitry Shostakovich before querying the importance of his compositions. The question has been posed with considerable force and regularity for more than fifty years, the facts and fictions surrounding the Russian composer's life often augmenting the discussion. Of course, it is never really sensible to take greatness on trust, and I must confess to considerable doubts regarding Shostakovich. But I do wish we could, for once, be allowed to consider his importance as a composer, rather than as a *Soviet* composer.

Audiences – and even most critics and musicologists – seem obsessed by the non-musical questions. Was Shostakovich a supporter of the Soviet regime under which he lived all his adult life, or was he a covert critic? The former view is very hard to sustain, but evidence can certainly be found in the music to support the latter. However, to be convinced by any of this evidence one must be prepared to read into the composer's music the sorts of things we wouldn't read into anyone else's. Because Shostakovich lived where he did and when he did, it seems his music must carry hidden meanings.

But how do we banish gossip and concentrate instead on Mozart and Shostakovich's music *as music*? It is difficult: the gossip is loud and insistent, and the music, in its own right, correspondingly hard to hear. Perhaps we can begin by dispelling some of the more persistent rumours. In Mozart's case these are hardly to do with the music at all, but with an often-sentimental view of the composer's short life.

As the whole world knows, Mozart had a glittering career as a child prodigy. He was on tour around Europe from the age of six, with his father Leopold in the role of manager and impresario. In the 1760s, instrumental virtuosi – including six-year-olds – appeared before small audiences in private homes, in clubs and in up-market shops, and while they would certainly have played the music of their contemporaries, they were also expected to play their own compositions, to improvise and perform clever tricks. These included adding a bass line to a given treble (and vice versa), sight-reading pieces provided by members of the audience and sometimes constructing instant sets of variations on themes hitherto unseen. It all sounds like the piano exam of one's nightmares. According to contemporary accounts, young Mozart was brilliant. The only evidence we can inspect for ourselves is his compositions of the time, and these are certainly brilliant – technically accomplished but spiced with compositional risk-taking. They are not especially profound or memorable, but why would they be when they are the work of a child?

A particularly persistent belief is that Mozart's music was divinely inspired. At his baptism, Mozart was given four Christian names, the last being Theophilus, which means 'a lover of God'. In German, this translates as Gottlieb (which turns up in a few contemporary documents), while the composer himself came to prefer and sign himself as the strangely macaronic (half-Latin, half-French) Amadé. History, of course, has preferred the fully Latin Amadeus. Render it as you may, God is certainly present in the composer's name, but it is rather harder for us to be categorical, one way or the other, about His presence in the music. The image of the giggling buffoon created by Peter Shaffer in his play *Amadeus* has only added to the popular myth. If *that's* what Mozart was like, we tell ourselves, then he can hardly have composed his more sublime music without assistance from some pretty inspiring source. He must have been taking dictation from on high.

There is little historical evidence that Mozart was a buffoon. Reading the composer's letters, particularly those to his father, we discover, it is true, a young man easily delighted by toilet jokes; but those same letters are far more concerned with the details of professional engagements, commissions and money than with scatological humour. The point is that you simply cannot produce more than 600 works in thirty years and be a stranger to hard work and seriousness of intent. Mozart was not some holy fool. And while we are scotching rumours, there is also no evidence that he was poisoned, or that he died a pauper. He was in considerable debt at the time of his death, but people tend not to lend money to paupers. Strip away the gossip, then, and you are left only with a very brilliant, very hard-working professional. Mozart composed music for money. That was his primary inspiration. He scarcely lifted a finger without the promise of a fee. The only astonishing thing about him is the sheer quality of his best works, which, *pace* Norman Lebrecht, has seldom been matched.

But how does one talk about this quality? How do we even begin to describe our feelings about Mozart's music without recourse to the gossip? For me, much of the greatness of Mozart lies with his melodic invention, which, often enough, seems to come in a continuous outpouring of lyricism. Even this composer's accompanimental figures can seem melodically inspired, giving his pieces a strong sense of unity, a profound structural integrity. And then there is what I can only call an *inevitability* about the way in which Mozart's music develops. This is almost impossible to speak about in any concrete way – I can't provide musical evidence, because I am really only describing a feeling in myself, though I know it is a feeling shared by many others. I think perhaps it may be what others describe as the music's predictable quality.

One often hears that Mozart's music is predictable. Strangely, it is a claim advanced by his admirers almost as often as by his detractors. It is easily disproved. With an unfamiliar piece of Mozart – especially mature Mozart – one may believe one can predict the next phrase, the next cadence, but one will invariably be wrong, because Mozart will have a surprise in store. The phrase will end sooner or later than expected; there will be another interpolated half phrase that springs from nowhere, appearing an octave lower than the rest of the melodic line; the cadence will be delayed or reached via a wholly unexpected harmonic route. The musical details are not in the least predictable, but once heard they do seem inevitable; you feel they could not have happened in any other way. Even now, writing those somewhat inadequate words, I can see how the struggle to describe this effect with any precision – let alone to account for it – would lead many people to settle for divine inspiration.

Of course, the foreshortening of a phrase or an unexpected bit of octave displacement are not at all the equivalent of Beethoven's introduction of a chorus into his last symphony or the syncopated stamping chord in *The Rite of Spring* – there is no 'shock of the new' here, and there wouldn't have been for Mozart's contemporaries, either. When Lebrecht insists that Mozart was not a composer who made a major difference to the course of musical history, he does have a point. Mozart may be said to have established the piano concerto as a compositional genre, but he didn't invent it. He gave woodwind instruments a new level of prominence in his orchestras, particularly in his piano concertos and later operas, but this is hardly the stuff of revolution. On stage, as David Cairns has pointed out in *Mozart and His Operas*, the composer found purely musical ways of suggesting complex characterisation: we hear the layers of humanity in the men and women (particularly the women) that populate his dramas. Cairns draws the parallel between Mozart's skill in characterisation and Shakespeare's, and the comparison does not seem forced. But none of this is really a musical innovation in the sense that Monteverdi, Beethoven, Wagner, Stravinsky, Webern or Steve Reich wrought stylistic and, one might say, 'technological' changes that affected so much of the music that followed.

Mozart's importance does indeed lie in his greatness. It is, shall we say, a subtler genius than that of those other composers, and we might learn to appreciate it for what it is. Rather like a consummate storyteller, Mozart knows how to keep us close to the edge of our seats. Perhaps we have to make more of an effort in this than did the audiences of the composer's day – the sound of this music is a little too familiar for us to find any major surprises – but by listening hard and attempting to enter the music's world, we can appreciate many of the same effects that Mozart's audience would have recognised, and perhaps a few they wouldn't. That is the other thing about a modern audience listening to an old composer. No matter how 'authentic' the performers of a Mozart symphony might try to be, the audience will remain resolutely and irredeemably inauthentic. We have heard Brahms and Bartók, the Beach Boys and Björk. How can we listen to Mozart in the same way as an eighteenth-century Viennese audience? And when we are fed by gossip from the Mozart industry – and if we believe his music to be a sonic panacea from God – we might well lose our ability to listen at all.

If popular myth and legend colour our appreciation of Mozart's music, then they effectively cloud our understanding of Shostakovich's. There is surely no other composer in history whose music is so connected in the public imagination to the times in which he lived. We imagine the benighted fellow writing his scores with Comrade Stalin peering over his shoulder, and based on this we brand the composer either as a boot-licking toady or a shrewd ironist, or – which is arguably even shrewder – both. But any of these interpretations severely limits our ability to respond to Shostakovich's music, and all of them present, at best, only partial explanations for the way that music sounds.

For one thing, Shostakovich's life was more complicated than many of his detractors and apologists will allow. Spending his early childhood in the final decade of Czarist Russia, he was something of a musical prodigy. Here, at least, there is a parallel with Mozart. Shostakovich's first symphony, a rather brilliant student work composed while he was still in his teens, is energetic, brightly coloured and apparently full of high spirits. This was in the early 1920s and the Russian Revolution was still encouraging its artists to experiment (not that Shostakovich was any more of an innovator – in Lebrecht's sense of pushing forward musical history – than Mozart was). It wasn't until 1936 and the second production of his opera, *The Lady Macbeth of the Mtsensk District*, that Shostakovich fell dangerously foul of the Soviet authorities. Stalin was less inclined than his revolutionary predecessors to welcome music that seemed to question the political status quo. The composer's reaction to *Pravda*'s criticism of his opera is well-enough known. He withdrew his as-yet-unperformed fourth symphony – a massive, hour-long structure full of noisy, hectic passion – and produced instead a seemingly more conventional, even classical, fifth symphony, kitted out, though not by the composer, with the subtitle 'A Soviet artist's response to just criticism'.

This may well have been the central event in Shostakovich's life. Certainly it has come to dominate all of our thinking about his music. There is a common tendency with Shostakovich to treat every one of his pieces as coded autobiography, indeed as coded protest. One thing that most music lovers seem to know about Shostakovich is that he made a motto theme of his initials. He used the first letter of his first name and the first three of the German spelling of his surname. In German musical notation, DSCH is D, E flat, C and B. This, we are told by those who view the composer as a hero, was his protest at a dehumanising totalitarian state that would destroy individuality. Well, Bach spelled out his name in his music. So did Robert Schumann. So did Alban Berg. In fact, the last two spelled out all sorts of people's names. As did Elgar. And I've done it myself. I wasn't being political. I don't think Bach or Schumann or the others were being political. Why, then, should we believe that in using this theme Shostakovich was intending a defiant musical stand?

When Shostakovich's music is militaristic (as in the first movement of his Symphony No 7, the so-called 'Leningrad' symphony) we are told this is the composer's defiance; when it is triumphant (for example, the finale of the fifth symphony), that triumph is generally dismissed as somehow hollow and therefore ironic; when the music seems desolate, as it frequently does in the later string quartets, this reflects the composer's barren daily existence, robbed of spiritual nourishment by a godless system. And so on. Shostakovich, it seems, could barely write a note without it having some extra-musical meaning. And postmodernist scholarship, inspired by *Testimony*, a decidedly dodgy publication claiming to be the composer's memoirs, and coupled with post-Cold War revisionism, has only exacerbated the tendency to read meanings into his music.

Nobody asks what Ravel's music means. No one seeks coded political messages in the music of Bruckner or Philip Glass. It is true that a few academics have been rather keen, of late, to prove that just about every note composed by Schubert reveals the composer's homosexuality. But this is not a global movement: most of the rest of the world believes these academics to be rather silly. With Shostakovich's music, however, the difficulty is in finding anyone who is prepared simply to treat the music as music.

And yet Shostakovich was, primarily, a composer, working with pitch and rhythm and timbre to create sonic art underpinned by musical logic. Most composers want to spend their days composing. For long stretches of time we need the outside world to go away and leave us alone. We crave a quiet life. We'd rather the phone didn't ring. This, it has always seemed to me, was behind the septuagenarian Strauss's attempts to keep his head down in Nazi Germany. I wonder whether this was also, primarily, Shostakovich's attitude to living in the Soviet Union. Richard Strauss, though an old man, had (and still has) his critics for attempting to survive under the Nazis, though I'm not sure what else he was supposed to do. Emigrate? Join the underground? But although Shostakovich stayed on in Soviet Russia under another of twentieth-century Europe's great genocidal monsters – and later joined the Communist Party and signed a letter denouncing Sakharov and Solzhenitsyn – he is forgiven because his music is one long coded protest. He is, indeed, a hero.

To me, it seems an intolerable burden on Shostakovich's memory that he be labelled a hero, a musical freedom fighter. And it is certainly more than the music itself can withstand. No music can do that job, and I don't believe Shostakovich intended his to do it. The military marches and passionate adagios that typify Shostakovich's symphonies are equally typical of Mahler. Indeed, Mahler was an important influence on the Russian composer. Was Mahler being political? Was Mahler a hero? Composers are composers, as flawed as any other human beings. And sometimes, when we are busy trying to compose and some appalling despot is disturbing us by noisily committing mass murder right outside our window, our characters can be even more flawed. Does it invalidate the music we are composing? Would it make our pieces better *music* if we possessed enough heroism to open the window and denounce the despot?

I doubt that Shostakovich's music will ever be rid of the accumulated gossip surrounding its composer's life. And, in the end, I am not arguing that we should try to forget the circumstances under which the music was composed. But if Shostakovich's music is great enough for us to be listening to it a hundred years after his birth and thirty-one years after his death, it is not because it represents a sustained attack on a communist dictatorship. It is because the music itself – the pitches and rhythms and timbres – is convincing in musical terms.

Finally, as we attempt to distinguish between musical greatness and biographical incident, we might spare a thought for those great composers of history who have no good stories to tell. In particular,

I am thinking of Mozart's contemporary and teacher, Joseph Haydn, a composer who really did change musical history, but whose long professional career was mostly (and happily) spent in the employ of the same aristocratic family. No childhood celebrity, no smutty jokes, no rumours, no scandals: just 104 symphonies, eighty-three string quartets and sixty-two piano sonatas. And at least twenty operas, all of them destined to be overshadowed by Mozart's.

Australian Financial Review, September 2006

Conducting for Hitler:
Furtwängler's musical soul

Perhaps what bothers us most in the story of Wilhelm Furtwängler is the thought that Nazis might have appreciated great art. We look at the photos and newsreel footage of the conductor's war-time concerts with the Berlin Philharmonic, and our attention is drawn, again and again, to the uniforms and armbands of the officers in the expensive seats. The images jolt us. The audience is giving rapt attention to the music of Beethoven or Brahms or Bruckner, the fruits of generous and creative German minds. And yet at least some of these same audience members, hanging on every note that Furtwängler draws from his players, moved, quite possibly, beyond words, must be war criminals. How many days has it been since one of them murdered or sanctioned the murder of an innocent human being? How could these people also love Brahms?

It is impossible to come to terms with the paradox, but there can be no doubt that it deserves regular consideration. And somewhere near the heart of the wider paradox is the conductor Furtwängler himself, a striking mixture of hero, culprit and victim. He cuts an authentically tragic figure, tragic in a way that both Aristotle and Shakespeare would have understood. There were plenty of other conductors who worked for the Nazis, not a few of whom were actually party members (which Furtwängler was not), but they are largely forgotten. Furtwängler's stature as an artist, allied to a personal aloofness, not to say pigheadedness, meant that his post-war humiliation by the Allies' de-Nazification board was all but inevitable. And his enduring greatness as a musician makes both him and his case impossible for us to ignore, even fifty years after his death.

Wilhelm Furtwängler's musical attitudes were every bit as controversial as his life. For him, great art was an 'orientation' for life, and on the podium he communed with it in a frankly spiritual manner. He seems seldom to have conducted a piece the same way twice. Some of his recordings – his great 1953 *Tristan und Isolde*, for example – have never been absent from the catalogue. But more recently there has been a flood of less familiar recordings, cleaned off and restored with the help of modern technology. Even this part of the Furtwängler story is paradoxical because the conductor did not like recording and entered the studio far less frequently than his contemporaries Otto Klemperer and Arturo Toscanini. Most of the Furtwängler CDs on the market today consist of German radio recordings taken from concerts, and consequently the sound quality is variable. What almost always shines through, however, is Furtwängler's commitment and his particular manner of shaping and phrasing the music.

When we watch film of him in action, the paradoxes only continue. On the podium he cuts a striking physical presence, tall, thin, slightly kinked in the middle with his pelvis pushed forward like a man contemplating limbo dancing. His body tends to quiver, and his beat is ungainly and often vague. As he begins Wagner's prelude to *Die Meistersinger* at a filmed concert in 1947, his arms move up and down, apparently providing two or three possible up beats for the orchestra. I have watched this moment many times and I still can't work out how the players know when to play. But they all do. Perhaps they were not watching Furtwängler's stick at all; perhaps they were looking at the conductor's eyes staring beadily from his bulbous head. The one thing we can be certain of is that the orchestras that played regularly for Furtwängler knew what he wanted and were happy to give it to him.

Perhaps above all what Furtwängler sought and generally achieved was a quality of sound. There is a translucence to it – it seems to glow

with inner life – but also a palpable weight. The bass line is rich and
clear and recognisably a product of this conductor, even on recordings
from the 1930s and 40s. You can hear through the hiss and crackle
just how good he made an orchestra sound. This is a further paradox,
because Furtwängler modified his tempos according to the acoustic
in which he found himself. In a dry acoustic, he might drive a particular passage harder than in a more reverberant space in which the
music required a slower tempo for the details to emerge. This is one
reason he disliked recording. On record, the acoustic rationale for
what he did was lost. So it is surprising that his recordings should
capture and communicate so much of his sound.

How did he create this sound? Werner Thärichen, the Berlin
Philharmonic's timpanist of the early 1950s, claimed that the orchestra's tone would alter in the presence of Furtwängler. Someone else
might be conducting a rehearsal, but if Furtwängler so much as
stepped into the room, the sound would change, drawn from the
orchestra by the mere fact of the players' seeing the great man. It
might seem to us an overly mystical explanation, but Furtwängler
would not have been the first to conduct with his personality as
much as his baton. Klemperer certainly lacked a classical technique
and towards the end of his life he sometimes appeared not to move
at all; Serge Koussevitzky, likewise, achieved results with sheer force
of character. The opposite of this was a conductor like Toscanini,
whose stick technique was legendary and whose beat (and performances) were extraordinarily precise. Furtwängler dismissed his
Italian colleague as a mere metronome, accusing him of 'ruthless
clarity'.

There is a 1952 recording of Brahms's first symphony that is one of
Furtwängler's slowest, yet it is absolutely thrilling. The physical excitement this recording generates down the decades is largely a function
of Furtwängler's sense of timing. The overall tempo might be slow,
but within any basic pulse this conductor was able to be especially
free and to pull the tempo around almost from phrase to phrase.

This is not to suggest that as a conductor Furtwängler merely conducted in the moment, incapable of seeing the forest for the trees. The composer Paul Hindemith once explained that 'Furtwängler possessed the great secret of proportion ... he understood how to interpret phrases, themes, sections, movements, entire symphonies and programs as artistic unities.' In other words, musical structure was important to Furtwängler on the large scale as well as the small, but the structure was always that of a living organism, the music capable of responding to the circumstances of its performance.

Brahms's Symphony No 1 begins with a pulse. The composer has written a steady beat for the timpani, and in most performances that is what we hear. But under Furtwängler's conducting, the Berlin Philharmonic's timpanist (presumably Werner Thärichen) is anything but steady. His tempo increases over the first five beats, settles into a regular pulse, then, at the end of this opening paragraph, grows louder and slower, before coming to a halt with a powerful thwack. From contemporary accounts, we know that this is how Brahms himself tended to perform his music and how he expected others to perform it. Tempo, he believed, should never be a straitjacket on the music. Brahms expected flexibility from moment to moment so that his music could find a natural ebb and flow.

We can sometimes forget that Furtwängler and others of his generation were themselves young contemporaries of Brahms. Furtwängler was eleven in 1897 when Brahms died, and while he might not yet have been conducting symphony orchestras, his early musical education was certainly underway. Furtwängler would have met musicians who remembered Beethoven and who had played for Wagner. More than a century on, perhaps this is what we find so compelling in his conducting – this personal connection with the Germanic musical tradition – and perhaps this is why Furtwängler's recordings still sell: he speaks for nineteenth-century composers with an authority that modern conductors simply cannot match.

This is truer still, of course, of the music of Richard Strauss, who was a far closer contemporary of Furtwängler, whose music had often been conducted by him, who also remained in Germany during World War II and who attracted just as much controversy for doing so. Strauss composed his *Metamorphosen* for twenty-three solo strings in response to the Allied bombing of German towns towards the end of the war, and in particular the destruction of the opera houses in Munich, Berlin and Dresden, where Strauss had so often conducted his own operas. Strauss felt the whole of German culture, its roots stretching back hundreds of years, was now under threat. First the Nazis had appropriated it and now the Allies had razed, indeed desecrated, many of its sacred sites. His *Metamorphosen*, then, was a lament for what had been lost. But it was also a gesture of hope and defiance, for as the music plays, the dotted rhythm that has been heard throughout gradually comes to dominate, before finally and with some inevitability turning into the funeral march from the second movement of Beethoven's Symphony No 3 in E flat, known, even by Beethoven, as the *Eroica* (Heroic). Strauss seems to be taking comfort that, while famous buildings might be destroyed, famous music remains. And of course this is not just any famous music; this is Beethoven.

It is a revelation to hear Furtwängler conducting *Metamorphosen* in 1947, only two years after it was composed. If the performance of the Brahms symphony seems unusually slow, the Strauss is swifter than any performance I have heard. The string playing is full of passion, *Metamorphosen* never having sounded so much like *Don Juan*, and not only passion but, to my ears, also anger. Strauss himself may have been present at the concert, but if not he was surely listening to the radio broadcast, and he must have realised that his piece had found, in Furtwängler, its ideal interpreter. We shouldn't be surprised. Strauss's *Metamorphosen* represents Furtwängler's own views completely. It summarises, in music, his reasons for remaining in Germany through the war. Writing in his *Notebooks*, which he kept from 1924 until his death thirty years later and never intended for public consumption, the conductor makes many attempts to put the same views into words. Some of his more successful attempts are from 1945, at the end of the war:

> The dishonouring of an entire and great people – a people whose inner nobility can compete with that of any other people, for it produced Goethe and Beethoven and innumerable other great men – it is not only dangerous, it is terrible.

This was essentially Strauss's view, too, which is why his piece quotes Beethoven. Strauss also shared Furtwängler's belief that Hitler had duped many Germans into believing the Nazis' view of the world, and duped the rest of the world into believing that all Germans were Nazis and so equally culpable for the Holocaust and the war.

'How could National Socialism claim to the world at large and finally even to the Germans that it was Germany?' Furtwängler asked in the *Notebooks*.

> It was not Germany but its opposite, at best a profoundly misunderstood Germany ... Those who became emigrants or demanded that one should emigrate, believed one thing of Hitler in particular: that he represented the German people. They believed that one had to leave a Nazi Germany. But this is precisely what is incorrect. Germany was never a Nazi Germany, but a Germany ruled by Nazis.

There would be many people, even today, who would find this line hard to swallow, and in 1945 the Allied command was having none of it. Furtwängler, who had ended the war in exile in Switzerland, was forced to go through the standard process of de-Nazification before being allowed to work again in public. This was a long process, its start delayed by the Nuremberg trials, but finally in December 1946 it began and Furtwängler was ultimately cleared of collaborating.

Surveying the evidence, there was not much to condemn him, though the case is by no means as clear-cut as many of Furtwängler's admirers might wish. Certainly, he refused to give the Nazi salute or to conduct in halls bedecked with swastikas, and he managed to gain at least temporary reprieves for many Jews in his orchestras. Himmler indeed believed that Furtwängler would stretch out his hand to any Jew, 'filthy as he may be', but that wasn't strictly true. As ever, Furtwängler was concerned with art, and so interested in saving artistically talented Jews. In other respects, he began to approach the Nazi line, approving of pre-war attacks on the Jewish domination of the press. He conducted in Adolf Hitler's presence, including a concert he was obliged to give in celebration of Hitler's birthday (once bitten, twice shy: thereafter, Furtwängler always ensured he had a doctor's certificate handy when the Führer's birthday came around). As much as anything, one suspects, the 'de-Nazifiers' were antagonised by Furtwängler's unshakable belief in German culture. In many of the Allied nations, German music had not been played during the war because it would have seemed a propaganda victory for the Third Reich.

Furtwängler's attitude to culture was deeply conservative. He conducted the music of Stravinsky (*The Rite of Spring*) and Schoenberg (the world premiere of the Variations for Orchestra Op 31), but it was from a sense of duty; his comments about these composers in the *Notebooks* are unfailingly critical. His criticism extends to Hindemith, whom he championed and over whom he nearly came to blows with the Reich, and even Richard Strauss. Bach, Mozart, Beethoven, Brahms, Wagner and Bruckner are the composers who mattered to Furtwängler. In the 1930s and during the war he believed himself to be a kind of caretaker for German culture. Hitler was only temporary, but these composers were forever; and when Hitler had gone, Germany – and the world – would have greater need of Bach, Beethoven and Brahms than before.

It is a compelling argument, in spite of its naivety, perhaps even because of it. In the years immediately after the war, this attitude, expressed ever more stubbornly, was nearly Furtwängler's downfall. Today it saves his reputation, not as a conductor (that was never in doubt), but as a human being.

Australian Financial Review, 2004

The Surprising Contents
of Toscanini's Mail

At the height of Arturo Toscanini's post-war fame, tens of millions of Americans tuned in each week to the direct radio broadcasts of his concerts. There is no equivalent mass audience today for classical music, yet somehow the name of Toscanini lives on in the public imagination.

There are perfectly sound reasons for this. Toscanini was a great conductor with a long and illustrious career. He had perhaps the most perfect conducting technique of the twentieth century, his standards were exceptionally high and his tastes were broad, encompassing newer scores by Stravinsky, Shostakovich and Copland, as well as baroque music. His later career, however, is firmly associated with direct and dramatic readings of the classics: the symphonies of Beethoven and Brahms, the operas of Wagner and Verdi.

Toscanini conducted the first performances of *La Bohème* and *I Pagliacci*, and he revolutionised the operatic repertory at La Scala, introducing Wagner, Tchaikovsky, Debussy and Strauss to Italian audiences. At the Italian premiere of *Tristan und Isolde*, there was nearly a riot when he insisted the house lights be dimmed. This was Wagner's own innovation, but it was unknown in Italian opera houses where the lights were always left up so the audience members could see each other and chat. Toscanini went on to become the first non-German to conduct at Bayreuth in the theatre Wagner himself had built to house performances of his music–dramas.

Three times Toscanini triumphed in New York, first at the Met from 1908 to 1915, then with the Philharmonic in the 1930s, and finally as founder (in 1937) and principal conductor of the NBC Symphony Orchestra in the 1940s and 50s. It was with the NBC orchestra that he made his famous broadcasts.

But of course none of that is why Toscanini is still so famous. Just as Einstein's name is invoked by people with not the slightest knowledge of physics, and 'Freudian slips' are remarked upon by those who have never read a word by 'the father of psychoanalysis', so Toscanini remains a byword for the figure of the great maestro. Thanks to him, in popular mythology all conductors have eyes burning with intensity, all are irresistibly charismatic and all are temperamental tantrum chuckers.

It is true, of course: Toscanini was a passionate man and a passionate artist. You can hear it in the recordings, you can see it in the photos, and in *The Letters of Arturo Toscanini*, compiled, edited and translated by Harvey Sachs, you can read it in his own words. This is passionate writing about passionate feelings.

Toscanini on conducting: 'Bruno Walter, Furtwängler, enjoy their work; you see them smiling, almost fainting, while they conduct. I, on the contrary – you can see me suffer … I'm like a <u>woman giving birth</u>!'

Toscanini on the *Adagio* from Beethoven's Symphony No 9: 'One ought to conduct it on one's <u>knees</u>. Do you know that at the modulation to E-flat I always conduct with my eyes closed? I see extremely bright lights far, far away; I see shadows moving around, penetrated by rays that make them even more disembodied; I see flowers of the most charming shapes and colors.'

Throughout the letters, Toscanini insists that he is not a sensualist, yet he continually demonstrates otherwise, and not least when it comes to his many affairs with women. In the conductor's letters to his lovers, more than a thousand sent to Ada Mainardi alone, passion and sensuality merge. Some of these letters, we are told in a throwaway footnote on page 200 of Sachs' collection, contained paragraphs written in Toscanini's own blood. Often enough blood was also the subject of the letters.

It emerges here that one of Toscanini's greatest passions was for oral sex, in which pursuit he believed it was more blessed to give than to receive. When unable to provide this service in person, most of his lovers being married (as of course was he), the conductor expected monthly tokens in the form of handkerchiefs dipped in menstrual blood. He calls them 'diaphanous veils' and 'holy shrouds'.

In his introduction to the letters, Harvey Sachs expresses his advance disappointment in reviewers who will inevitably make more of Toscanini's love life than of his conducting. I find his complaint a touch disingenuous. He reminds me of those tabloid editors who first show us something outrageous and titillating and then pretend to take a disapproving attitude. Not only does Sachs devote a huge amount of space to Toscanini's love letters (those written to Ada dominating the middle of the book), but the letters themselves contain the volume's principal surprises.

We already knew that Toscanini was an idealist, a perfectionist, a martinet; these letters merely provide further evidence, as we read, for example, that the conductor is hoarse from screaming at his orchestra all morning. We also knew that Toscanini had a strong political conscience, refusing to appear first at the Bayreuth Festival and then at the Salzburg Festival after the Nazis took them over, and meanwhile travelling, at his own expense, to conduct dozens of exiled Jews in the Palestine Orchestra (later the Israel Philharmonic). The letters document these actions, too, the only real surprise being the acute sensitivity of Toscanini's political radar when it came to knowing when to leave a place. He is furious with Ada when she attends a performance at Bayreuth: 'You are in contact with a people that has never known a <u>sense of the ridiculous</u> ...' (Nazism in a nutshell!)

What we did not know about was the affairs, at least not the nature of them. It's the love letters that lodge in the memory and for more than just their sexual explicitness. It is significant that Toscanini should refer to himself as 'Artù' when he writes to Ada. For Italians, this form of his name conjures images of King Arthur, and Toscanini, the devoted Wagnerian, was especially attached to the composer's Grail opera, *Parsifal*. Later in the correspondence he takes to signing himself 'Adartù', combining his name with Ada's just as Tristan and Isolde combined their identities. Reading these letters, one senses that Toscanini's affairs sustained his artistry. Even the bloody hankies apparently served an artistic purpose.

'I received our <u>Holy Shroud</u> just as I was going up the stairs in the Musikverein,' Toscanini writes to Ada from Vienna in November 1936. 'I conducted the concert with it jealously hidden in my pocket, and it was a real inspiration.'

Nearly all of the letters collected by Sachs were previously unpublished. Indeed, it was once commonly believed there were no letters worth publishing. Sachs himself wrote in his 1978 biography of the conductor that Toscanini's letters were 'relatively few and often uninformative'. Well, now we know different.

Sydney Morning Herald, 2002

What Makes an Opera Singer?

This year has marked the thirtieth anniversary of the death of Maria Callas, who, many would argue, was the most important opera singer of the twentieth century. She brought a remarkable passion to her performances, vocally and theatrically; indeed, it was often difficult to tell where the acting stopped and the singing began. She threw herself into her roles so fully – it was perhaps as close as opera has ever come to method acting – that she would occasionally sacrifice beauty of tone for dramatic effect. After all, what justification can there be for trying to sound beautiful if your character is not behaving beautifully or feeling beautiful? When Tosca stabs Scarpia or when Carmen goads Don José into stabbing her, the soprano who aims for beauty of tone is cheating emotionally and dramatically. More than anyone else in modern times, Callas brought singing and acting together with shocking effect, and she made roles such as Tosca, Norma, Violetta and Medea her own. In the process she became the biggest-selling female opera singer on record, which she remains thirty years after her death.

According to the website of BBC Wales, 'the fastest-selling female opera singer since Maria Callas' is Katherine Jenkins. From that claim, one might infer that Ms Jenkins has sold a great many records and that she is, as Callas was, an opera singer. The first part is true, but the second part isn't: Katherine Jenkins is no more an opera singer than I am. If the definition of a cricketer is one who has taken part in quite a lot of professional cricket matches, it follows that an opera singer should have sung in a good few operas. But unless she is hiding the fact from her assiduous web-biographers and failing to mention it even at her own website, then Ms Jenkins has never sung in an opera. She has sung in Westminster Cathedral at a Mass for Pope John Paul II, in various sports arenas (she is the official mascot of the Welsh Rugby team), in Trafalgar Square on the sixtieth anniversary of VE Day (she sang 'We'll Meet Again') and before huge outdoor audiences in parks the length and breadth of Britain – but never on an opera stage.

It is true that her CDs contain a handful of popular numbers from operas. There are soprano arias by Puccini such as 'Un bel dì' from *Madama Butterfly* and 'O mio babbino caro' from *Gianni Schicchi*; there are also 'Nessun dorma' from *Turandot* and 'Va', pensiero' from Verdi's *Nabucco*, neither of which is a soprano aria. The former, as every soccer fan knows, is for a tenor voice, while the latter is actually a chorus. Of course Jenkins's versions are simply studio recordings of the music; there's no acting involved, which is rather a pity in the case of 'Va', pensiero', because one would like to see the young Welsh singer impersonating a large party of Hebrew slaves.

But more than the occasional aria, Jenkins's CDs are full of hymn tunes and pop songs, including '(Quello che farò) Sarà per te' and 'L'amore sei tu'. You don't know them? In fact, you probably do, though they are more recognisable called by their English titles: '(Everything I Do) I Do it for You' and 'I Will Always Love You'. Is a Bryan Adams song less of a Bryan Adams song because it's been translated into Italian? Is a Dolly Parton song thus magically turned into an aria?

Katherine Jenkins has been around for a few years now, but this year she has been joined on the celebrity singer circuit by 'opera singer' Paul Potts. Potts, who has a pleasant tenor voice, won a talent quest on British television, singing – you can predict the next two words – 'Nessun dorma'. Unlike Jenkins, Potts does have a small claim to being an opera singer. He sang in four productions for Bath Opera. This is an amateur company in the west of England and, by his own admission, he was paid nothing more than petrol money, and not for every show.

Paul Potts has an album out. On it, you can hear him sing 'Ognuno soffre' (otherwise known as 'Everybody Hurts' by REM), 'Por ti sere' (that's Secret Garden's 'You Raise Me Up' in Spanish) and, best of all, 'A mi manera'. You can work that one out for your-selves. Frank Sinatra had a hit with it and it's big at funerals.

And on the subject of funerals, Luciano Pavarotti hadn't even had his, before 'opera singer' Russell Watson was rushing to eulogise him. Well, here anyway was a real opera singer (Pavarotti, obviously, not Watson), and a truly great one, at that – an operatic superstar in the old-fashioned sense of Caruso and Gigli and Björling, Tetrazzini and Callas and Sutherland. It is true that by the time he became an authentic household name, courtesy of the 1990 Football World Cup and the first 'Three Tenors' concert, his best singing was behind him, but he still possessed a great instrument. It is also true that after these huge successes, he spent less and less time in operas, preferring to be behind the microphone in a 100,000-seater stadium. The microphone benefited his declining voice and the 100,000 people in the audience made him incredibly wealthy. As Tom Sutcliffe pointed out in his *Guardian* obituary, the acclaim and the money meant it was hard for Pavarotti to retire.

Like a lot of opera singers, Pavarotti was naturally musical and his voice was as much of a gift as his ebullient personality. His rep-ertoire was always narrow – really just a dozen or so Italian operas from the nineteenth century, plus Puccini and a little Mozart – but in the roles in which he specialised, he had no real rivals. You listen to recordings from the 1960s and 70s – his Rodolfo, his Nemorino, his Duke in *Rigoletto*, his Edgardo (to Joan Sutherland's Lucia) – and the singing is extraordinary. The voice is big, yet lithe and flex-ible, and the music emerges with something close to inevitability, always illuminating the text. Visually, he wasn't much of an actor, but vocally he was peerless and, like Callas, it's hard to tell the dif-ference between his singing and his acting.

When in 1997, at the height of his stadium-fame, it was revealed that Pavarotti couldn't actually read music, some people sneered as though this fact condemned him and the music he sang. Others regarded the news as a vindication of their belief that anyone who knew the words to 'Nessun dorma' could be an opera singer, in much the same way that anyone in the United States can rise to be president. In fact, Pavarotti's musical illiteracy wasn't so very newsworthy. There have always been opera singers who have needed to have the notes dinned into them. This does not mean that anyone can be an opera singer.

The BBC television series *Operatunity* and its ABC spin-off certainly traded on the assumption that a person with a nice voice and some personality just needed a break and they could be like Pavarotti. Years of training hardly entered into it: opera singers were born, and for their careers to take off they were merely awaiting discovery. Telephonists and electricians, computer programmers and check-out operators were all just an 'operatunity' away from being stars. (It is an important part of the mythology surrounding Paul Potts and Katherine Jenkins that the former was a car-phone salesman and the latter a schoolteacher.)

'Opera' is a loaded word. It divides people. I am not thinking so much of those people who actually attend performances in opera theatres: I'm thinking about the vast majority who do not. They fall into two camps: those who believe opera is something to aspire to and those who think it's a despicable bourgeois conspiracy. Both groups equate opera with high status. For fans of Katherine Jenkins and Paul Potts, it is important that the singers are 'opera singers'. Apparently, the term bestows a seal of credibility.

The other side of this coin – and it is *exactly* the same coin – is represented by something I recently read by a young composer. I've forgotten her name, but as part of her entry to a competition for new operas, she had, as requested, provided an artistic credo. In it, she explained that she disliked most opera because it is so elitist. She didn't elucidate. People who use the word 'elitist' never do.

For some, then, the term 'opera' brings cachet; for others, it's stigma. Writing his Pavarotti obituary, Tom Sutcliffe points out that when most people mention 'opera', they mean nineteenth- and early twentieth-century Italian opera, not Wagner or Strauss or Benjamin Britten. Italian opera was always a form of popular entertainment. It still is. Sit in the cheap seats up in the 'gods' in the Rome opera or at La Scala, and you will see whole families, often with quite small children, unpacking food, loudly whispering to each other, and cheering or booing the singers. There is nothing elitist here, and nothing especially elevated (except the seating).

Then there are the operas themselves. Italian opera plots are mostly ridiculous – either wildly melodramatic or stupefyingly trivial or just plain incredible. Subject it all to even half-hearted scrutiny and you can't take it seriously. The music tends to be straightforward and even rather obvious. Remember, this was popular entertainment, so there are good tunes that you can sing along to, hum on your way home, and (a hundred years ago, at least) hear the following evening played in a café. The tunes have simple accompaniments (lots of rippling arpeggios and throbbing strings and oom-pah basses) and at the climaxes of the more heroic numbers the singers always have long-held high notes. Elitist? You must be kidding. Something to aspire to? Well, maybe.

Because there are those nights when it all comes together. It doesn't happen every time, but when it does – even for a while – it reminds you why you go to the opera in the first place. Maybe you arrived tired or fractious. You were late and couldn't get a drink. Someone had misread the information on his ticket and was in your seat. The man in front of you is too tall, the woman behind is wearing far too much perfume and you seem to be in the one seat in the theatre from which you can't see the surtitles.

But then it happens. The curtain goes up. An inspired conductor is at the helm, pacing and shaping the music; the orchestra is on top form; a remarkable singer–actor is in the lead; it's a great production, with great sets and great lighting; the stars align, the music and drama seem one, disbelief is suspended and grown men weep. On nights such as this, opera can indeed seem an elevated art form, or, to put it more accurately, it can elevate its audience.

Take the drama out of the music and you have not opera, but songs. Fine songs, of course, great songs, often, but only songs. What is the man in 'Nessun dorma' singing about? 'None shall sleep!' he commands. Yes, everybody knows that. But why shall none sleep? And until when? And anyway, who says so? Out of its dramatic context, Puccini's aria loses quite a bit.

Right from the start, and certainly since the days of Caruso and Tetrazzini, opera singers have performed their favourite highlights in concert. But that's not what made them opera singers. They were opera singers because they sang in operas.

If you've only heard Katherine Jenkins or Paul Potts, it's time to try the real thing.

Sydney Morning Herald, 2007

The Long Reach of Franz Liszt

Composers' anniversaries come and go. They provide excuses for performers and concert promoters, record companies, radio producers and music journalists to trade on the birthday in question, dusting off the composer's greatest hits and summarising the anecdotes from a life. But the 200th anniversary of the birth of Franz Liszt offers a bigger opportunity, for it is hard to think of a major composer less appreciated, less well-understood and less often performed.

Liszt was born on 22 October 1811 in Doborján (or Raiding, to give it its more familiar German name) in Hungary, and two centuries later his name remains famous enough, but the composer's reputation rests on what we have heard of his flashy virtuosity at the piano and his unusually full sex life.

As a boy genius, he took composition lessons from Mozart's contemporary and sometime rival Antonio Salieri, and piano lessons from Carl Czerny, who had studied with Beethoven. He was introduced to both Beethoven and Schubert, and was one of the fifty composers invited by the publisher Anton Diabelli to contribute to the 'Patriotic Anthology' of variations based on Diabelli's waltz. Liszt was still only twelve.

During the course of his relatively long life, Liszt would come to know (or at least meet) all the great composers of the mid nineteenth century, in many cases actively promoting their music. Paganini, Berlioz and Chopin were important early influences on him, while Liszt's later influence on Wagner can scarcely be overestimated. Liszt died in 1886 at the age of seventy-four, but not before he had met and advised Grieg, Borodin, Busoni and Debussy.

So Liszt is right at the heart of nineteenth-century music. But there remains the problem of his reputation: Liszt the superhuman performer, Liszt the inexhaustible rake, Liszt the diabolist, Liszt the priestly mystic. 'Lisztomania', we should remember, was a term coined not by the film-maker Ken Russell for his lurid 1975 biopic, but by the composer's contemporary, the poet Heinrich Heine.

Is it possible to reassess Liszt's reputation based on his music? Apart from anything else, there is so much of it, and no one – not even Humphrey Searle – would deny that the composer's achievement was uneven. Besides being a composer himself, Searle was the cataloguer of Liszt's music. Where Mozart's works have K-numbers (after the musicologist Köchel), Liszt's have S-numbers – 768 of them. More than half these opuses are transcriptions, paraphrases, fantasies and 'reminiscences' taken from, based on or inspired by the works of other composers, and here is where much of our misunderstanding of Liszt begins.

It is often maintained that pieces such as the *Grand Concert Fantasy on La Sonnambula*, the *Concert Paraphrase on Rigoletto* and *Réminiscences de Don Juan* were simply packages of favourite arias done up as vehicles for Liszt's prodigious talent as a pianist. It is true that these works are dazzlingly virtuosic, but we should not dismiss them so lightly. *Réminiscences de Don Juan* in particular is far more than a flashy showpiece. In a little over fifteen minutes, Liszt distills the very essence of Mozart's *Don Giovanni* (nineteenth-century Germans called the opera *Don Juan*) with recourse only to a duet, an aria, elements of the overture and, right at the beginning, the climactic confrontation between the Don and the talking statue of the Commendatore, whom he has earlier murdered.

Liszt conflates this encounter with the stone guest's later arrival at the Don's dinner party, underpinning the latter with the swirling minor scales from the overture. Then he introduces the duet 'Là ci darem la mano'. This is the Don's sweetly reasonable seduction of Zerlina, from Act One of the opera, in which he invites the servant girl to take his hand, but in Liszt's version the refrain 'Andiam, andiam, mio bene' ('Come, come, my dearest') is underpinned by disquieting harmonies from the statue scene, reminding us of where all this will lead. Moreover, as the musicologist Richard Taruskin reminds us, Liszt's juxtaposition of the duet with the statue scene draws our attention to their similar diction. The Don's invitation to Zerlina matches the statue's solicitation to the Don as he invites him to dinner in hell ('Dammi la mano in pegno' – 'Give me your hand in pledge'). After this, the 'Champagne' aria with which Liszt concludes his piano 'reminiscence' has a hollow ring to it, the Don very much whistling in the dark.

So far from providing a compilation of hits from Mozart's opera, Liszt approached his job almost as a critic, uncovering dramatic as well as musical themes in *Don Giovanni* and recasting them to throw new light on the story and on Mozart's treatment of it. In George Bernard Shaw's words, if you know Mozart's opera *'au fond'*, Liszt's fifteen-minute fantasy will seem 'a stroke of genius'.

On a much more modest and subtle level, there are also revelations in Liszt's transcriptions. The composer made a great many of these, often as favours for friends and colleagues. One of the most famous was his transcription of Berlioz's *Symphonie fantastique*, which he often played in concert and which did much to increase interest in Berlioz and appreciation of his work. The nine symphonies of Beethoven were also transcribed, Beethoven's publisher encouraging Liszt in his endeavour when the project seemed to be flagging. It seems odd from our standpoint that Beethoven's symphonies should ever have required such advocacy, but in the century before sound recordings, getting to know orchestral music was difficult if you didn't play it at home on your piano.

Not even a pianist of Liszt's calibre could play the whole of a Beethoven symphony. Even beyond the sheer number of notes that an orchestra can produce compared to those that lie within reach of a pianist's ten fingers, there is also the matter of tone colour.

Beethoven – and, more so, Berlioz – made great use of instrumental timbre. Set beside the kaleidoscope of colours on offer from an orchestra, the piano is a monochrome thing. So a transcriber must make choices. Notes must be left out, solutions found for instrumental effects, and in making his choices Liszt, time and again, uncovers cross rhythms, harmonic details and the workings of inner parts that we miss in orchestral performances. His piano version of Beethoven's ninth symphony, in which a single pianist conjures not only an orchestra but a choir and four soloists, is both a *tour de force* and an education.

But there was surely another reason behind Liszt's inveterate making of transcriptions and paraphrases, something to do with the whole business of giving recitals. Along with Clara Schumann, Liszt invented the public piano recital. Before the nineteenth century, and even during it, piano music was composed to be played in the home. In grander homes, perhaps, friends might be invited to hear a particularly talented pianist play, but the public concert did not properly exist until the nineteenth century.

Early concerts had typically consisted of long and varied programs, with vocal items and orchestral works, and plenty of 'novelties'. It was at one such concert that the young Liszt first encountered the violinist–composer Niccolò Paganini and vowed to acquire a piano technique to rival Paganini's on the violin. Such concerts had been backed by a private sponsor or by selling subscriptions, but now the rise of the bourgeoisie brought with it a musical public willing to walk in off the street and buy a ticket at a box office. This public wanted a show and Liszt was eager to provide one. But it was going to be a solo show: that was the point. In his *Oxford History of Western Music*, Taruskin quotes Vladimir Stasov who attended Liszt's debut in St Petersburg: 'Liszt appeared alone on the stage throughout the entire concert … What conceit! What vanity! … And in such an immense hall! What a strange fellow!' This was 1842.

The fact that Liszt routinely included orchestral transcriptions and operatic paraphrases in his recitals was a way of bridging the gap between himself as a solo performer (albeit with two pianos in St Petersburg) and an audience used to hearing and seeing singers and orchestras. Liszt would show them that he could be all this and more. We may view public concerts as an escalation of the domestic recital, but it was also something grander: one pianist taking on the concert hall, being the embodiment of music – songs, orchestral works, operas, the lot.

Public concerts brought with them other developments in the history of music. Undoubtedly the most significant was the invention of the very notion of 'classical music', of a repertoire of works, old and new, and in time a classical canon. Liszt's transcriptions and paraphrases were a significant contribution to this, bringing the works of dead composers into his recital programs. Another invention was the music critic: if concerts were now to be public events, they would be written up in newspapers and they would be compared to each other. And artist management began here, too; Liszt was among the first performing musicians to have an agent.

He was also the first pianist to have groupies. At the height of his performing career, Liszt criss-crossed Europe giving up to four recitals a week. Wherever he went he filled halls not only with his own compositions, and with his versions of the orchestral works and operas of others, but also with adoring women who fought over his silk handkerchiefs and velvet gloves, frequently tearing them to shreds. Here was Heine's 'Lisztomania'.

If there seemed something impious, not to say devilish, about the powers of a man who could have such an effect, Liszt did little to dispel the perception. Significantly, Berlioz's *Symphonie fantastique*, which featured so regularly in Liszt's concerts, concluded with a witches' sabbath, while Paganini, who had been the pianist's inspiration, had done a Faustian deal with the Devil in exchange for his violin technique – everyone knew that! And now here was

Liszt with similarly prodigious skills. And what's more, Liszt's own works included a set of virtuoso piano studies based on Paganini's compositions.

It is tempting to divide Liszt's career into two, the first half full of performances, women, wild behaviour and a morbid obsession with death and the Devil, the second characterised by composition and sober religious contemplation. But in fact Liszt had been devout for most of his life and had contemplated the priesthood as a young man. The photographs of the elderly Abbé Liszt, tonsure and all, shouldn't fool us into thinking he had some late conversion. In any case, the majority of the composer's diabolic music also comes from his later years, the *Totentanz*, the *Mephisto Waltzes* and the *Faust Symphony* were all written after the end of his concert career. The diabolic and the devout were twin sides of his personality as surely as were the performing virtuoso and the composer.

As it happens, it was one of Liszt's adoring female fans, the Princess Carolyne zu Sayn-Wittgenstein, who finally persuaded him to give up touring and concentrate on composition. Even the mother of his children, Countess Marie d'Agoult, had not been able to achieve this. On the contrary, in the later stages of their relationship, Liszt had toured in order to escape her. But Princess Carolyne was an experienced confidante of composers (she had had a long correspondence with Berlioz, who dedicated his opera *Les Troyens* to her), and she convinced Liszt that composition was a more noble activity than playing the piano in public and that, in any case, travelling and composing were scarcely compatible. And so in 1847, aged thirty-five, Liszt retired from the concert platform to settle down with his manuscript paper (and the princess).

He didn't cease production of his operatic paraphrases, however, and one of his singular achievements was to bring together those apparent polar opposites of nineteenth-century opera, Verdi and Wagner. In the first year after retiring from concerts, Liszt produced a paraphrase on Verdi's *Ernani* and transcriptions of both the overture and Wolfram's 'Song to the Evening Star' from Wagner's brand new *Tannhäuser*. And he would go on to provide the same advocacy for more of their operas, from *Simon Boccanegra* to *Don Carlos*, from *Rienzi* to *Parsifal*.

But it is Liszt's original music of these later years that is his most important achievement of all and the B minor piano sonata of 1853 is a watershed in his style. The only work to which he allocated this generic title, the half-hour piece plays without a break and, while it lacks nothing in virtuosity, it also contains passages that have a new starkness. Creeping melodic lines, unadorned by accompaniment, hesitant to the point of seeming fractured, offer an extremely unsettling experience. Doubtless they owe something to the composer's extensive knowledge of the music of Berlioz, but they now became a hallmark of Liszt's mature music, along with ever more chromatic harmonies.

That same summer of 1853, Liszt visited Wagner in Zurich, playing him his latest completed works together with ideas for his yet-to-be-written *Faust Symphony*, replete with yet more stark textures, chromatic harmonies and dark-hued orchestration. It was only weeks later that Wagner began work in earnest on *Der Ring des Nibelungen*. As he worked, he continued to receive scores from Liszt – particularly his new symphonic poems – and Wagner continued to absorb them.

'When I compose and orchestrate,' Wagner wrote to Liszt, 'I think of you alone ...'

The opening of Wagner's *Tristan und Isolde* (1857–59) is unimaginable without the example of Liszt (as well as Berlioz's *Roméo et Juliette*). After it, Wagner wrote to the conductor Hans von Bülow that his knowledge of Liszt's use of harmony had affected his own very greatly, indeed that it had changed him. Von Bülow, who was married to Liszt's only surviving daughter, Cosima, conducted the premiere of *Tristan* in 1865, by which time Cosima was having an affair with Wagner, bearing him three children and eventually leaving the conductor for him. In 1870, Wagner became Liszt's son-in-law.

Liszt's late music is in many ways his most remarkable. There is religious music, including the austere yet beautifully limpid *Via Crucis*. There are a handful of late orchestral works, most notably the radiant symphonic poem *Von der Wiege bis zum Grabe* (*From the Cradle to the Grave*). But perhaps above all, there are some strikingly gnomic piano miniatures such as *Unstern!*, *Nuages gris* and the two versions of *La lugubre gondola* in which the composer has a premonition of Wagner's death in Venice. And there is one astonishing little waltz, known as the 'Bagatelle without Tonality', which just as Liszt's musical experimentation seems to be drawing to a close, pushes things a little further. Composed in 1885, the year before his death, this attempt at atonal music serves as an embryonic manifesto for the second Viennese school of Arnold Schoenberg, Anton Webern and Alban Berg. We must remember, however, that at the time Schoenberg was only eleven, Webern two and Berg newly born.

Summing up Liszt's achievement in 1954 at the end of his wise and concise monograph on the composer, Humphrey Searle, who himself had studied with Webern, put it very well: 'Liszt was born two years after the death of Haydn; he died a year after the birth of Alban Berg, and in a way he may be said to bridge the gap between those two musical worlds.'

Liszt's bridge leads right to our own time. We are absorbing his influence still.

Australian Financial Review, 2011

Edward Elgar, the Dreamer of Dreams

A survey of the literature about Edward Elgar reveals a curious tendency among commentators to dwell on his appearance. This is particularly true of those writers from the middle of the last century, exclusively English, most of whom agree on one thing: Elgar didn't look like a composer (as though we all know what one of those looks like). As evidence, they usually refer to the visit to Elgar's home in 1901 by the composer Arnold Bax, then a seventeen-year-old student. In his memoir, *Farewell, My Youth*, Bax would later write of his surprised impressions of the older man:

> Hatless, dressed in rough tweeds and riding boots, his appearance was rather that of a retired army officer turned gentleman farmer than an eminent and almost morbidly highly strung artist … He was very pleasant and even communicative in his rumbling voice, yet there was ever a faint sense of detachment, a hint – very slight – of hauteur and reserve.

In other words, Elgar looked like a stereotypical English country gent, which was not how a composer – certainly not a great one – should look. Neither was it how a composer should sound: composers were meant to have foreign accents. It might have been a German who invented the phrase 'the land without music' to describe the British Isles, but it was the English who took it to heart.

These days, the image of Elgar is familiar enough: the somewhat sad face retreating behind a shaggy handlebar moustache; piercing, almost otherworldly eyes peering out from beneath the brim of a bowler or Homburg; and, yes, the tweeds. But surely no one wonders any longer about whether he looked like a composer, because we all know he wrote the *Enigma* variations and the *Pomp and Circumstance* marches, and these contain tunes most people can hum. Anyway, there have been plenty of other English composers since – that in itself is not so strange a concept. But doubts still dog Elgar's music.

The one thing everyone appears to be agreed upon is that Elgar's music epitomises Englishness, although no one is able to say with certainty how or why that is, or even what it means. But where does Elgar fit in musical history? Was he a reactionary? Most people would say yes, but his German contemporary Richard Strauss called him a progressive. Was Elgar's music genuinely great? Again, there's no broad agreement. It was in and out of favour even during the composer's lifetime and it has been ever since. Does it 'travel'? Well, there is a long list of non-English conductors that at one time or another have championed Elgar's music, including Arturo Toscanini, Pierre Monteux, Eugen Jochum, Yevgeny Svetlanov, Leonard Bernstein, Zubin Mehta, Giuseppe Sinopoli and Daniel Barenboim. But so often their performances seem to come with special pleading. Recently, Sakari Oramo, the Finnish chief conductor of the City of Birmingham Symphony Orchestra, wrote an article in the *Guardian* lamenting the fact that Elgar is not played more often or taken more seriously outside the British Isles.

Oramo's orchestra played a significant role in Elgar's career. Since the composer himself was a West Midlands man, the CBSO was his local orchestra. Indeed he conducted its first concert in 1920, with a group of players, some of whom had played in the first performance of his oratorio *The Dream of Gerontius* at the Birmingham Festival twenty years before. That concert, conducted by the great Wagnerian Hans Richter, had been a disaster.

Elgar was forty-three at the time of the premiere. With the *Enigma* variations, given its premiere (also by Richter) just the previous year, the composer had enjoyed a popular breakthrough. Late starts by composers would become quite common in the twentieth century (Michael Tippett, Elliott Carter, Witold Lułostawski and Franco Donatoni were all in their forties when they discovered their musical voices), but in the nineteenth century it was unusual if not unprece-dented for a major composer to emerge so late. No one knew this better than Elgar, who had begun to believe he had missed the boat. So the success of *Enigma* delighted him and gave him the confidence to move ahead with *Gerontius*, into which, he said, he put 'the best of me'. Elgar, who was a Catholic, though seldom a devout one, took his text from the poem by Cardinal Newman in which the elderly figure of Gerontius contemplates his death, prays for salvation and is reconciled with his god. It is not hard to think of the piece in terms of the composer's own religious struggles and there is a tempting parallel with the Schoenberg of *Jacob's Ladder* and *Moses and Aaron*, both of which, significantly, were left incomplete. But Elgar finished *Gerontius*, and that very day his wife wrote to a friend, 'He has written his Dream of G. from his very *soul*.'

Then came the performance, badly played, badly sung, out of tune, full of wrong tempos and wrong notes. Elgar told Bax, a year later, 'The fact is neither the choir nor Richter knew the score', but his immediate response following the performance was altogether more bitter.

'I always said God was against art,' Elgar wrote to his publisher, '& I still believe it ... I have allowed my heart to open once – it is now shut against every religious feeling and every soft, gentle impulse *for ever*.'

The premiere of *Gerontius* really should have done for the piece, and it might have done for Elgar, too. But something curious hap-pened. The work received good reviews. Critics were able to hear past the inaccuracies in the performance to the music beyond. Further performances were arranged and these were triumphs. Indeed, it was after a performance of the work in Düsseldorf just eighteen months later that Strauss proposed his toast to 'the welfare and success of

the first English progressivist [*sic*], Meister Edward Elgar'. Elgar
appreciated the 'Meister'.

The next years were full of success for Elgar. In 1901 he composed
the first of his military marches, entitled *Pomp and Circumstance* –
the one with the tune that became 'Land of Hope and Glory' – and
it was an immediate hit. There quickly followed three more marches,
as well as the concert overtures *Cockaigne (In London Town)* and *In
the South (Alassio)* and the *Introduction and Allegro* for string quartet
and string orchestra. In 1908, at the age of fifty-one, he produced his
first symphony, which was a huge critical and popular success at its
Manchester premiere where it was conducted by its dedicatee Hans
Richter ('true artist and true friend'), now long forgiven for the
Gerontius debacle.

God was forgiven, too, the largest-scale works of this period
being two more religious oratorios, *The Apostles* and *The Kingdom*.
These now formed a trilogy with *Gerontius*. But it was the symphony
that became the composer's calling card, receiving more than a hundred performances at home and abroad during the twelve months
that followed its premiere. Elgar's glorious decade culminated in
Fritz Kreisler's premiere of the violin concerto, a work of a scale and
quality that invited (and received) comparisons with the violin concertos of Brahms and Beethoven.

But then everything went wrong again. In 1911 a second symphony was performed, and unaccountably nobody seemed to understand it. Certainly it was a less obvious work than the first symphony,
which had begun with a long tune (played twice) that returned at the
very end. Structurally and texturally the second symphony is denser,
richer and rather unpredictable. It was only at the end of World War
I, when Adrian Boult revived it, that the second symphony was
enthusiastically received. Elgar wrote to Boult the next day:

> With the sounds ringing in my ears I send a word of thanks for
> your conducting of the Sym: I am most grateful to you for your

affectionate care of it & I feel that my reputation in the future is in your safe hands.

From a musical point of view, Elgar's confidence in Boult was well-placed, but in fact his 'reputation in the future' has had the same ups and downs the composer himself experienced. Today his music is played very regularly in the United Kingdom, but mostly ignored on the European continent. Even in other English-speaking countries, it often seems that the music's reputation is something to be lived down. In his *Guardian* article, Sakari Oramo suggested the problem was that foreigners associated Elgar's music with the English upper classes, embodying its clichés of the 'stiff upper lip' and 'emotional constipation'. They hear the composer's name and recall 'Land of Hope and Glory', with its celebration of empire:

Wider still and wider shall thy bounds be set.
God, who made thee mighty, make thee mightier yet.

It colours their attitude to Elgar's music and to the composer. Both are dismissed as arrogant and hopelessly old-fashioned.

'What an extraordinarily ironic fate,' Oramo wrote, 'for this deeply romantic son of a piano-tuner.'

And, one might add, what an ironic fate for a composer with such ambivalent views about English society. For Elgar's patriotism was sentimental rather than belligerent. He disliked the words to 'Land of Hope and Glory'. His politics were conservative in the way that those of the provincial middle classes often are, but as a Catholic he always felt an outsider. And anyway, in Arthur O'Shaughnessy's phrase from 'The Music Makers', set to music by Elgar in 1913, he was, first and foremost, a dreamer of dreams.

Elgar's own performances of his orchestral works, as they've come down to us in recordings, have a devil-may-care quality. The instrumental ensemble is often ragged in quicker passages and tempos are generally swift. Was he perhaps attempting to compensate for the sentimentality, for the dreaminess? In recent years conductors have used these historical recordings as benchmarks for their own performances, ratcheting up the tempos to match the composer's. But the raggedness that affects these recordings from the 1920s and 30s affects most other orchestral recordings of the era. It was the style of the day: short notes were shortened, dotted notes over-dotted and lines of semiquavers lightly skated over. When a whole violin section does this, it can – and to our ears does – sound ragged. As for the speeds, the era of 78 rpm records was subject to the restrictions of the four-minute side. It would be a brave person who stated unequivocally that Elgar's fast tempos in the studio were simply his preference.

But what of the music itself? Does it really sound English? And if so, why? The composers who most inspired Elgar were all Europeans, and Germans at that. In Elgar's music, one readily hears the phrasing and rhythmic verve of Schumann, the symphonic logic – especially with regard to the working out of melodic motifs – of Brahms, and a multitude of harmonic and orchestral touches from Wagner (*Parsifal*, of course, lies behind *Gerontius*, in its prevailing mood of radiant calm as much as anything). Strauss, too, is an important model, those concert overtures of Elgar's resembling the German's symphonic poems on so many levels, while it is hard not to hear *Falstaff* as an older, fatter version of *Till Eulenspiegel*. And yet, Elgar is his own man, his music as recognisable as that of any of his Teutonic counterparts. So what is different about his work?

It is partly a matter of orchestration – for Elgar never sounds more Elgarian than in his orchestral works. The examples of Wagner and Strauss are certainly present, but the brass writing in particular is distinctive and – dare one say it? – quite English. Brass instruments provide the signature sound of Elgar's orchestra, not so much in the form of a brass section as a brass band, there at the heart of everything and always wanting to take charge. Far from inspiring the marching of soldiers, this band is entertaining Edwardian families in deckchairs. It is ubiquitous. Even the lyricism of the violin concerto is regularly energised by the welling up of the brass band within. But this is probably as 'English' as the music gets.

Elgar's harmony is also distinctive. In comparison with the music of the above-mentioned German composers, Elgar's is surprisingly diatonic, which is to say harmonically more straightforward, less tense, less meandering. The long opening tune of the first symphony is a perfect example of this, walking along in A flat major, accompanied by chords that firmly support its untroubled progress. The great 'Nimrod' from the *Enigma* variations is a celebration of E flat, while it's hard to think of a composer since Handel who made D major sound brighter than Elgar does in his *Introduction and Allegro*. None of which should suggest that Elgar's attitude to harmony is simpleminded. The opening melody of the first symphony over, the music jolts us from that blithe A flat major into the dark, tritonally-related key of D minor. The same symphony's slow movement keeps lapsing into a tonally ambiguous *Tristan*-like lethargy. Uncertainty threatens Elgar's music just as it threatened his peace of mind. But in the music, tonal clarity always triumphs.

Is this English? It could be the influence of English hymnody; perhaps it's English folksong. But it's probably neither. Given Elgar's troubled relationship with organised religion, the former is hard to believe, while his views on folk music were perfectly clear: any composer including a folk tune in a piece of music was simply being lazy.

Like any good art, Elgar's music is totally personal. That is its mystery and its strength. If it sounds 'English', perhaps this is simply a matter of the associations – with the British Empire, with armies on parade, with the flag wavers at the Last Night of the Proms. Whether these are the correct associations is another matter. Given what we know of Elgar himself, it is hard to believe they are.

Australian Financial Review, 2007

Delius: The components of a style

The English composer Frederick Delius did not care for every note by his Nordic contemporary Jean Sibelius, but he admired a lot of the music and he liked the man himself. Of course, he had never read the Finn's diary, in which he is described as a snake and a slanderer (there is no evidence of slander), and in which Sibelius gloats over bad reviews of Delius's music.

There was a time when the two composers' names were frequently linked. Both were widely considered poets of nature. Both were outside the classical mainstream. Their countries of birth alone would have guaranteed this at the start of the twentieth century, but additionally each composer had a unique and distinctive voice, neither traditional nor obviously modernist, that had come to him relatively late. Both were also surprisingly popular in their lifetimes, so much so that they rated a mention in the Cole Porter song, 'Red, Hot and Blue':

> I can't take Sibelius,
> Or Delius,
> But I'd throw my best pal away
> For Calloway.

At least some of that popularity came down to the work of one man, for Delius and Sibelius shared a tireless champion in the conductor Thomas Beecham, and one suspects that Sibelius's unflattering opinions of Delius were provoked by a twinge of jealousy. Did he feel Beecham was spending too much time with his other favourite?

He need not have worried. The popularity that Sibelius's music enjoyed during the composer's lifetime shows no sign of fading. German orchestras, it's true, play the music less than most, and the French don't seem to understand it at all, but throughout most of northern Europe and in all English-speaking countries, Sibelius's name fills concert halls. In recent years, moreover, he has received considerable critical attention and acclaim. It is generally agreed he was a great composer, and some now think of him as a modernist after all.

Delius is another matter. Few would suggest that he was a true great, and these days his music is anything but popular. It was always hard to know where to place him. Because Sibelius's early works were composed at the time of Finland's struggle for independence, he could be branded a nationalist, no matter how much his later work might refuse the label. But with Delius, it was barely possible even to locate him in one country. Was he actually really English?

Frederick Delius was born Fritz Delius in 1862 in Bradford, Yorkshire. His parents were Germans who owned a wool business there. When it became clear that Fritz had no interest in joining the family firm he was packed off to Florida, finding himself, aged twenty-three, the manager of an orange plantation at Solano Grove near Jacksonville. Music had always been one of his passions, but now hearing African-American spirituals, as well as work songs on the plantation, he suddenly felt driven to compose. From Florida he moved briefly to Danville, Virginia, then to Continental Europe where he began formal studies in Leipzig. This is where he first met Sibelius and also the Norwegian composer Edvard Grieg who recognised Delius's talent and offered him support. After Leipzig, Delius lived the good life in Paris, before finally settling down, with his German wife Jelka, at Grez-sur-Loing on the edge of the forest of Fontainebleau. They married in 1903. Delius was 41 and about to embark upon writing his greatest works.

However, after World War I the composer began to experience the effects of the syphilis he had contracted in his Paris years. By the late 1920s, he was blind and paralysed and unable to work. Reading of Delius's plight, an English student named Eric Fenby wrote to the composer offering himself as amanuensis, and it was thus that a number of late pieces were dictated to the young man between 1928 and the composer's death in 1934.

That year is generally regarded as a bad one for English music, for Edward Elgar and Gustav Holst also died in 1934, and yet Delius sits oddly in such company. All his life, he spoke with a strong Yorkshire accent, but, as more than one of his biographers have recognised, he was an unusually cosmopolitan figure. And that is how the music sounds, too. If Delius was a 'poet of nature' (and that label, at least, attaches more convincingly to him than to Sibelius), it was not an English pastoral scene he evoked so much as a philosophical one.

Summer Evening, Winter Night and *Spring Morning* (1890), *Songs of Sunset* (1907), *In a Summer Garden* (1908), *Summer Night on the River* (1911), *On Hearing the First Cuckoo in Spring* (1912), *A Song before Sunrise* (1918), *A Song of Summer* (1930): these are by no means all of Delius's season-related titles. They make him sound like a pagan or pantheist, but in fact his attitude to nature came filtered through the philosophy of Friedrich Nietzsche. Avowedly unsentimental, Delius saw humanity as part of nature, dwarfed by it, inspired by it, buffeted by it, and finally absorbed by it.

There is nothing triumphant here, and there is no optimism. Delius's music, at its greatest, is characterised by a sad inevitability. It is made explicit in some of the texts he chose to set. These are by Nietzsche himself in both *A Mass of Life* (1905) and the atheist *Requiem* (1916) dedicated 'to the memory of all young artists fallen in the war'. He also set Walt Whitman in *Sea Drift* (1904), James Elroy Flecker (the opera *Hassan*), and English 'decadents' Ernest Dowson ('I have been faithful to thee, Cynara! in my fashion') and Arthur Symons.

In his poem 'On Craig Ddu', Symons describes the sensation of looking up from a mountain crag in North Wales.

The sky through the leaves of the bracken,
Tenderly, pallidly blue,
Nothing but sky as I lie on the mountain-tops
Hark! for the wind as it blew,
Rustling the tufts of my bracken above me,
Brought from below
Into the silence the sound of the water ...

In 1907 Delius took Symons's pale symbolism, creating a musical setting of the words for an unaccompanied six-part chorus, subtitled 'An impression of nature'. It is a small miracle of chromatic close harmony. Setting off in an airy G major, immediately disrupted by dissonant notes, the music rises and falls through all manner of tonally remote added-note chords until the final words ('Blue, through the bracken, softly enveloping, / Silence a veil') bring the piece to rest on a poignant chord of G minor with an added A that hangs there in a sweet harmonic limbo, as we hope it will never resolve. When it does settle into G minor proper, we feel a disappointment.

And there it is: Delius's art in miniature. And perhaps it offers a clue to the problem of Delius and audiences. For while a song like 'On Craig Ddu' is a ravishing gem, the same technique – the same rootless harmonies meandering across a far longer time span – can have a disorientating effect that is unlikely to engage wide sympathies. Even Eric Fenby, in his memoir of working with Delius, admits that '[it] would have been so refreshing if, after a hard day's work, one could have listened for a while to music that was just a little less chromatic in character'.

So what does it consist of, this style that is so personal and so instantly recognisable? And where does it come from? The most obvious source of chromatic harmonic writing at the turn of the twentieth century was Wagner. Any composer coming after Wagner had to deal with the legacy of his music. You could be for it or against it (both, if you were Debussy), but you could not ignore it, and for a young man with German ancestry and an interest in Nietzsche it was inevitable there should be some influence.

But Delius's melodies are not Wagnerian. At their simplest, they recall composers such as Borodin (the popular 'La Calinda' from the opera *Koanga* [1895] is redolent of the Russian's *Polotsvian Dances*) and Delius's mentor Grieg. Indeed, Grieg's influence on Delius was as great as it was on Percy Grainger. Grainger himself, a frequent visitor to Delius in France, was more an admirer than an influence on the older man (Grainger once maintained that the three greatest composers in history were Bach, Delius and Duke Ellington), but the two shared a profound emotionalism in their music, an over-the-top quality that is not for the squeamish. All those notes piled on top of each other, those complex chromatic chords: they are there to wring intense feeling out of the music.

As for Delius's exact contemporary, Claude Debussy, in whose country the Englishman took up residence, there are themes and interests in common – nature, painting and symbolist poetry, for example – but surprisingly few musical connections. The two might have shared a fastidious ear for instrumental detail, but Debussy's orchestra is translucent, while Delius's so often seems opaque.

Is it, then, all a matter of personal idiolect? Is the distinctive sound of Delius the result simply of an individual imagination? There is one more influence we must not forget. Those spirituals and field hollers back in Florida were much more than the inspiration for a life in music; they left their impression on Delius the composer and affected his whole musical language.

Delius had a great love of so-called 'Lombard rhythms', sometimes known as 'Scotch snaps' for their prevalence in bagpipe music. These rhythms have a short accented note followed by a longer note, and they are very common in spirituals. Think of 'Go Down Moses' and the line 'Tell old Pharaoh to let my people go': 'Tell old' and 'people' are both Lombard rhythms and so is the first syllable of 'Pharaoh'. Delius's melodic lines are full of these rhythms.

Then there is the more significant matter of harmony. He would not have called them this, but there are 'blue' notes all through Delius's music, flattened or raised pitches that decorate and disrupt the key of the music. They would have been typical of the singing Delius heard in Florida, and when you have enough of these notes, they add up to an extremely chromatic harmonic palette. This is true enough of Delius's work, but it is also a function of a lot of voices singing together yet independently: workers on a plantation, for example. Called heterophony, it can be heard today in pentecostal churches throughout the southern United States: a single melodic line sung by many voices, never quite together and each with its own repertoire of spontaneous blue-note ornaments and elaborations. The result is chromatic and dense, and that describes the choral and orchestral music of Frederick Delius. It may not sound like spirituals on the surface, but Delius's music remained true – in its 'fashion' – to the sounds that first inspired it.

Australian Financial Review, 2012

Landscape and God

There's a song by the Elizabethan lutenist and composer John Bartlett (or Bartlet) in which fourteen individual birds are invoked and their songs impersonated. Topping the bill, just before the end, comes the red kite:

> *The kite tiw whiw whiw whiw full oft cried soaring*
> *Up aloft and down again returned presently*

The 'tiw whiw whiw whiw' is sung at a piercingly high pitch in emulation of the kite's voice, while the bird's soaring is represented by passages of ascending notes ('Up aloft, up aloft, up aloft, up aloft') and descending notes ('and down again, and down again, and down again'). A cadence, naturally, accompanies the words 'returned presently'.

But as chance would have it, it is not a perfect cadence, which would have implied a homecoming, and sadly this is fitting because, presently, the kite did not return. In Tudor times, the red kite was considered a threat to livestock, especially to sheep. When Bartlett composed his song, then, just at the end of Elizabeth's reign, there had already been a bounty on the head of the bird for several decades and baits were routinely set. By the nineteenth century, the kite was extinct in England and Scotland, making especially poignant Bartlett's words:

> *O might I hear them ever*
> *Of straines so sweete, sweete birds deprive us never.*

These days, thanks to more benign human intervention, the red kite is making something of a comeback in the British Isles. But Bartlett's 400-year-old song retains its power to move and inspire, and this is because it is more than just an example of one composer's love of nature, or even of the influence of birdsong generally on composers. It is, to employ Wilfrid Mellers's term, a piece of musical 'ecology'. The kite itself might have vanished for about a hundred years and more, but its voice was preserved in Bartlett's song.

Wilfrid Mellers, composer, teacher and writer about music, founder of the music department at the University of York in England, and mentor, informally, to Peter Sculthorpe, is eighty-eight years old, but he remains a vital figure in the understanding of music. The idea that music might be a medium for ecology is raised in the subtitle of Mellers's book, a collection of essays entitled *Singing in the Wilderness: Music and ecology in the twentieth century.*

Throughout history, the use of birdsong has been the composer's most obvious debt to nature, not least because you can so clearly hear the birds. There they are in the madrigals of Janequin and Morley, in the keyboard pieces of Couperin and Rameau, in the concertos of Vivaldi and Handel, and the operas of Verdi and Wagner. Often it is not even a matter of generalised twittering in the high woodwind; you can actually identify specific birds. At the end of the slow movement of Beethoven's *Pastoral* symphony we hear three common European birds one after the other: a nightingale (flute), a quail (oboe) and a cuckoo (clarinet). Olivier Messiaen carefully listed all the birds you could hear in his pieces. In *Catalogue d'oiseaux*, a series of solo piano pieces running to seven volumes, the voice of one bird at a time is explored in almost scientific detail.

Landscape, too, is present in music. Once again, the movements of the *Pastoral* symphony will serve as examples. Their titles refer to happy feelings upon arriving in the country, to a scene by a brook, to peasants making merry and offering thanks to God after a storm. All that's missing from this Teutonic bucolia is a forest. Forests have been important to German culture for centuries. The Roman historian Tacitus recognised their significance when he wrote his *Germania* at the end of the first century. Very frequently in art, and in music, forests provide the backdrop to mysterious or supernatural occurrences. The magical events of Weber's *Der Freischütz* occur in a forest, while in Wagner's *Siegfried*, the wood bird appears with advice for the eponymous hero in the clearing of a 'murmuring' forest. It is a wood dove that flies to King Waldemar with news of the death of his lover, in Schoenberg's *Gurrelieder*. Schoenberg, indeed, seems to have been especially drawn to the imagery of forests. The two lovers in *Verklärte Nacht* walk through a moonlit forest, and it might as well be in the very same forest that the frantic woman in *Erwartung* searches for her man and stumbles on his bloodied corpse.

Mellers discusses the snow-covered forest of Sibelius's *Tapiola* and the fairytale forest where the action of Leoš Janáček's opera *The Cunning Little Vixen* occurs. He takes us to the imaginary forests in the mind of Charles Koechlin and to the jungles of Heitor Villa-Lobos's Brazilian homeland. Throughout, Mellers is thinking about far more than the Western composer's traditional love of nature. Chirruping birds, babbling brooks and murmuring forests might provide musical inspiration, and they certainly make apt symbols and metaphors, as do mountains and oceans and prairies and deserts, but the essays in *Singing in the Wilderness* concern still more fundamental issues. Mellers is interested in composers whose music has a strong identification with place, music that is grounded in the dirt.

He describes Peter Sculthorpe, for example, as an 'aboriginal' composer for his achievement in creating something from nothing – the apparent emptiness of the outback certainly, but also, one suspects, the emptiness of Australian classical music before him. The American Steve Reich went in search of a literary desert as a means to musical renewal (in his choral setting of William Carlos Williams, *The Desert Music*) and discovered a flowering of melody. The expatriate Frenchman, Edgard Varèse, fascinated by rock and crystal formations, entered the Arizona desert during a twenty-year period of compositional silence, finally emerging with the score of *Déserts* (1954) one of the very first works to employ music composed with and played back via the newly invented tape-recorder. Even before this, Varèse had invented a musical language from the ground up. Leaving European music quite literally behind him, in 1915 he had made his home amid the modern din of New York City and created, in Mellers's words, 'a revolutionary music that abandoned Western progression and development in favour of quasi-architectural blocks of sound'. Composing with a tape-recorder was a natural extension of this technique, and so Varèse had emerged from his period in the wilderness, more himself than ever.

In returning to nature, in discovering his or her *own* nature, a composer leaves the mainstream to become, in at least one sense, an artist *in extremis*. Although Mellers doesn't make the precise claim, one senses in these pages his strong conviction that these are the most interesting artists of all. He is also fascinated by the difference between art and nature, between calculation and spontaneity, between artfulness and what comes naturally.

Throughout his career, Mellers has been drawn back, again and again, to pop music, to jazz and the blues, and to folkloric music in many other forms. His study of the Beatles, *The Twilight of the Gods*, was the first book-length analysis of their art; *A Darker Shade of Pale* placed Bob Dylan's early songs in the context of all that had inspired them. Mellers has written and lectured about Hebridean mouth music and Native American chant, about Big Mama Thornton and Billie Holiday, about Louis Armstrong and Charlie Parker and John Coltrane. In *Singing in the Wilderness*, a long chapter deals with Duke Ellington and an epilogue explores the music of Abdullah Ibrahim.

Spontaneity is as important to Mellers as tradition, and he believes it is important to art, not least as a source of creative renewal. Writing about one of his own large-scale musical compositions,

Yeibichai (1969), for singers, speakers, chorus and orchestra, Mellers says that the issue is 'the intermittent necessity for a return to the instinctual life'. Again, what he is describing is a confrontation with nature, with human nature. And to the extent that it is ecological, this kind of music preserves the human spirit.

Which, I suppose, is where God comes in. Wilfrid Mellers might be in his late eighties, but *Singing in the Wilderness* is not his only book to appear in 2002. Closely following this study of the music of nature and the nature in music, was the yet more ambitious *Celestial Music?: Some masterpieces of European religious music.* Covering 800 years of compositional endeavour, from the Abbess Hildegard of Bingen to John Tavener and Arvo Pärt, via Bach's B minor Mass, Beethoven's *Missa solemnis*, the Requiems of Berlioz, Brahms and Verdi, the book considers (in the words of its subtitle) 'some masterpieces of European religious music'.

What is fascinating about a comparison of the two books, is the extent to which chapters are almost interchangeable. A section about Messiaen's music, for example, which includes discussion of both *Quatuor pour la fin du temps* (*Quartet for the End of Time*) and *Chronochromie*, might easily have turned up in *Singing in the Wilderness*. The quartet, composed in 1940 in a German prisoner of war camp, contains the first instance of Messiaen's use of birdsong; in one movement of *Chronochromie* (1960), eighteen solo violins are each allocated the song of a different bird, chirping away simultaneously in a sort of dawn chorus. But in fact this chapter appears in *Celestial Music?*, Messiaen himself having, from the start, tied his love of birdsong and nature in general to his Catholic faith.

Similarly, Aaron Copland, the gay, Russian-Jewish, Brooklyn-born, Paris-trained inventor of 'cowboy' music, seems to belong in *Singing in the Wilderness*. Mellers himself points out that Copland composed only one overtly religious work in his life, while if anyone drew strength from landscape and nature it was surely the creator of *Appalachian Spring*. But no, Copland creeps in at the end of *Celestial*

Music?, an American interloper at this European party, and with Emily Dickinson on his arm, what's more.

Copland's *12 Poems of Emily Dickinson*, composed in 1950, deal as we might imagine and as Mellers suggests with 'first and last things', as much through the 'plainness' of Copland's musical response as through the elaborate grammar and over-elaborate punctuation of Dickinson's verse.

Frederick Delius, too, merits attention in *Celestial Music?*, the punctuation in Mellers's title acquiring more significance all the time. What is celestial? Delius might have composed both a Mass and a Requiem, but it was *A Mass of Life*, Nietzsche's words replacing the Roman liturgy, and a 'pagan' Requiem, 'a Mass of death' composed during and at least partly in response to World War I.

'The proud spirit casts off the yoke of superstition,' wrote the atheist Delius, 'for it knows that death puts an end to all life and therefore fulfilment can be found only in life itself.'

Wilfrid Mellers, in the preface to his earlier book, *Beethoven and the Voice of God* (1983), explained that he was not then, nor had he ever been, a Christian, and so far as I am aware there has been no late conversion. In other words, the author approaches music from something like the same standpoint as Delius. You might think, then, that Mellers would have little sympathy with the unequivocally religious – some would say religiose – music of the so-called 'Holy Minimalists'. Yet he devotes a chapter to Arvo Pärt, Henryk Górecki and John Tavener, placing their music alongside that of the considerably less minimal James MacMillan and Michael Finnissy. Reading the chapter, one begins to see that, at bottom, Mellers's two books are complementary. What the author admires in the work of these five living composers is not their apparent faith, so much as the musical renewal that faith has brought about. Call it faith, call it ecology; call it nature, call it God: it has sent these composers to new extremes, into themselves and, significantly in a global age, into the places, geographical and spiritual, to which they belong. The first chapter of *Celestial Music?* looks at 'oneness' in the *Symphonia armo-niae celestium revelationem* of Hildegard of Bingen. Even the title of her 'symphony', uniting harmony and heavenly revelation, points to a sort of 'oneness'. More significant, in terms of underlining the one-ness of Mellers's two books, is the fact that in addition to being a composer and a theologian, the Abbess of Bingen was a naturalist.

There are those who argue that all music is about other music, and you do not have to be a card-carrying postmodernist to feel there might be some truth in the statement. It would be hard to imagine a human being composing music without ever having heard any other music, if only, perhaps, birdsong. Equally, there are plenty of pieces of music that bear generic titles: preludes and fugues, sym-phonies, concertos and sonatas have, on the face of it, little connec-tion with either heaven or the wilderness. But the impulse to compose music must come from somewhere. As children we learn languages by imitating the noises that others make – that is *how* we learn to talk – but *why* we learn is another matter. There is a need in us to communicate. By the same token, a composer's music might relate to or respond to or be influenced by other music, but communica-tion is surely its main motivation. And music can help us communi-cate our most important feelings about 'first and last things', even if we did not actually compose the music ourselves.

'For most people the origin of life is a sound,' Mellers suggests. We hear the creation of all human life 'latent in the cry of a new-born babe'. The baby's cry, in turn, gives way to the more sophisti-cated composition of language, though the sounds of our 'instinctual life' return intermittently and of necessity. When we laugh or grieve or love or warn of danger – when we are *in extremis* – we often abandon words entirely, we return to being instinctual and musical.

The communality of music – all music, not just folk music – is what connects it so strongly to what some people experience as God and others as a belonging to a place or group. That is why music can soothe and comfort us or rouse us as no other art can. That is also why books such as these by Wilfrid Mellers, books that illuminate the humanity from which music arises and to which it speaks, ultimately make us hungry for its inspiration and its balm.

Australian Financial Review, 2002

To Be a Pilgrim: The music of Ralph Vaughan Williams

The English composer Ralph Vaughan Williams was a passionate man with a famously short fuse. Few things provoked his ire more than others' attempts to explain the meanings of his symphonies.

'Does it never occur to these people that a man might just want to write a piece of music?' was the composer's typically bluff response to one critic's post-apocalyptic theory regarding his sixth symphony, completed in 1947.

In a way it is odd that Vaughan Williams should suffer from the curse of interpretation. There have been composers throughout history whose music seems to demand the search for extra-musical motives or meanings. When was the last time anyone discussed Shostakovich's work without mentioning his strained relationship with Stalin or Khrushchev? Can we listen to Benjamin Britten's music – in particular his operas, with their alienated protagonists – and forget that the composer was a homosexual pacifist in mid twentieth-century England? The music of Leoš Janáček's final decade, which includes his greatest works, is nearly impossible to hear without remembering his one-sided love affair with a much younger woman. This, mind you, is Janáček's own fault (or maybe the woman's), because he wrote to her (and she kept) 700 letters in which he outlined the connections between his passionate feelings and the music he was writing, going so far as to claim that the one had inspired the other. But Vaughan Williams? Old Uncle Ralph? Surely he is just English music incarnate, and that's an end of it.

In fact the problem starts with that very image of him as harmless and avuncular. The most commonly accepted interpretation of his music is that it celebrates the English countryside, evoking some sort of rustic bliss. If you knew only his most popular scores – *The Lark Ascending*, *Fantasia on Greensleeves* and *Fantasia on a Theme by Thomas Tallis* – and perhaps also knew that he had composed a piece entitled *A Pastoral Symphony* – it would certainly be possible to arrive at that conclusion. A contemporary critic, Philip Heseltine (who was also the composer Peter Warlock), called *A Pastoral Symphony* 'a cow looking over a gate'. A composer from the next generation, Elisabeth Lutyens, dismissed Vaughan Williams and his colleagues as the 'cowpat' school.

But a purely pastoral interpretation of those four pieces misses the point of at least three of them, and if one digs only a little deeper into the work of this prolific composer, it quickly becomes clear that they are scarcely typical of him. In a long life, Vaughan Williams composed a great deal of music in all genres: operas and ballets, concertos and other orchestral works, some chamber music, a lot of songs and choral works, hymn tunes and film scores. But at the heart of his output are nine symphonies, the last five of which he wrote after his seventieth birthday. And it is these symphonies – in particular, the middle pieces – that have been the subject of the greatest interpretive speculation.

In a sense, Vaughan Williams only had himself to blame for the rush to read meaning into his music. Each of his first three symphonies had not a number, but a descriptive title. The first was *A Sea Symphony* (1910), a big hour-long choral work, setting words by the American poet Walt Whitman. There followed *A London Symphony* (1914) and *A Pastoral Symphony* (1921). So when, on 10 April 1935, Adrian Boult conducted the first performance of a new Vaughan Williams symphony entitled merely 'Symphony No 4 in F minor', people quite reasonably wanted to know what this one was about. It was not simply the absence of a descriptive title that made them curious. The new symphony was a turbulent, frequently violent creation, beginning with the whole orchestra blaring out grinding dissonances. At the time, the composer's friends told him they heard the piece as a self-portrait, the *Scherzo* in particular redolent of his 'poisonous temper'. But it wasn't long before the work came to be accepted as a response to the rise of fascism in Europe and a premonition of World War II. Similarly, the radiant Symphony No 5 in D ('dedicated without permission to Jean Sibelius'), which was begun in 1938 and finally premiered at the London Proms in 1943, has generally been heard as a vision of peace.

By the time the sixth symphony appeared in 1948, a war-time triptych appeared to have taken shape. The sixth contained a slow movement in which trumpets played an insistent repeated-note fig-ure that reminded early audiences of the stuttering sound of anti-aircraft guns still fresh in their memories. But it was the work's Epilogue that inspired those theories of a landscape after an apoca-lypse. This is really unprecedented music. For one thing, the move-ment, which lasts around twelve minutes, is practically devoid of themes. The music drifts and meanders through a succession of chromatic harmonies as though in search of a home key, but finds it impossible to settle. There is often a hint of an 'Amen', but it is never conclusive. And also the whole movement is played at the threshold of audibility. Vaughan Williams marks the first bar *pianissimo* – very quiet – and the only other indication of dynamic is an occasional reminder not to get louder – *senza crescendo*. At the end, it simply fades to nothing. If you had to attach an image to it, a post-war wasteland would do very well.

Perhaps because of the theories that quickly sprang up, Vaughan Williams produced his own extra-musical image in a letter to the critic Michael Kennedy. He said that when he composed the Epilogue he had had in mind Shakespeare's *The Tempest* and Prospero's valedictory lines:

We are such stuff
As dreams are made on; and our little life
Is rounded with a sleep.

A few years later, in 1951, the composer set those same lines to music in his *Three Shakespeare Songs*, the words drawing from him on this occasion music that is even more chromatic than that of the sixth symphony, although this time the 'Amen' properly resolves.

That Vaughan Williams, in old age, might be attracted to the disillusioned magus, Prospero – the central figure (one can hardly say hero) of Shakespeare's final play – is surely not surprising. But those lines about 'our little life' being surrounded by nothing more than sleep – death – is perhaps more significant still. Although he composed a Mass and a *Magnificat* and a *Te Deum*, and set Biblical texts to music over and over again; though he even took religious themes for his ballet *Job* and opera *The Pilgrim's Progress*, Vaughan Williams was not himself a believer. He was an atheist who, according to his second wife Ursula, sometimes 'lapsed into agnosticism'.

Vaughan Williams died on 26 August 1958, and the fiftieth anniversary of his death has prompted new recordings, opera revivals and concerts. There have also been two new documentary films, and in this regard it is arguably Ursula Vaughan Williams's death – as recently as October 2007 – that has been the more significant. Rather suddenly, we are becoming aware that most of our theories about the composer's music – and this includes the composer's own protestations that it was *just* music – might need to be reconsidered in the light of new revelations about his private life.

Ralph Vaughan Williams was born in 1872, the son of a provincial vicar who died when the boy was two years old, but the family was well-connected. On his mother's side, Ralph (pronounced 'Rafe') was related to the Darwins and the Wedgwoods. So he had science, design and business acumen in his blood, and a healthy dose of nonconformity, too. Through the Darwins, Vaughan Williams was also related to the Keynes family. The historian Geoffrey Keynes would develop the scenario of Vaughan Williams's ballet, *Job*, and his brother, the economist John Maynard Keynes, financed it. But the truth is that money was never much of an object for the composer.

After Cambridge, where his friend Bertrand Russell introduced him to Whitman's poetry – an enthusiasm that would last his whole life – Vaughan Williams was married, in 1897, to Adeline Fisher, a cousin of Virginia Woolf. From early in the marriage, Adeline began to suffer from something like arthritis, which finally crippled her so severely that she was confined to a wheelchair. The marriage lasted 54 years, until Adeline's death in 1951, and Vaughan Williams cared for her devotedly throughout, always anxious to return home to Surrey after a concert in London, rather than leave her alone for the night.

This much we already knew. What was not known – not for sure – was that Ursula Wood, the 'music assistant' whom the composer married in 1953, had been his lover for the previous fifteen years. In 1938, as a young drama student, she had written to him hoping to interest him in a ballet scenario entitled, somewhat prophetically, *The Bridal Day*. At first he wasn't interested, but Ursula persisted, and finally they met. She was 27, he was 65. It seems to have been love at first sight.

In Tony Palmer's documentary *O Thou Transcendent*, there is the suggestion not only that the affair began immediately, but also that during the war Ursula became pregnant to the composer and had an abortion. Some of Palmer's talking heads take this further, suggesting that the anger of the fourth symphony, far from being the composer's response to a premonition of war, was really directed against Adeline and their passionless marriage, while the *Serenade to Music*, first performed at Henry Wood's Golden Jubilee concert in October 1938, and one of the most sublime works Vaughan Williams ever wrote, owed its wistful radiance to more than just the composer's admiration for the distinguished conductor. And while the fifth symphony, begun in 1938 but not completed until five years later, for the most part shares the radiance of the *Serenade*, it has at its heart a slow movement of great lyrical beauty and almost unbearable sadness. Was this the abortion?

Another film, by John Bridcut, spells out the relationship between Ursula and Ralph in more detail, confirming the suggestions in Palmer's film. Ursula had apparently wanted the truth told after her death.

When they had met that first day in 1938, Vaughan Williams took Ursula to lunch. In Bridcut's film, she explained what happened in the taxi afterwards: 'Ralph clutched me in his arms and gave me a terrific kiss. I said: "Well, I'm not used to this!" He said: "Well, you will be soon!"' Ursula was instantly smitten ('I fell in love absolutely fully'), and early the following morning she was unable to restrain herself from telephoning the composer. Vaughan Williams dropped everything and rushed over, arriving on her doorstep with half his face still unshaved.

The ensuing affair was made difficult by the fact that not only was Vaughan Williams married, but so was Ursula. When her husband, an army officer, died in 1942, Vaughan Williams invited her to come and live with him and his wife. Willingly or not, Adeline seems to have accepted the situation. In 1944, at the height of the V2 flying-bomb raids on England, at least one night passed with Vaughan Williams and his wife in twin beds, Ursula lying on a mattress between them holding their hands.

That Vaughan Williams led a double life while he composed some of his greatest works would not have surprised the late musicologist and composer, Wilfrid Mellers. Throughout his book *Vaughan Williams and the Vision of Albion*, Mellers discusses the composer as a 'double man'. He was not referring to the composer's personal relationships but to the many contradictions in his music and other work. In contrast to his private life, these were mostly in plain view.

Though born with what he called 'a very small silver spoon' in his mouth, Vaughan Williams was a lifelong socialist. This manifested itself in several ways. He refused a knighthood when one was offered, just as he had refused to buy himself a commission in the army, a common enough practice among others of his class. Since the composer was almost forty-two when the Great War broke out, he need not have served at all, yet he enlisted as a private in the Royal Army Medical Corps, was made a 'wagon orderly', and was shipped off to the Somme where his job was to drive an ambulance on to the battlefield each night and bring back the dead and wounded. For the rest of his life he refused to speak of this experience.

Although he did not write much music during the war, *A Pastoral Symphony* was brewing and this is a good example of the contradictory nature of his work. The piece can be listened to with nothing but its title for a guide – presumably this is how the critic Heseltine listened – but one would have to wonder at the gently botched attempts at 'The Last Post' heard in the slow movement. In fact this moment was inspired by a real experience, the composer in his barracks on Salisbury Plain hearing a bugler practising and repeatedly fluffing the top note. Vaughan Williams said that if he had any particular landscape in mind it was the 'Corot-like' scenes he saw in France; he also admitted that the piece was 'really a wartime symphony'.

Naturally, this knowledge makes us hear the music differently. 'The Last Post' was never hard to spot, but now the piece brings other associations. Suddenly, we are hearing the 'bugles calling ... from sad shires' in Wilfred Owen's 'Anthem for Doomed Youth'. If it's merely a *pastoral* symphony, then the wordless soprano in the final movement is some shepherdess or milkmaid. But if it's a war-time symphony, then another line from Owen's poem suggests itself: 'The pallor of girls' brows shall be their pall ...'

This is precisely the sort of speculation that irked Vaughan Williams, but perhaps it is inevitable when a great composer is also a popular composer. And being popular was important to Vaughan Williams, not in the commercial sense, but in terms of being a man of the people. It accounts, in part, for his early work as a folksong collector – one of the first serious composers to be so engaged. Contrary to common belief, few folk tunes turn up in his music, but there can be no doubt that traditional music affected his melodic writing and, perhaps even more, the strongly modal nature of his harmonic thinking.

He also seems genuinely to have liked the elderly farm labourers who sang him their songs, and perhaps there is a connection here with his work on behalf of amateur singers, conducting their choirs, adjudicating their competitions, attending their committee meetings. In 1905, in the Surrey town where he lived, he was asked to conduct the first concert of the Leith Hill Music Festival, a coming together of local choirs. He continued to conduct their concerts for the next forty-eight years, alongside his professional work.

Most striking of all in Mellers's 'double man', is the paradox of an atheist accepting the editorship of the *English Hymnal*, and taking to the task with enthusiasm. Perhaps Vaughan Williams regarded this as another aspect of amateur music (he accepted the job a year after he took on Leith Hill). Although it wasn't part of the brief, he composed a few new tunes himself ('Come Down, O Love Divine' is one of his, and so is 'For All the Saints'). He included folk tunes, fitting John Bunyan's words ('To Be a Pilgrim') to a stirring Sussex melody collected from Mrs Harriet Verrall of Monk's Gate, and replacing the mawkishly sentimental tune of 'O Little Town of Bethlehem' with one called 'Forest Green'. He also dug back into English history to find forgotten hymns, and it was in this way he came across the tunes that Thomas Tallis (1505–85) had composed for Archbishop Parker's Psalter. One of them gave him the theme on which he wrote his famous fantasia. Just as his experience of folk music changed him, so did this. Tallis's block chords, often moving in parallel, became a feature in Vaughan Williams's music: *Fantasia on a Theme by Thomas Tallis* sounds as bright and fresh and original today as it must have done at its first performance in 1910, and crucially it signifies a break with the Germanic domination of English music that had continued for a hundred years and which even Elgar had been unable (or unwilling) to dispel. There is no Brahms here, and no Wagner.

Ambiguity is a hallmark of great art. A work of art may be strong and vivid and clear, and we may read or look or listen with acute sensitivity: even so, the best art leaves itself permanently open to a range of interpretations. This is certainly true of Vaughan Williams's music, and if further proof were needed, there is a curious little book by the right-wing British journalist Simon Heffer, entitled simply *Vaughan Williams*, in which the author sets out to bend the composer to his own view of the world. The *Tallis* fantasia, far from being fresh or radical, 'is explicitly reactionary'; the composer only turned down the knighthood because he was proud of his doctorate and enjoyed being called Dr Vaughan Williams; and all this talk of him being a socialist and an atheist is really an exaggeration: he was 'never ... ideological', always seeking the mystical.

The last bit is true. You might argue that this is what all composers do – that music, by its abstract and intangible nature, is the most mystical of the arts – but in Vaughan Williams's case it was more than that. His first mature choral work, which was his first use of Whitman, is entitled *Towards the Unknown Region*, and it sets the tone for what is to come. Another choral work, *Sancta Civitas* – his favourite out of twenty such works – takes words from the Book of Revelation. His ballet *Job* – he called it 'a Masque for Dancing' – concerns the Old Testament prophet asked to praise a God that visits upon him one calamity after another. His opera *The Pilgrim's Progress* – he called it a 'Morality' – is about one who seeks and finds the Heavenly City, but only after encountering a myriad discouragements. Significantly, Vaughan Williams changed the name of Bunyan's 'Christian' to 'Pilgrim'.

What was Vaughan Williams seeking? Perhaps something like a common good, something like social equality through music. Wilfrid Mellers – always imaginative, canny, making connections – drew a parallel between *The Pilgrim's Progress* (a project that occupied Vaughan Williams, off and on, for most of his creative life) and *Sinfonia antartica*, which draws on the music he composed for the film *Scott of the Antarctic* (1948).

The latter is regularly accorded low esteem – film music cobbled together to make an ad hoc symphony – but Tony Palmer tells a different story. For *O Thou Transcendent*, he spoke to Roy Douglas, who was Vaughan Williams's editor, and Jill Balcon, daughter of the producer Michael Balcon. Both told him that when Balcon commissioned the music for *Scott of the Antarctic*, the film had not yet been made. When Ealing Studios came back with the rough cut, Vaughan Williams politely asked if he could play Balcon some music 'to see if it suited'. Apparently it fitted like a glove, not only in mood, but also often in actual music cues. There is no doubt that the score was revised to make it fit precisely, and revised again to make it into a coherent whole as a symphony. But, equally, there is no doubt that the basic score was written in advance of the film.

Could this film score – a genre to which the composer was introduced in his seventieth year with Powell and Pressburger's *49th Parallel* (1941) – really have been so significant that he wrote the music ahead of the film and later turned it into his seventh symphony? Yes, according to Mellers.

The 'unknown region' of the Antarctic was the ultimate 'waste land'. And if Bunyan's pilgrim was the seeker that dominated the composer's imaginative life, Captain Robert Falcon Scott – explorer, hero, failure – formed a potent symbol for the composer in old age. Words from Scott's final diary entry stand as an epigram at the head of the last movement of Vaughan Williams's *Sinfonia antartica*.

I do not regret this journey … We took risks, we knew we took them; things have come out against us, therefore we have no cause for complaint.

The fact that Vaughan Williams's music is sung and played today more than ever, and that he is one of the most frequently recorded composers, suggests that things did not 'come out against' him. Unlike Scott, perhaps the composer did not expect to find anything at the end of his explorations – certainly not God. Or perhaps he hoped simply to find himself (which he surely did) and, through his music, to help his listeners and performers find themselves.

Australian Financial Review, 2008

Holst, the Mystic

Everyone knows *The Planets*, the orchestral suite by Gustav Holst. At least everyone knows the opening movement, 'Mars, the Bringer of War', and the famous tune in the middle of 'Jupiter', which is sometimes sung as the patriotic hymn, 'I Vow to Thee, My Country'. So it may come as a surprise to learn that when Holst composed the former in 1914, it had nothing to do with Mars or with war – indeed, the original title of the entire work was 'Seven Pieces for Large Orchestra' – and also that the words of the hymn were at odds with his beliefs. Equally surprising is his own poor opinion of *The Planets* as a whole, a judgement shared by his daughter and biographer, Imogen Holst.

When it comes to matters of longevity in music, popular opinion is seldom wrong. There is a lot of great music that eludes the average concert audience, largely because it is seldom heard, but the famous works – the 'warhorses' – are nearly always famous for good reason. A brash novelty might catch the attention of a first-time audience, but brashness alone will not secure a lasting place in the repertoire: only quality will do that. And whatever its composer might have had you believe, *The Planets* is full of quality. Said to be the most performed piece of English orchestral music, it has been recorded by many of the world's famous conductors, and even by Bernard Herrmann and John Williams, *The Planets* evidently a piece that speaks to film composers. In fact, there are more than sixty different commercial recordings of the orchestral suite, and this is to say nothing of the versions by Rick Wakeman and Keith Emerson, King Crimson and Manfred Mann, or the countless arrangements for organ, piano, two pianos, brass band and military band.

So what else, you may ask, did Holst compose? And the fact that you ask is the nub of his ambivalence about the work. He felt not only misunderstood, but also aggrieved that he should be known just for *The Planets*, and his response was to downplay its worth.

Gustavus von Holst was born in Cheltenham, on the edge of the English Cotswolds in 1874. His father (also English-born) was a church organist. His grandfather, who as child had come to England from Riga with his family, was a pianist, teacher and composer of salon music. His great-grandfather had taught harp to the Czar's children in St Petersburg. Earlier still, the family had come to Russia from Germany.

Holst was in poor health all his life. He was asthmatic, prone to bouts of depression; his eyesight was poor and he suffered from neuritis, making it painful to write – he was sometimes forced to dictate his music to an amanuensis. For all that, Holst was industrious. He taught at St Paul's Girls' School from 1905 until his death in 1934, and busied himself in a range of musical activities in the wider community, so that composing had to be done in the evenings, at weekends and during holidays. Still, he was quite prolific, writing operas, orchestral works, concertos and a great deal of choral music. But the only other piece that was (and is) as popular as *The Planets* is a setting of Christina Rossetti's poem 'In the Bleak Midwinter', and most people who sing Christmas carols don't bother looking for the name of the composer. So for the broad public – and for most concert-goers – Holst remains a one-hit wonder.

In the Bleak Midwinter is the title of Tony Palmer's film about the composer, following on from studies of Walton, Britten, Stravinsky, Orff, Malcolm Arnold and Vaughan Williams. Most of Palmer's composer documentaries share concerns about neglect and rejection, decline and death. You could argue that his films are death obsessed. So the figure of Holst – regularly ill, convinced he was a failure, dead at fifty-nine – provides Palmer with the opportunity to revisit some favourite themes. Unlike his Vaughan Williams film of 2007, *In the*

Bleak Midwinter contains few revelations, but it offers a timely reminder that there was more to this man than *The Planets*.

Perhaps the most surprising connection made in Palmer's film is between Holst and Conrad Noel, the 'Red Vicar' of Thaxted. In the middle of World War I – and in the middle of composing *The Planets* – Holst and his family moved to the village of Thaxted in rural Essex where Noel, in Imogen Holst's words, became a 'firm friend'. Imogen doesn't have much more to say on the subject, though one senses that she liked Noel and approved of him. But Palmer makes a meal of the relationship.

To enter Noel's church was to find the red flag of socialism hanging beside a green flag representing the downtrodden Irish, both of them alongside the English flag of St George. What you would not have seen in Thaxted Parish Church was the Union flag, which Noel considered a symbol of imperialism. By the end of the war, the green flag had been replaced with the Irish tricolour. Meanwhile on the noticeboard, you might have read that 'The Bell will Toll at Noon For Those Slain by Empire' or, on Empire Day itself, '24 May. Prayers in the Parish Church at Noon for the Victims of Imperial Aggression. May They Rest in Peace.'

Palmer's view is that, for Holst, Noel was more than a 'firm friend', he was a 'soul mate'. Certainly, Holst considered himself a socialist and, before arriving in Thaxted, had trained the Hammersmith Socialist Choir. He had also taught at Morley College in London, a workers' education centre where he ran the Can't Sing Choir, with whom he gave concerts for the poor of the East End. Like his lifelong friend Vaughan Williams, Holst had a love of amateur music-making, making no distinction between conducting the London Symphony Orchestra and encouraging his non-singers. He believed that music brought people together, that it was a force for good in society. Holst also shared with Vaughan Williams an enthusiasm for English folksong, the people's music – indeed, it had been on a song-collecting expedition with his friend that he had found Thaxted.

But before we brand the composer a political extremist, we should set his beliefs and attitudes in a fuller context. A socialist he might have been, but the composer of 'Mars, the Bringer of War' was no pacifist and, at the outbreak of war in 1914, he had attempted to enlist. Already forty and with his various debilitating ailments, he was rejected. As Imogen pointed out, the army would have 'had little use for a man who could hardly hold a fountain pen, let alone a rifle, and who was unable to recognise his own family at a distance of more than six yards'. So Holst sat out the war in Thaxted, continuing work on *The Planets* while assuring his neighbours and the occasional police officer that he was not German. He finally changed his name by deed poll, losing the 'von'.

The other important piece of context that qualifies Palmer's insistence on Holst's radical socialism is the matter of the hymn fitted to the 'Jupiter' tune:

> *I vow to thee, my country, all earthly things above,*
> *Entire and whole and perfect, the service of my love;*
> *The love that asks no question, the love that stands the test,*
> *That lays upon the altar the dearest and the best;*
> *The love that never falters, the love that pays the price,*
> *The love that makes undaunted the final sacrifice.*

The sentiments would have jarred with Noel, particularly the notion that young lives – 'the dearest and the best' – might willingly be laid 'upon the altar' of imperialism, but in 1921 Holst not only allowed the melody's use, he came up with the idea, making the necessary alterations to it so the words would fit. He even called the hymn tune 'Thaxted'. Palmer's film doesn't tell us this, only that the words were 'the opposite' of what Holst believed.

Palmer badly wants Holst to be a political radical, and on some days most likely he was. But that's the trouble with composers and with artists in general: they seldom behave consistently, however much their biographers might wish them to, and those who are consistent are seldom interesting.

In the end, it is the art that remains and the art that really matters, and it is *in* the art that we find the artist. So that, you might think, is precisely why Holst requires a film such as Palmer's. If most people know only *The Planets*, how will they ever gain a true picture of this composer and his rather large body of music? Palmer's film fills not a few gaps in our knowledge of Holst's music, but although it doesn't explicitly make the point, in returning again and again to *The Planets*, it underlines the truth that, after all, those 'Seven Pieces for Large Orchestra' offer a very clear portrait of the composer and his work as a whole. However much Holst himself might have down-played the achievement, *The Planets* are completely typical of the man and his musical imagination.

Holst was particularly open-minded and acquisitive. While he and Vaughan Williams might have shared a fascination with folk-song, their responses to it were different. Like the Hungarian Bartók, Vaughan Williams seems to have absorbed folk music into his own style. His music is imbued with its melodic contours, its modal harmonies, its very essence, but it seldom quotes its sources. Folk-song left its mark on Holst's music too, but in general the surfaces of his works are more European, more modernist than Vaughan Williams's.

At the end of the nineteenth century, Holst had become extremely interested in Hinduism, not only the stories of the *Ramayana*, but the religion itself, which he regarded as more 'rational' than others. He learned Sanskrit and made his own translations of the mystical hymns from the *Rig Veda* which he then set to music. And he found in the *Bhagavad-Gita* a philosophy that accorded strongly with his own feelings about humility. Holst hated being famous – perhaps another reason he was keen to put some distance between himself and *The Planets* – and anyone who wrote to him seeking his autograph was sent a politely formal card explaining that he could not oblige (he carried a supply of these to hand out to those who approached him in person).

It would be stretching the truth to say that India entered his music stylistically. The *ostinato* figures – repeating melodic and rhythmic figures – that became common in his music (think of 'Mars') have their roots in English folk music more than the music of India, but he certainly drew on other non-Western cultures in his music. There are Japanese melodies in his *Japanese Suite* – though otherwise the piece does not sound remotely Japanese – and *Beni Mora* is full of the musical sounds of north Africa.

Beni Mora is a remarkable piece, and it has a remarkable origin. Early in 1908, Holst was exhausted, depressed and his neuritis was particularly bad in the cold English weather. His doctor ordered a holiday somewhere warm, so Holst took it into his head to go bicycling in the Sahara. Vaughan Williams gave him the money for the trip and off he went, spending Easter in Algiers. There, in his notebook, he jotted down a fragment of melody. He wrote next to it: 'oboe tune in procession. 5AM (they had been at it all night).'

The short melody Holst heard was repeated, unvaried, for two and a half hours – you begin to see why it made such an impression – and two years later the tune surfaced in the final movement of *Beni Mora*, where it is repeated, mainly by a low flute, for 163 bars. Holst's original sketch for this is entitled 'Nocturne', but eventually he named the movement 'In the Streets of the Ouled Naïls' – the street of dancing girls. It was a daring experiment, and at its premiere in London's Queen's Hall it did not please everybody, one critic writing: 'We do not ask for Biskra dancing girls in Langham Place.' Still, it is an early, pre-'Mars' use of a relentless *ostinato*, and it is interesting that it should have come to Holst as a musical 'found object'.

The opening minute of 'In the Streets of the Ouled Naïls' is hardly less striking, and no less predictive of Holst's later music. That discarded title of 'Nocturne' set the tone, for the atmosphere of the opening might well be a still, sultry night. Dark, chromatic chords drift gently. The music suddenly stops, then the chords continue, the solo flute trying out a few notes of its tune. The mood is mysterious, even *mystical*, and there is perhaps no better word to describe a certain type of music typical of the mature Holst.

When we think of *The Planets*, it is likely the rumbustious music we think of first: the belligerence of 'Mars'; the joyous, buoyant swagger of 'Jupiter'; the impish strut of 'Uranus, the Magician'. But there is as much quiet, slow music as extroversion. 'Venus, the Bringer of Peace' is appropriately serene, while 'Saturn, the Bringer of Old Age', though it irrupts with a shocking polytonal clamour of bells, is for the most part a weary trudge (it was Holst's favourite movement). Finally, 'Neptune, the Mystic' is a slow drift into nothingness – literally, because the piece has no ending: an off-stage six-part chorus of women's voices gradually takes over from the orchestra, which eventually falls silent. The voices repeat their final phrase over and over, an ethereal version of the dancing girls, until they gradually fade from our hearing and the piece is over.

In between completing *Beni Mora* and starting *The Planets*, Holst had heard both the world premiere of Schoenberg's Five Pieces for Orchestra Op 16, and the London premiere of Stravinsky's revolutionary ballet score, *The Rite of Spring*. They both impressed him, and their influences can be heard in his suite. In particular, 'Saturn' has a close affinity with the strange, soft, repeating chords of 'Farben', the central piece of Schoenberg's five, while the drifting chords of 'Neptune' recall the glacial opening of the second half of *The Rite*. No other English composer of Holst's generation responded so positively or so quickly to the new music coming from Europe in those years before World War I. Holst might not have gone down Schoenberg's atonal path any more than he adopted the more radical rhythmic language of Stravinsky (the timpani cross rhythms in 'Uranus' come close), but both examples were noted and both left their mark on him.

The piece that Holst believed to be his finest, the little tone poem *Egdon Heath* (1928), inspired by Thomas Hardy's novel *The Return of the Native*, brings those influences together. The landscape is open, barren and unforgiving, and the music reflects this. As with 'Saturn' and 'Neptune', the harmony drifts and the pace is slow. Tiny details make themselves heard, like rocky outcrops or the speck-like figure of Hardy's reddleman crossing the heath, but all the time something seems to be missing. The music is crying out for a tune – a solo oboe or a clarinet, a pair of flutes, perhaps – playing something plaintive: perhaps something from the west of England, from Hardy's country, something like 'A Rosebud in June', which had featured in the *Somerset Rhapsody* of twenty years before? But it never comes. We hear only an opening phrase, tossed around until, in anger, it violently self-destructs. Later, the solo wind instruments do appear, but their lines are fractured. They refuse to turn into tunes. The absence is keenly felt, yet the piece takes strength from it. Holst's music has what the poet Keats called 'a negative capability'.

Those desolate landscapes – from Egdon Heath to the Sahara, from Saturn to Neptune – are completely typical of Holst. They reflect the man, his demeanour – his very body – as much as his personality. Staunch, yet frail; modest, yet imaginative; down to earth, yet mystical – almost fey. *The Planets*, those 'Seven Pieces for Large Orchestra', have nothing to do with astronomy, which is why our Earth is not among them. Holst himself attributed the planets' characteristics, the bringers of war and peace, jollity and old age, the magician and the mystic: it is surely not fanciful to detect autobiography in these titles, though the composer himself would have shrunk from the thought.

In one of his last works, the twelve songs to words by Humbert Wolfe, completed in 1930, Holst turned his attention to the heavens once more, this time leaving the solar system. Wolfe's poem 'Betelgeuse' reads as though it were written not only for Holst to put to music, but as an explanation of his musical aesthetic.

On Betelgeuse
the gold leaves hang in golden aisles
for twice a hundred million miles,
and twice a hundred million years
they golden hang and nothing stirs,
on Betelgeuse.
Space is a wind that does
not blow on Betelgeuse
and time – oh time – is a bird,
whose wings have never stirred
the golden avenues
of leaves on Betelgeuse.

Holst had grown increasingly interested in astronomy in middle age, and was impressed that the second-brightest star in Orion should be so vast and also so distant – in time as well as space. Imogen Holst writes that this summoned 'an answering remoteness in his music', captured in slow, spare octaves that in a tolling *ostinato* delineate the rising fourths of C/F and B/E – pitches that are side by side on the keyboard yet distant in terms of tonality.

As the reddleman is dwarfed by Egdon Heath, nature engulfing man, so Wolfe's poem ends with lines that put humanity properly in its place.

... and the God, of whom we are
infinite dust, is there
a single leaf of those
gold leaves on Betelgeuse.

And with that, Holst's music, as so often, simply fades away.

Australian Financial Review, 2011

William Walton:
A twentieth-century Romantic

It was not at all William Walton's fault that, halfway through his career, both he and his music became unfashionable. The fault was all with the twentieth century. But then Walton's is a quintessentially twentieth-century story. It is the story of a composer who went, in fifteen years, from being the musical figurehead of an avant-garde circle of artists – albeit a self-conscious and very English version of the avant-garde – to writing a march, *Crown Imperial*, for the coronation of George VI. A meteoric rise you might think, but a twentieth-century artist had to be wary of the wrong sort of success. By the start of the century's second half, the newly knighted Sir William was hard at work on a second coronation march and his career was headed south.

William Turner Walton was born in the Lancashire mill town of Oldham in 1902 and he showed considerable early promise. This was confirmed by his acceptance, aged ten, into the choir of Christ Church, Oxford; his admission, aged sixteen, into that same college as an undergraduate (he was one of the youngest ever to enter Oxford University); and his subsequent 'adoption' by the Sitwell family with whom, aged eighteen, he went to live in bohemian Chelsea.

The Sitwells, Edith and her younger brothers Osbert and Sacheverell, were a slightly less talented version of the Bloomsbury group, their hearts firmly set on shaking up the philistine bourgeoisie of Britain. They were admiring of the latest trends in Europe and, perhaps a little childishly, courted the kind of *succès de scandale* that habitually attached itself to the Continental avant-garde.

Something approaching the public brawl on the opening night of *The Rite of Spring* would be good.

Sacheverell had met and liked Walton at Oxford and the other Sitwells quickly took to him as well. The young Walton's good looks, small stature and what remained of his flat, Northern vowels gave him something of the quality of an exotic house pet in the Sitwells' home, but his talent was spotted too, and it was quickly harnessed for the avant-garde cause. For the next fifteen years, Walton was to be the Sitwells' composer in residence, his first collaboration with the family a series of musical settings of Edith's somewhat ostentatious poetry in *Façade: An entertainment*. Walton wrote the music astonishingly quickly, spurred on no doubt by Edith's threats that if he didn't, she'd invite Constant Lambert to do it instead. But one also senses something of the young man in a hurry about the score. There is real brilliance here, and if the public unveiling in 1923 failed to provoke the longed-for fisticuffs, it certainly managed to ruffle some bourgeois plumage: 'Drivel They Paid to Hear', harumphed a headline in the *Daily Graphic*.

Undoubtedly the response was prompted less by the music than by Edith Sitwell's poems and the manner of their presentation. Edith always intended her poetry to be heard as much as read, and in *Façade* she selected words for their sounds more than their meanings. At the premiere, the reciter and six instrumentalists were hidden away behind a stage curtain, the poems delivered somewhat monotonously via a megaphone poked through a hole in the curtain's centre. *Façade* was always going to fail as the new *Rite of Spring*, but it was trying very hard to be the new *Pierrot lunaire*. Schoenberg's score, first performed in Berlin in 1912, the year before *The Rite* had its scandalous premiere, was almost as notorious as Stravinsky's, and, in terms of its appearance and structure, it was a model for *Façade*.

Both works have poetry recited (rather than sung) to the accompaniment of a small mixed ensemble of instruments. Both works, also, are in twenty-one short movements, arranged into three groups of seven in the case of *Pierrot*, seven groups of three in *Façade*. In fact, *Façade* did not find its finished structure until much later, and Sitwell and Walton composed many numbers for it that were performed early on but failed to make the final selection. Nevertheless, when Oxford University Press came to publish the work, and the three-by-seven design was fixed in print, the *Pierrot* connection can have escaped no one's attention.

Perhaps more important than these structural matters, however, was the very nature of the words and the music. Just as Schoenberg, in *Pierrot lunaire*, had based each of his movements on an existing musical model, often popular in nature, so *Façade* is full of parody. There's a waltz, a foxtrot and a furious bit of ragtime; 'Tango–Pasodoble' quotes the music-hall song, 'I Do Like to Be Beside the Seaside'; 'Jodelling Song' quotes Rossini's *William Tell*. And the piece is also full of references to the modern music of the day, to Debussy and Ravel, and particularly to their 'Spanish' music. In 'Lullaby for Jumbo', Walton and Sitwell adopted the title Debussy thought he was using in *Children's Corner*, when his faulty English actually led him to write '*Jimbo's* Lullaby'. (Edith's words also draw on the art of *fin-de-siècle* France. In the eleventh number of *Façade*, entitled 'By the Lake', she virtually paraphrases lines from Verlaine's poem, 'Colloque sentimental'.)

Walton's parodies were dazzling and witty and this probably accounts for the fact that *Façade* remains his best-known piece, its later arrangement for orchestra (minus the poetry) bringing in sufficient royalties to keep the wolf mostly from the composer's door. But *Façade* was also the beginning of Walton's later problems, because it got him off on the wrong footing. Here he was, twenty-one years old, the Sitwells proclaiming him an *enfant terrible*, while anyone who heard *Façade* would have assumed him to be a brilliant pasticheur. In truth he was never the former and much more than the latter. To quote the subtitle of one of the books published for his centenary, Walton was actually a 'romantic loner'.

The twentieth century didn't set much store by Romanticism. Romanticism was a nineteenth-century aesthetic and the modern world felt no need of it. Even if we allow that Walton's music was romantic, rather than Romantic, the fact remains that it is lush and emotional and frequently in very good spirits. By the 1930s, such musical tendencies displayed a want of sophistication; by the 1950s, they clearly belonged to another era altogether. And this, I think, explains the second word in that title: ultimately Walton had little option but to be a loner.

For all the witty pastiche of Ravel and Debussy and early jazz evident in *Façade*, Walton's role model in larger-scale works was Sibelius. The Finnish composer was a great favourite with audiences, particularly in Great Britain and the United States, but nobody would have considered him a trendsetter. In any case, by 1931, when William Walton began work on his first symphony, Sibelius had already sunk into the so-called 'silence of Järvenpää' that continued for the last thirty years of his life. He might have been composing his Symphony No 8, but the world would never hear it. In many ways, Walton's Symphony No 1 is the nearest thing we have to Sibelius's eighth, so close is the similarity between the styles of the two composers (though to be fair, it is the Finn's earlier symphonies that Walton's first most resembles). The rather sinuous themes of Walton's first movement, the pulsing rhythms that drive the music forward, the slow-moving harmonies that simultaneously try to restrain it, the resulting tension: these are all characteristic of Sibelius.

And yet even if he found it easier to compose than Sibelius now did, this music did not come to Walton with the fluency that the surging first movement might suggest. By 1934, three years after he had begun work on the piece, Walton's symphony still had no final movement and it was in this truncated, three-movement form that it received its world premiere. The finale was written the following year, but the struggle to bring big pieces to completion would be a recurrent problem for its composer. It was not that he had lost his earlier ability to produce music quickly – he seems to have dashed off his scores for Laurence Olivier's Shakespeare films in the 1940s – but perhaps he was already beginning to feel the loneliness of the twentieth-century romantic.

It is difficult to describe Walton's musical style. The word 'Italianate' frequently crops up, but one wonders whether this is based on Walton's fondness for the country and the fact that he spent the later part of his life on the island of Ischia. His harmonies are unfailingly rich, nearly always tonal, but with all manner of chromatic added notes that seem to come from jazz rather than, say, Wagner. Increasingly, however, the composer's use of the orchestra was sparing. The first symphony had been rather densely scored, but beginning with the violin concerto composed for Jascha Heifetz in 1939, there is a marvellous translucence about Walton's orchestration. It's a striking combination, this limpid presentation of lush harmonies. Coupled with Walton's characteristically long, seemingly meandering melodic lines and a rhythmic tautness born of the composer's love of syncopation, his compositions are wholly distinctive. Even today, his music is unmistakable.

As his talents matured, however, Walton's fortunes began to wane. Before the war, although finally recognised as the comparatively conservative composer he always was, he had at least been Britain's *top* conservative composer. Now, suddenly, following the 1945 premiere of the opera *Peter Grimes*, that mantle had passed to Benjamin Britten, leaving Walton to be the conservative 'also ran'. After *Grimes*, Walton wrote a generous letter to Britten (included in Malcolm Hayes's *Selected Letters*) and he remained more than cordial to his young rival, but privately (as we can also read in Hayes's book) he was often bitter. He got straight to work on an opera himself, *Troilus and Cressida*, but it was to be a project riddled with frustrations. Probably it was the wrong project altogether; next to Britten's stage works it is dramatically limp and flabby. It bombed at its Covent Garden premiere in 1954 and, two decades later, revised and partly rewritten, it bombed all over again.

To make matters worse, the modernist push was all the time growing in strength and critics increasingly derided music with recognisable tunes and tonal harmonies. After the war, composers such as Pierre Boulez and Karlheinz Stockhausen ('that ghastly man', as Walton described him in a letter to Malcolm Arnold) were in the ascendancy. Increasingly, they were more commissioned, more written about and more broadcast.

Around that same time, Walton seems to have suffered a crisis of confidence. The second symphony, begun in 1957, was a commission from the Royal Liverpool Philharmonic, and its composition caused Walton nearly as much trouble as the first symphony had done, although on this occasion he quickly settled for three movements. At the technical level, the second symphony is far more accomplished than the first. The orchestration is absolutely masterful, displaying a wonderful lightness of touch. Themes are lithe, sophisticated, urbane, and they crop up with apparent spontaneity throughout the composition. Even the main theme of the finale, a twelve-tone row – perhaps a sop to the avant-garde, more likely a joke – seems effortless. But something is missing: the second symphony is simply not as memorable as the first.

Walton's crisis continued. Inasmuch as its source was his failure to be up-to-the-minute in musical style, this was old news: remember, the Sitwells had wanted him to be modern, too. But the twentieth-century obsession with 'progress' cannot alone account for the slow stagnation into which Walton descended. Walton always responded well to being the centre of attention. He never produced music faster than when he was being the Sitwells' clever boy or when he had the world's most famous actor/director on the phone demanding a score for his new film or, as he frankly admitted in a letter, when he was being paid in US dollars. Stagnation did not set in completely – 'the silence of Ischia' never eventuated – but one seldom senses with Walton the irresistible drive to create that fuels the work of other artists.

The last images of Walton are of the physically feeble composer living amid beautiful surroundings, the wicked-uncle sparkle in his eye not quite extinguished but sadness and disillusionment evident behind it. Walton's final works are correspondingly thin on the ground. They include a surprising number of fanfares for one event or another, suggesting that if the occasion were suitably grand, a two- or three-minute musical celebration could still be whipped up. Listening to them today, what is so striking and so moving about even these slimmest of offerings is the fact of instant recognition. They could have been composed by no one else.

There's a poignant if amusing story that Walton himself told about the only time he met Edward Elgar. It was in the interval of a concert in Hereford Cathedral during the 1929 Three Choirs Festival. Walton, just twenty-seven and still the bright young hope of British music, was there to conduct his new viola concerto; the 72-year-old Elgar was conducting *The Music Makers*. The composers met upon emerging from adjacent cubicles in the gents' toilet, brusquely acknowledged each other, and that was that.

By the time of their meeting, it had been a decade since Elgar had completed a major work. With some justification he felt as though he was already part of English music's past, and one imagines he was in no mood to strike up friendly conversation with its future. Walton himself, who knew and loved every note of Elgar's music, would likely have been too tongue-tied to respond in any case.

What makes the story especially touching is that this meeting was like a premonition of Walton's own later career. In Humphrey Burton and Maureen Murray's book, *William Walton: The Romantic loner*, there is a photograph of Walton on his seventieth birthday, taken in London's Royal Festival Hall, together with a group of younger composers including Peter Maxwell Davies, Richard Rodney Bennett, Thea Musgrave and Nicholas Maw. They have contributed to a jointly composed birthday tribute for the venerable Sir William – somewhat unimaginatively, a set of variations on 'Happy Birthday to You' – and here they all are, together with the conductor André Previn, the birthday boy himself looking a tad sheepish. Walton described the occasion as 'A real tribute from the avant-garde to the almost buried and dead', and we can be sure he was only half joking. And now, of course, it's *Sir* Peter Maxwell Davies and *Sir* Richard Rodney Bennett, and doubtless, if it hasn't happened already, history will soon be repeating itself. Perhaps artists who live long lives are doomed to watch themselves being replaced by younger men and women; perhaps the element of fashion inherent in contemporary success ensures that outcome. But now that William Walton is neither fashionable nor contemporary, now that his century is over, perhaps his music can be judged on its own merits, irrespective of its place in history.

Probably Walton was not an *important* composer in the twentieth-century sense of the word – he forged no new musical language, he founded no dynasties – but his pieces continue to inspire affection. There are days when I find I need to listen to Walton; that no other composer will do, because no other composer's music is just like his. Almost certainly, this wouldn't have been enough for the composer himself, but you know it's still quite a lot.

Australian Financial Review, 2002

Thinking of Michael Tippett:
A centenary essay

The other weekend I attended a performance of Michael Tippett's war-time oratorio, *A Child of Our Time*. It was a particularly involving account of the piece by performers for whom it was anything but repertory. As it ended, I found myself glancing over to the stage entrance, half expecting a rangy old fop in patchwork jacket, yellow pants and pink trainers to emerge and take a bow. Towards the end of his life, Tippett liked to dress outrageously.

Tippett's centenary has come too soon for me. It doesn't feel right. Eight years ago he was still alive; eleven years ago he was still composing. Surely, it is too early for the cool consideration of his life's work that the present year-long retrospective seems to invite. I still have difficulty remembering he's dead.

A Child of Our Time was performed by the Sydney Philharmonia Choir under its conductor Brett Weymark. There was generous commitment, passion even, from the singers, and hearing the piece seemed to crystallise a number of nagging suspicions I've had ever since the day of the centenary itself.

I spent that January day driving to Melbourne from the New South Wales Southern Highlands where I live. It was stinking hot, the sun was dazzling and, since eastern Australia was and still is in the grip of drought, the landscape didn't look a lot like the Home Counties. It was flat and dusty and there were dead wombats and kangaroos along the side of the road.

In the car I was playing CDs in preparation for my participation in the National Music Camp run each summer by the Australian

Youth Orchestra. One of the works to be rehearsed and performed was Tippett's *Fantasia Concertante on a Theme of Corelli*, and as I dodged the mashed marsupials I listened to that piece and the Concerto for Double String Orchestra, in performances conducted by the composer himself. They are rather direct readings of two of Tippett's most familiar scores. He wasn't an especially good conductor, not technically, and he made these recordings when he was old and his eyesight failing.

As you listen, you're aware of a tendency to push on regardless where more skilled interpreters might have been inclined to linger, moulding a phrase here, delaying a cadence there. Tippett was a self-confessed sentimentalist, but these are far from sentimental performances, and so I was rather surprised, at the end of the *Fantasia Concertante*, to find that behind my sunglasses there were tears. As I listened, it occurred to me how English this music sounded.

In terms of its form, Tippett's piece is a sort of baroque *concerto grosso*. It's based on a theme by a seventeenth-century Italian, and at one point it quotes a fugue by Bach (itself based on a theme of Corelli). Nothing very English about that. But there's a pastoral quality to the music, a sense of nostalgia that is strongly redolent of England, or at least of an idealised Englishness. Above all, perhaps, there's an oddness – I am tempted to call it eccentricity – that sets it apart from the European mainstream.

The piece's immediate model is surely Vaughan Williams's *Fantasia on a Theme by Thomas Tallis*. Like Vaughan Williams's piece, Tippett's is a free-wheeling fantasy about music from another time. With the Vaughan Williams, that other time is obviously Tallis's Tudor England, and oddly enough it's also Tudor England with the Tippett. Nominally, the piece might celebrate the three-hundredth anniversary of the birth of Arcangelo Corelli, but the sprung rhythms of Tippett's string writing and the knotted lyricism of his counterpoint owe less to the European baroque than to Elizabethan and Jacobean composers of madrigals and consort music. The fantazias of William Byrd and Orlando Gibbons were always close to Tippett's heart, and their presence is felt here, while the harmony of this piece is often in thrall to Henry Purcell, especially in that 'pastoral' interlude just before the end. This was the bit that sounded so 'English' to me as I motored down the Hume Highway to Victoria that sweltering day in early January. But still none of it accounted for the tears.

Was it homesickness that unmanned me? I have lived in Australia for twenty-two years without pining much for England. And anyway, it wasn't the incongruity of that music in this landscape that struck me at all, rather the opposite. There seemed to be a curious fit between Tippett's piece and the wide expanses of scrubland and bush.

I think part of my response to the music was linked to the prospect of hearing the same piece played a week later by the group of student musicians. Tippett was always interested in young people. In some ways he had a childlike attitude to life. He certainly regretted having no children of his own, although, since he was gay, that was never going to be a simple project. On the conductor's podium in front of a youth orchestra he was immediately at home – more at home than before a professional band – his enthusiasm communicating itself instantly to the young players, who invariably gave him their best efforts. Although Tippett came to Australia a few times and was liked and admired by audiences, few of those about to play his *Fantasia Concertante* last January would have been of even school age when he made his final visit. One or two of them probably weren't even born. Tippett, who still felt like such a presence in my own life, was, at best, going to be a historical name to these kids.

But there was an advantage to this. Because they didn't know Tippett or his music, the players at the AYO National Music Camp also didn't know that the *Fantasia Concertante* was supposed to be difficult. In 1953, the BBC had booked Malcolm Sargent to conduct the first performance of the piece at the Edinburgh Festival. But the conductor saw the score and turned tail. He contacted Tippett's publisher, complaining of the music's 'intellectualism', which he said was exactly the sort of thing he was hoping to eradicate from English music. In the end, Tippett conducted that first performance himself, but for years afterwards the piece had the reputation of being both tricky to play and challenging to listen to.

Sargent's charge of 'intellectualism' says more, I fear, about the conductor than about Tippett's music. Now when one hears this piece, it is the unbridled lyricism that seems most remarkable. Tippett mostly wore his heart on his sleeve, and nowhere more than in this piece. Difficult? Intellectual? I don't think so. As for being tricky to play: well, these Australian teenagers didn't find it too daunting. The performance was fine and full-blooded, and it provoked the same response in me as it had when I'd listened to the recording in my car.

What I think the student musicians responded to and projected so well in their performance was the same quality that moved me each time I heard the piece. There is an openness in Tippett's best music, a freshness, a candour even, that suits the young and, as I discovered, suits expansive Australian landscapes. Candour might not be the first quality one associates with Englishness, but it's worth remembering that Tippett was a countryman. He spent his childhood at Wetherden in Suffolk, his early adult life in Oxted on the North Downs, and he lived out his old age in Wiltshire. Moreover, he was proud of and always insisted upon his family's Cornish heritage. He thought of himself as a Celt.

Ultimately, of course, it's far too glib to say that Tippett's music is 'open' or 'fresh' or 'candid'. What's important (and much more difficult) is to try to explain how it is those things, and why.

In many ways, Tippett's compositional technique – like his conducting technique – was home-spun. That's not to say he lacked a musician's education, though he was always an unconventional pupil. He attended the Royal College of Music where he studied composition with Charles Wood (who had taught Vaughan Williams), and after Wood's death, almost as though Tippett himself knew that his technique needed bolstering, he took lessons from the decidedly conservative harmony teacher, C.H. Kitson. The end product of all this was a young composer whose music we would not recognise today. All that formal training had failed to unearth Tippett's real voice, and, after a concert in 1930 at which his major works to date were performed, Tippett decided he must start again.

In his late twenties, he signed up for lessons with the contrapuntalist R.O. Morris. It might have been an act of desperation, but it was a wise move. Tippett's best music would always be distinctively contrapuntal, and his lessons with Morris seem to have kick-started something. Finally, at the age of thirty, Tippett produced his String Quartet No 1. In it – seemingly overnight – there appeared most of the recognisable characteristics of his mature style: the elaborate counterpoint, the rhythmic verve, the lyricism, the rather modal harmony, and a flair for the grand gesture. Very clearly it was hard won – there were moments of awkwardness amid the exuberance – but these too would remain a hallmark of his music.

Unlike his friend and contemporary Benjamin Britten, Tippett was never especially fluent. But he was every bit as musical and, I think, more original. He certainly strove for more in his music. Much of the perceived difficulty of his scores for players – sometimes regarded by them as a lack of professionalism – was, as much as anything, the result of Tippett's fondness for irrational rhythms and long lines. The irrational rhythms one finds in Stravinsky – in a work such as *The Rite of Spring* – are the result of adding together small rhythmic cells. If you can count to five, you can play Stravinsky. But Tippett was not so interested in small cells. Tippett was a melodist; he wanted his lines to go on and on. And so they do, tripping across the bar lines, stressing the 'wrong' beats, frequently at odds with the conductor's three or four in a bar. Playing this music is a balancing act. Done well – with the confidence of an Australian teenager – it sounds nearly effortless, but any hint of doubt among the players can bring the whole thing crashing down. In 1958, the first performance of his second symphony fell apart and had to be restarted.

Of course in the best and truest sense of the word, Tippett was indeed an amateur. He loved music – a lot of different sorts of music (from Beethoven to Bessie Smith) – and for all its distinction and originality, his own work was in constant dialogue with other music, often inviting it in. This was part of that openness. There are lots of examples, among them the five spirituals in *A Child of Our Time*. Although it's a war-time piece, the oratorio is really a response to the violence in Germany in the years leading up to the outbreak of World War II. Tippett began work on it the day after war was declared.

The composer keenly felt his place in society ('whether society has felt music valuable or needful') and that his job was to speak, as far as possible, on behalf of a 'collective unconscious'. So, he reasoned, his oratorio required music that came from that same place, music that his audience would know. When Bach had composed his Passions (models of sorts for *A Child of Our Time*), he had included Lutheran hymns for this very purpose. Tippett thought that the mid-twentieth century equivalent of those hymns might be American spirituals, and so he imported five of them into his piece.

Far from being the musical 'patches' this might suggest, they are vital to the success of the oratorio; they hold it together. And they are successful because they are so seamlessly woven into the piece. In part one, 'Steal Away' creeps in beneath a long held soprano note without disturbing the musical flow, while at the very end, the first note of 'Deep River' arrives as the simple, inevitable resolution of the previous five minutes of ecstatically hopeful singing. It is not the mere presence of the spirituals that is so moving here, it is what Tippett did with them, and how he made them – for the duration of the piece – his own.

These appropriations are everywhere in Tippett, from the folk-song 'Ca' the Yowes' in his First Piano Sonata (1937), to 'Auld Lang

Syne' in *New Year* (1988), his final opera. Another particularly successful instance is the moment in his third opera, *The Knot Garden* (1970), where the African-American homosexual Mel sings a duet with the disfigured freedom fighter, Denise, which turns momentarily into 'We Shall Overcome'. On paper, it looks like an appallingly ham-fisted idea, but it's actually rather subtle. Again, the tune creeps in – it's half over before we really notice it (when Mel, mid duet, finds himself singing the words 'Oh, deep in my heart') – and again its success is a matter of what Tippett brings to it, this time high violins that beautifully stretch the tonality of the familiar song.

But if Tippett's love of other music produced many of the most beautiful moments in his work, it also led him into that vale of tears that is artistic relevance. I think great art is always relevant, whereas bad art is always irrelevant. I don't imagine Tippett would have disagreed, after all he esteemed the music of Beethoven more highly than anything. But partly in his eclecticism and partly in his desire to seem trendy, his music would sometimes lapse into archness.

Most obviously this affected his opera librettos, which he always wrote himself. In his fourth opera, *The Ice Break* (1977), the many musical felicities can easily be overwhelmed by a text that relies on what sounds like warmed-over lines from old episodes of *Kojak*. Tippett sought out what he considered up-to-the-minute American slang for this opera ('What's bugging you man? / Cool and jivey once; / Now touchy and tight. / You're a drag, Hanna's with it!'), though by the time it reached the stage of the Royal Opera House some of it was already out of date. (One doubts they noticed in the Crush bar.)

The other side of Tippett's openness and candour was its inclusiveness, which is a fine quality if it is discriminating. In his later pieces – really from *The Knot Garden* on – popular music forms recur with some frequency, and Tippett didn't always understand them well. You felt as though he was dragging those boogie-woogie basses and electric guitar lines into his music without fully absorbing them as he had the spirituals in *A Child of Our Time*. Perhaps he was to some degree seduced by his growing fame in the United States. He was certainly drawn to what he recognised in Americans as their own openness and candour. The last time I met him, he told me this is what he liked about Australia, too. But I wonder if in courting these new audiences, he allowed some of his own candour to slip away. There was a tendency, in his last pieces, towards unwitting self-parody. And the yellow pants didn't quite compensate.

I met Tippett three times, and liked him enormously. On the first occasion, still living in England, I was an undergraduate at Lancaster University's music department, and Tippett visited for a week-long residency in 1977, during which he collected an honorary degree. He gave me perhaps the single most useful piece of advice I ever received from another composer. I told him about my latest piece of which I was rather proud. It was a stupidly overworked twelve-tone double canon that had taken me all term to write from an elaborate set of charts. Tippett said, 'Just use your ears, love.' He called every-one 'love'.

The second time, in 1984, he came to Wollongong University, where I was teaching, and afterwards I drove him and his partner Meirion Bowen to Sydney. It was night time and Tippett was a nervous passenger, not I think because of my driving, but because of something to do with his poor eyesight and the headlights of the oncoming cars. He sat flinching in the passenger seat for most of the journey.

The last time I met him, I interviewed him in a Brisbane hotel room during his final visit to Australia in 1990. By the end of that meeting, I felt I knew him very well.

Now let it be said immediately that Tippett would not even have known my name. He was always meeting people, and he had no reason to remember me. Yet I felt close to him (and still do) and I am sure there must be hundreds of other people around the world who, after similarly brief meetings, also felt they knew Tippett well and continue to feel close to him. Tippett was that sort of person – the sort of person Britten wasn't – who let one look right inside him. His best music is exactly the same.

Will it last? That's the question one is meant to ask on occasions such as centenaries. Will we all be back celebrating his 150th birthday with similar gusto?

A Child of Our Time will surely live on. So will the double concerto and the *Fantasia Concertante*. They're already repertoire pieces. I think the string quartets are very fine and certainly deserve to live. The operas are more problematic, but *The Knot Garden* appears to have been given a new lease of life in Britain this year, while the 'Ritual Dances' from his first opera *The Midsummer Marriage* will surely remain, even if the oddness of its sub-Jungian plot perhaps rules out a permanent place for the opera itself.

What is not speculation is the uniqueness of Tippett's music. You would never mistake a piece by him for the work of another composer. That degree of individuality is pretty rare, and often makes itself indispensable.

The Independent on Sunday, 2005

The Letters of Michael Tippett and Robert Lowell

The publication of collections of letters by famous men and women will soon be impossible. First the telephone replaced the regular writing of letters, and then, when the letter-writing art – if 'art' is the word – made an unexpected return in the form of emails, it did so in a manner permitting the instant destruction of correspondence at the touch of a button. Letters on paper could be destroyed, too, sometimes theatrically – cast into the flames or torn into a hundred pieces – and the English composer Michael Tippett seems to have destroyed nearly all those that were sent to him, though how theatrically we don't know. Judging by some of Tippett's self-dramatising letters to others, quite a few of those that came his way would have been dispatched with a flourish.

Why do we read artists' letters? Why are they so compelling? Is it that we expect revelations of a personal nature, or are we hoping for explications of the artist's art? Tippett's letters provide both, although reading about the composer's private life occasionally proves discomforting. For that matter, reading about the progress of his music is not always easy, so great is the struggle to create it. He confesses as much to the writer Edward Sackville-West in a letter of 1948 concerning the progress of his first opera, *The Midsummer Marriage*.

'It will be another 2 years before completion,' Tippett warns (in fact it was to be another four). Then he adds, with something of a pout one feels, 'I have not the genius to toss works off like some of my colleagues. I must needs plod.'

He is, of course, referring to his younger contemporary, Benjamin Britten, who, by the time Tippett finally got to the end of his first opera, had composed and produced seven of his own, including *Peter Grimes* and *Billy Budd*, as well as a modern version of *The Beggar's Opera*. Sackville-West was also Britten's friend and correspondent – some fascinating letters from 'Ben' to 'Eddy' may be found in the third volume of Britten's *Letters from a Life* – and so it seems likely that Tippett knew his comments would reach the other composer. This knowledge surely colours the way we read Tippett's words, but you won't hear about it from the editor of *Selected Letters of Michael Tippett*, Thomas Schuttenhelm.

In any case, Britten was also one of Tippett's correspondents and, in 1950, still stuck in Act 2 of *The Midsummer Marriage*, Tippett writes to Britten himself in a similar vein: 'I have never kept so long at one huge continuous invention ... I sigh all the time for your wonderful ease of composition, and what I can steal I do.' And he goes on to tell Britten that 'a lovely phrase' from the latter's opera *Albert Herring* has found its way 'into the most splendid aria I've written yet – for the heroine Jenifer'. I haven't been able to spot this borrowing, and if Schuttenhelm attempted it, he also failed – or at least failed again to mention it in his editorial notes. This editor's explanatory notes are thin indeed.

The reader of this book is very much at Schuttenhelm's mercy. Identified on the cover as both editor and transcriber of this corre-spondence, Schuttenhelm is also, as he explains in his introduction, a selector. Tippett wrote a lot of letters ('I seem to be letter mad!'), but only about a fifth of them appear in this 450-page book. The majority of these contain editorial ellipses. So a lot is missing, and we're not told what. But the most frustrating aspects of the book are caused by the editor's decision to group those letters that did make the final cut according to their recipients, rather than the date on which they were written. So all the letters to the BBC (1937–72) form a single chapter, all those to Tippett's publisher (1939–81) form another, and it is the same with individual people such as Britten (1942–65). Even here, we never find out why certain letters are missing. Did Tippett, for example, really not write Britten a letter during the final eleven years of the latter's life? Relations between them cooled, but to that extent? It is the only inference one can take from this book. Tippett must surely have written to someone at the BBC at some point between 1972 and 1998, but the letters stop just as the Controller of Music there is planning a Tippett festival at the Proms. What happened? Knowing the answers to questions such as these would have provided some much-needed perspective for those letters we are fortunate enough to be able to read. But the chief frustration with Schuttenhelm's arrangement of the letters is that the reader is unable to follow the chronology of Tippett's life.

Concurrent with my reading of Tippett's letters, I have been living with (and that surely is the appropriate expression) the 850 pages of *The Letters of Robert Lowell*. Again, it is a selection, even if the book's title doesn't mention the fact, and again there is something left to be desired by the editing, although happily Saskia Hamilton prints Lowell's letters in the order in which they were written. This is particularly helpful when it comes to recognising the onset of one of the poet's severe manic spells, which Lowell himself referred to as his 'periodic mix-ups' and bouts of 'enthusiasm' (the inverted commas around 'enthusiasm' were Lowell's own). You can sense the episodes coming and going, even when he does not refer to them directly. When he does mention his illness, it is often poignant.

Writing to T.S. Eliot in 1964, Lowell apologises for 'plaguing' the older man with phone calls at the end of 1963: 'When the "enthusiasm" is coming on me it is accompanied by a feverish reaching out to my friends. After it's over I wince and wither. Fragments of the true man, such as he is, are in both phases.' Both these Lowells are much in evidence in his letters.

Michael Tippett's century-spanning life easily encompassed Lowell's. Lowell (1917–77) was born twelve years after Tippett and died twenty-one years before him, but the two men had much in common. Eliot, for one, was a friend and mentor to them both, though there are no letters from Tippett to Eliot in the *Selected Letters*. Lowell (like Eliot) was an American drawn to England; Tippett was an Englishman attracted by the United States. Both Tippett and Lowell were briefly imprisoned as conscientious objectors during World War II and they continued to speak publicly, and sometimes controversially, on political matters. Both were much preoccupied with the state of their own minds, although the Jungian analysis and self-analysis undertaken by the essentially stable composer scarcely equate with Lowell's regular hospitalisation. While both Tippett and Lowell produced work that listeners and readers (and critics) considered unnecessarily difficult, each later came to be regarded as something of a guru for the next generation. And the reputation of each has faded somewhat since his death.

In 1969, it seems Tippett was contemplating setting to music one of Lowell's most famous poems. He wrote to his biographer Ian Kemp, 'I've accepted a commission from [the conductor, Georg] Solti for [the] Chicago [Symphony Orchestra], for Dec. 72 – a setting of Richard [*sic*] Lowell's poem "For the Union Dead". But I'll tell you about that later when it gets a bit nearer.'

My guess is that Tippett was probably drawn to Lowell's poem via Charles Ives's *Three Places in New England*, which Tippett had conducted in the United States just a few months before his letter to Kemp. The first movement of Ives's orchestral triptych is entitled 'The "St Gaudens" in Boston Common', a reference to Augustus Saint-Gaudens's bas-relief commemorating the 54th Regiment of Massachusetts Volunteer Infantry, the first African-American regiment in the Union Army of the Civil War. Lowell's poem is also about this:

Two months after marching through Boston,
half the regiment was dead;
at the dedication,

William James could almost hear the bronze negroes breathe.

Their monument sticks like a fishbone
in the city's throat.

Tippett's musical version of 'For the Union Dead' never came off. Instead he wrote Solti a fourth symphony (1977) and, much later, a setting for soprano and orchestra of W.B. Yeats's 'Byzantium' (1991), which is far more appropriate territory for a composer with his own mystical tendencies. Yet it isn't hard to see the appeal of Lowell's poem. Not only was 'For the Union Dead' an apt text for a composer with a social conscience at the end of a decade passionate about civil rights (Lowell had written the poem at the start of that decade), but also there was, as in much of Lowell's writing, a tendency to verbiage with which Tippett must surely have identified.

Whether in his articles and radio talks, in his five opera librettos or even in his letters, Tippett's writing style usually involved a degree of verbosity. At its worst this can seem arch; at its best it is as though we hear (or read) Tippett's thought processes. But sometimes, and especially in these letters, it just poured out of him. He knew it, too. He even apologised for it, writing to the composer Alan Bush, 'Don't be worried by these rows of letters. I get into the habit of writing a whole batch to someone and then stop for a bit.'

Drawing the reader's attention to this in his foreword, the composer and Tippett biographer David Matthews suggests that Tippett is implying this 'someone' could be anyone at all. The important thing was that another person was listening to his outpourings, which were mostly about Tippett himself and not infrequently in the third person, especially later in his life: 'Bill has had to do a short para on T[ippett] and America for the exhibition,' he writes to Kemp in 1977.

Tippett's obsession with himself in these letters can read like monomania, and when you met him you found he also talked about himself most of the time. But in the flesh this was engaging –

charming even – and here in his letters, while perhaps less charming, it is nonetheless full of revelations. Reading Tippett's first thoughts and off-the-cuff remarks gives us a powerful insight into Tippett the composer. It is not only what is said – a mixture of certainty about his self-worth and the importance of his music, and a regular bemoaning of how hard it is to get the work done – but also the way in which it is said. Typically he writes like a flibbertigibbet, using dashes to separate the disparate thoughts that come to him mid-sentence. When, in a very revealing letter, he complains that although he has plenty of time to compose, he seems to spend much of it day-dreaming, you know just what he means. You see the evidence for it in the letters themselves. In some of his later pieces, too, the lack of concentration is audible as the music jumps from one thing to another with little obvious logic.

Lowell's tendency to verbosity is slightly different. His poetry is wordy and sometimes difficult to understand. He recognised this himself, and tried to clarify. He became famous indeed as a reviser of his work, often publishing the same poem more than once (in some cases more than twice). One of the attractions of Lowell's poetry is that you can see the writer's mind working through the drafts. These letters add to that experience. He discusses his work and his working methods, but the very manner of his letter writing – as with Tippett's – also throws light on his art. The letters, one assumes, are first drafts and intended for an individual reader; yet they demonstrate the writer's craft, and his art.

Like Tippett, Lowell knew his worth and was prepared to tell others. As it happens, both these volumes begin with exercises in ingratiation. The 26-year-old Tippett, sounding almost like a schoolboy, writes to Adrian Boult, apologising for bothering him, but wondering if the conductor might find the time to peruse a score. Lowell was more precocious, and we find him, at nineteen, robust in his approach to Ezra Pound. He admits his letter might seem 'impudent and presumptuous', but then gets right down to business, asking to come to Italy to study with the great man. It is a remarkable letter in many ways. It displays a degree of self-knowledge ('All my life I have been eccentric according to normal standards. I had violent passions for various pursuits …'), and more than a little determination:

> I pray you to take me! I can bring sufficient money to support myself, in a few year[s] I'll have to make my own living and am glad of it … Your *Cantos* have re-created what I have imagined to be the blood of Homer. Again I ask you to have me. You shan't be sorry, I will bring the steel and fire, I am not theatric, and my life is sober not sensational.

Pound didn't take him but became a friend and correspondent, and Lowell stood by him even after the older poet's arrest for treason in 1945. But the search for a mentor went on and, less than a year after his approach to Pound, Lowell was living in a tent on Allen Tate's lawn. Much later there was a falling out with Tate, but Lowell patched it up and they also remained correspondents. Indeed the majority of Lowell's letters were to fellow poets – to Eliot, Pound and Tate, but also to William Carlos Williams, John Berryman and, above all, Elizabeth Bishop. Bishop was a very different sort of poet to Lowell – less declamatory, more domestic, perhaps, in the end, just plain better – yet their friendship was long and deep and honest, and reading Lowell's letters with a copy of Bishop's own letters (many of them to Lowell) open beside you is to gain a privileged insight not only into that relationship, but also into the minds of two of America's more important twentieth-century writers.

Bishop's most famous letter to her friend is the one in which she told him – tentatively, painfully, regretfully, though ultimately refusing to pull her punch – that there was a want of morality in his poetic use of extracts from letters written by his estranged second wife, Elizabeth Hardwick. The extracts, some of which involved little more than the poet adding line breaks to verbatim quotes, would appear in *The Dolphin* (1973), though in 1971 and '72 we read Lowell assuring Hardwick, who like Bishop had seen the poems in draft, that they will not be published at all. And now we can also read Lowell's replies, both to Hardwick's original letters imploring him to return to the marriage, and to Bishop's objections.

'Now Lizzie's letters?' Lowell writes to Bishop. 'I did not see them as slander, but as sympathetic, tho necessarily awful for her to read.' There's something about the word 'necessarily' that suggests Lowell had no alternative but to quote from his wife's epistolary pleas.

'The trouble is the letters make the book, I think, at least they make Lizzie real beyond my invention.' It's another insight into the poet's mind, and an uncomfortable one. Where Tippett's music took over his life to the extent that he could write about little else, Lowell's life took over his art.

There are intimacies in letters that are not for the public gaze – this was Bishop's point about Hardwick's letters – and towards the end of Tippett's published correspondence are letters to Meirion ('Bill') Bowen that are particularly difficult to read. In 1962, Bowen was a 22-year-old student when he wrote to the 57-year-old composer about his music. By 1964 the relationship had become sexual, but Tippett was living with another man, Karl Hawker, who also acted as the composer's personal assistant. So we read here a series of letters to Bowen containing plans for meetings in hotel rooms and instructions about when to ring and which story to tell if caught out. One feels somehow implicated in this deception. And when 'the inevitable' (Tippett's expression) happens and Karl Hawker sees a garage bill mentioning a taxi for Bowen, we want to look away.

We feel more uncomfortable still at these words to Bowen: 'K.'s nightmare (no quarrelling) is a terrifying fear that you are waiting so to speak to step into his shoes. He knows rationally this isn't true ...' In fact, it was perfectly true. When Tippett and Hawker finally parted, as late as 1974, the composer was not only free to appear publicly with Bowen, but to make him his new personal assistant.

The trouble with reading letters intended for others' eyes, whether published or not, is that although one may learn plenty about the way the writer thinks, in the process one will surely be caused embarrassment. That is certainly the case here. It is a salutary reminder not to confuse the art with the artist, however close they might turn out to be.

Australian Financial Review, 2005

Britten and the Poets

Benjamin Britten's music is perhaps the most literate ever composed. First, there is the sheer quality of the words that Britten chose to set to music; second, there is the place that word-setting occupies in his musical output. Put simply, it dominates his work.

Consider the range and nature of his catalogue of music. It is extremely uneven for a major composer. There is really no solo piano music worth mentioning, though Britten himself was a pianist of great natural gifts; and there is surprisingly little important chamber music beyond the three mature string quartets and the cello sonata for Mstislav Rostropovich (Britten also composed, for Rostropovich, three solo suites and a concerto in all but name). Since Britten's summer months were spent playing chamber music at his own Aldeburgh Festival, it is remarkable that there are so few pieces by him in this genre. As for orchestral works, even if one includes on that list the pieces for chamber orchestra and for strings alone, there are still only eleven stand-alone items. That's only one more than the list of Britten's full-length operas.

In fact there are fifteen operas in all, counting the two children's operas and the three one-act 'church parables', but when it comes to Britten's text setting, these dramatic works represent just the tip of the iceberg. Setting words to music was Britten's habit. And like Mahler before him, songs formed the core of his art. Britten composed songs for solo voice and piano, solo voice and harp, solo voice and orchestra, unaccompanied chorus, chorus and instruments, chorus and orchestra: in all, more than 360 individual poems set to music: many, if not most of them, words of literary distinction.

And here is what truly sets Britten apart from other composers. Yes, Schubert set Goethe's words to music, Schumann set Heine, Wolf set Mörike and Mahler set Rückert; but the majority of the texts these composers set were undistinguished, and sometimes egregious. In contrast, Britten's literary standards were almost impossibly high. Shakespeare, Donne, Blake, Wordsworth, Shelley, Keats, Burns, Hardy, Sitwell, Auden and Eliot: the list of literary sources is impressively extensive, and I will not be alone in having come to know much English poetry through listening to Britten's songs.

In this regard, the composer's 'anthology' pieces remain especially close to my heart. These are works that take poems with a common theme by a range of different writers from different centuries. For example, the *Serenade*, for tenor voice, horn and string orchestra, is a song cycle about evening, its poetry stretching from the pastoral ruminations of Charles Cotton's 'Evening Quatrains' ('The day's grown old, the fainting sun / Has but a little way to run'), via Tennyson, Blake and Ben Jonson, to Keats's mock-Elizabethan sonnet 'To Sleep': 'Turn the key deftly in the oilèd wards / And seal the hushèd casket of my soul'. The later – and possibly even greater – *Nocturne* concerns itself with night and dreams, beginning with Shelley's Prometheus drowsing 'On a poet's lips' and ending in deep REM sleep with Shakespeare's Sonnet 43: 'All days are nights to see till I see thee, / And nights bright days when dreams do show thee me'.

In contrast, the choral *Spring Symphony*, which, though virtually unique in its optimistic outlook, is my single favourite piece of Britten's music, starts in the grip of winter with an anonymous seventeenth-century plea to the sun to 'Shine out ... with all your heat'. Spring is welcomed, with Edmund Spenser's 'merry cuckoo' its herald, and then considered from many angles (courtesy of Thomas Nashe, John Clare, Milton, Auden, Blake and others), until finally, in a speech from Beaumont and Fletcher's play, *The Knight of the Burning Pestle*, Ralph, the 'May-lord', directs our attention to the first signs of summer and a children's choir suddenly bursts out with the mediaeval lyric 'Sumer is icumin in / Lhude sing cuccu', the tune fitting miraculously on top of the main choir's swirling waltz. Such moments always raise the pulse (think of the scene at the Capulets' ball in Berlioz's *Roméo et Juliette* or the colliding march and tarantella in Debussy's *Fêtes*), but part of the thrill in this case is Britten's bravura ability to mix and match evocative words.

These are the questions, then: What sort of poetry did Britten respond to? And just how, musically, did he couch those responses?

I suspect that Britten's breadth of reading was rather more than just a pastime to satisfy his own curious mind. My guess is that Britten also felt he had something to prove. Intellectually he was not especially brilliant, and certainly not of the calibre of his friend W.H. Auden. As a young man, Britten was much impressed by Auden, and it was the poet who provided the composer with one of his first really typical sets of words for a song cycle, a mini-anthology for *Our Hunting Fathers*, beginning and ending with words by Auden himself that frame poems from Elizabethans. Auden didn't invent the anthology approach (Britten had discovered that for himself in the Christmas choral cycle, *A Boy Was Born*), but Auden's selection of verse had a distinctly recherché quality that seems to have been designed to show off his knowledge to an impressionable young composer. I think it worked, and that Britten's later devotion to English poetry – lasting long after he and Auden had ceased being close friends – was always partly an attempt to impress his older, far more worldly, mentor.

In this task, Britten was doubtless helped by his long-standing relationship with the tenor Peter Pears. Seven years older than Britten, at an age when such things still matter, Pears also came under Auden's sway. In New York, the composer and singer lived together under the same roof as the poet, along with Paul Bowles and Gypsy Rose Lee. But Pears was less easily impressed than Britten, and also probably better read, so he was able to guide the composer's reading to some extent when Auden himself was no longer on the scene.

Pears, of course, was usually the first to sing Britten's new vocal works – indeed most of them were tailor-made for him – but the singer also often had a hand in selecting the words.

Another element in Britten's word-setting was undoubtedly political. Britten believed from an early age that composers should make themselves useful to society, coming down from their ivory towers to write music for public occasions, for amateurs and for children. His setting of every imaginable sort of text was, in part, a practical demonstration of that. Britten's music could serve Shakespeare, but it could also serve folk poetry. It could turn the Bible into song, but also Brecht.

Britten was a fearless setter of texts and he took on the greats. Schubert and Schumann did not turn so much poor poetry into song because they knew no better. On the contrary, a feeling for great poetry might very well lead a composer to conclude that adding music is a redundant and potentially risky business. You either destroy the poem or you duplicate the poetry's own devices, adding, as it were, mere sound effects.

Britten does not appear to have suffered from any such qualms and, possibly because he failed to recognise the dangers, he seldom comes a serious cropper. There are really very few places in which Britten's music attempts to illustrate the words he is setting – far fewer, to be sure, than in Schubert's lieder with all those babbling brooks and mill wheels and galloping horses. One instance in Britten's work – and it is considerably less literal than any of those Schubertian examples – comes in the final song of the *Serenade*. Keats's 'lulling charities' are allocated an especially lulling melodic line, while the phrase 'burrowing like a mole' is set to a slow trill as though the mole in question ('curious conscience') is not so much burrowing as boring its way into the last waking moments of the would-be sleeper.

Is it too much? Well, it's not 'word painting' on a grand scale – for that we still turn to Schubert – but anyway, as the poet Peter Porter once pointed out to me, Keats's sonnet is itself an exercise in artificiality. Perhaps Britten merely recognised it for what it was and responded accordingly.

Setting words to music can be a fraught business. How should a composer do it? Does one respond to the sound of the words – the *music* of the words, one might say – or to their meaning? Composers have to be aware of both qualities in a poem, and Britten was. There is little word-setting in Britten's music that goes against the flow of the original text, and this is very much to do with the sound the words make. Certain vowels are better sung high than others. For example, it is hard to sing 'ee' on a high note. It's virtually impossible for a soprano to do it – the vowel simply changes into something like 'uh' – and even with a male voice one seldom ends up with an attractive noise. Of course that in itself can be useful. (I once set the word 'freeze' for a tenor on a high E, the resulting sound adding colour to the word – it sounded 'cold'.) The point is that composers have to know about these things, and Britten undoubtedly did.

He also knew about the rhythm of language. As far as English goes, he learned a good deal from the music of Henry Purcell, who was one of the first composers to set the language in a natural manner. English is full of trochees – words in which the final syllable is thrown away, usually on a schwa or neutral vowel. If one extends these syllables or stresses them, one immediately begins to lose intelligibility. This never really happens in Britten. When the composer does want to extend a syllable, he takes those trochees into account, Ben Jonson's Diana in Britten's *Serenade* being a 'Goddess e-e-e-e-e-e-e-EX-cel-lent-ly bright'.

So much for English diction. Britten's ear for subtleties of colour also allowed him to set other European languages idiomatically, even though he was not fluent in them. Following the early cycle of French poems by Arthur Rimbaud, *Les Illuminations* (1939), came the *Seven Sonnets of Michelangelo* (1940) in Italian, the *Sechs Hölderlin-Fragmente* (*Six Hölderlin Fragments*, 1958) in German, and finally,

and most audaciously – for Britten spoke not a word of Russian –
The Poet's Echo (1967) to poems by Alexandr Pushkin. These were
written for the great Russian soprano Galina Vishnevskaya, and she
maintained that Britten's settings of the language were as idiomatic
as any songs by a Russian composer.

*

It has become harder and harder to discuss Benjamin Britten's music
without also discussing his life. Just as the popular press cannot refer
to Wagner's operas without mentioning Nazis, so Britten's name
now tends to live in the shadow cast by questions about the propriety
of his relationships with boys.

There's certainly not much evidence of impropriety – this is the
subject for another article – but questions will probably always be
asked. What is clear, from Britten's music and from the words he
chose to set, is that he was strongly attracted to boys in many ways
that were *not* sexual. Childhood in general was a powerful metaphor
in Britten's work, and particularly when set alongside adulthood.
Children are innocent, though that innocence is destined to be
destroyed; and children's association with adults destroys it.

These themes run through Britten's operas from *Peter Grimes*
(1945) and *Billy Budd* (1951) to *The Turn of the Screw* (1954) and *Death
in Venice* (1973). But the songs are no less concerned with it. There
they are, in the *Hymn to St Cecilia* (1942) to words by Auden, those

> *dear white children casual as birds,*
> *Playing among the ruined languages,*
> *So small beside their large confusing words,*
> *So gay against the greater silences*
> *Of dreadful things you did.*

They keep turning up when you least expect them. In *Winter Words*
(1953) to poetry of old age by Thomas Hardy, there are constantly

'children who ramble through' the songs, their innocence causing pain, until, at the cycle's close, the poet and composer beg for an end to 'the disease of feeling': 'Ere nescience shall be reaffirmed / How long, how long?'

And the children are still there in the final song cycle for Pears to sing with Britten at the piano. This time the words (some of them in Scots dialect) are by the poet William Soutar, and the title asks the pertinent question, *Who Are These Children?* (1969). An oak tree threatened by an 'axe-man' – lost innocence, again – is the central image of this cycle, but it is not the one that sticks in the mind. In this case, the children appear in a post-apocalyptic landscape, sullenly confronting the 'ladies and gentlemen' who ride on horseback 'through the village street' dressed in hunting pinks with the bright red of 'blood upon the coats / And on the women's lips'. Nothing could be clearer. It's as though the children are the hunters' quarry.

What one finds very seldom in all these words that Britten set to music is love poetry.

It isn't totally absent, the most obvious example of it being in the *Seven Sonnets of Michelangelo*. This was the first song cycle specifically composed for Peter Pears's voice, and the lyrics – though in Italian – are about as explicit a confession of love as Britten would ever manage in a song cycle. Another especially beautiful example of a love lyric is the Shakespeare sonnet that ends the *Nocturne*.

But these moments are rare, and since nearly all Britten's solo vocal music after the *Michelangelo* sonnets was composed for Pears to sing, with Britten either accompanying at the piano or conducting the orchestra, the dearth of love songs is striking. For Britten, it seems, homosexual love was nothing to be celebrated, at least not publicly. Perhaps Britten's sexuality was, for him, a symbol of his own lost innocence. For most of his life, it was also illegal.

As it happens, *Who Are These Children?* was composed two years after the British government finally legalised homosexual acts between consenting adult men. But the cycle ends in despair. The 'axe-man' wins. The tree is felled.

> *The auld aik's doun:*
> *The auld aik's doun:*
> *We were sae shair it wud aye be there,*
> *But noo it's doun, doun.*

Australian Financial Review, 2007

Percy Grainger: The objections

Benjamin Britten's final orchestral work, completed in November 1974, was his *Suite on English Folk Tunes: 'A Time There Was ...'*, dedicated 'lovingly and reverently' to the memory of Percy Grainger.

Both the title and the dedication are significant. Although Britten had previously made arrangements of folksongs for voice and piano, describing Grainger as his 'master' in that enterprise, this was the first time he had used such tunes in a purely orchestral guise, something Grainger had done a great deal. So the dedication was not just poignant but fitting.

However, the quotation that forms the second part of the title comes from Thomas Hardy's poem, 'Before Life and After', which posits a time 'Before the birth of consciousness, / When all went well'.

It continues:

None suffered sickness, love, or loss,
None knew regret, starved hope, or heart-burnings;
None cared whatever crash or cross
Brought wrack to things.
If something ceased, no tongue bewailed,
If something winced and waned, no heart was wrung ...

In using Hardy's words in this context, Britten seems to have been associating folksong with simpler, more innocent times, a world devoid of knowledge and even feelings, particularly painful feelings.

But if this was Britten's idea of folk music, it was not Grainger's. And it was not what Grainger admired in Britten's folksong arrangements either. Writing of Britten's version of 'O Waly, Waly' (better known as 'The Water is Wide'), Grainger remarked on the 'tragic & inspired' chords. The key word here is 'tragic'.

It is often said that Percy Grainger is misunderstood, but that doesn't quite cover it. It is more that the man and his music were objected to, and in some quarters still are. The objections are not hard to understand. Much of what Grainger did was arguably in poor taste, and whether you consider this reprehensible will depend very much on your views about artists and their art.

Grainger was prodigiously talented. He was a brilliant pianist, a good conductor and a capable player of a range of other instruments. He also spoke ten or eleven languages. But immediately we run up against a paradox, for Grainger himself would not have agreed that these things were a matter of talent. Grainger felt that his abilities were the result of his own hard work and the encouragement of his mother, Rose.

He was born in Melbourne in 1882 and played his first piano recital there aged twelve. The following year, with Rose, he left Australia to further his studies in Frankfurt (he never lived in Australia again). Even as a boy, his preference was for inventing music over playing the piano and he quickly came to dislike and eventually detest both concert-giving and the instrument itself. In his lifetime, however, he was known primarily as a virtuoso performer, and many of his best-known compositions were piano miniatures made for his own recitals, generally arrangements or adaptations of folk music or original pieces that sounded like arrangements or adaptations of folk music. *Country Gardens* and *Shepherd's Hey* come into the former category, *Molly on the Shore* and *Mock Morris* are in the latter. The composer would grow to dislike these pieces, especially *Country Gardens*, which made him famous at the expense (or so he believed) of his more 'serious' music.

After his studies in Frankfurt came to an end, he lived in London until the start of World War I, moving to the United States (still with his mother) in order to avoid conscription. There, in 1917, he joined an army band (playing soprano saxophone), becoming a US citizen in 1918. From his concert appearances and the publication of pieces such as *Country Gardens*, he became famous and wealthy.

In 1922, Rose Grainger – half-mad with syphilis and believing she stood accused of an incestuous relationship with her son (for which there is no evidence) – stepped out of a window on the eighteenth floor of New York's Aeolian Hall and dropped to her death. Six years later, Grainger married the Swedish artist Ella Ström at the Hollywood Bowl before an audience of 20,000 while a large choir and orchestra gave the first performance of his new composition *To a Nordic Princess*. The Graingers lived at White Plains in upstate New York until the composer's death from prostate cancer in 1961.

Even from a public point of view, then, Grainger's was a colourful life, and respectable Australians had plenty of reasons to disapprove of him. In the mid twentieth century, Rose's suicide – even without the suggestion of incest – might have been sufficient reason for the stigma attached to the composer and his music. But Grainger's views on life and how to live it, expressed with vigorous candour, provided many more opportunities.

There was, for example, the suspicion of racism clinging to the composer. There still is. Certainly there are pronouncements in his letters and published writings that will always raise eyebrows, particularly on the subject of racial purity, though he was equally adamant about '[t]he worthwhileness of all races & all cultures'. One aspect of his thinking on these matters was a life-long commitment to 'blue-eyed English', his crusade to rid the language of what he believed to be the pernicious influence of Latin and Greek, replacing those words with pure Nordic equivalents. In the 1930s and 40s, an insistence on 'pure', 'Nordic', 'blue-eyed' anything was always going to look dodgy, and Grainger's zeal in the matter didn't help.

An energetic man, Grainger never walked if he could run – literally: on a concert tour of South Africa, he ran hundreds of miles between venues. But this was his attitude to everything: to physical fitness, to studying languages, to collecting folksongs, to designing and making his own (towelling) clothes, to friendships, to sex, to documenting his life as truthfully as possible in words, objects and images, and to displaying these in the museum he built for the purpose in Melbourne. In spite of his US passport, he always insisted on his Australianness, and there was never any doubt in his mind that the city of his birth should be home to his 'hoard house' (in 'blue-eyed English'), whether it wanted it or not.

An enthusiastic flagellant (at both ends of the whip), Grainger did not shrink from documenting this either. It was an important part of his life and a vital part of his creative personality, so why should he hide it from the world? Accordingly, the museum was sent whips of various sorts and a collection of photographs of Grainger and his partners, naked and bleeding. However in 1956, the year Sydney shunned its former musical hero Eugene Goossens following the discovery of a suitcase full of porn by airport customs, Grainger evidently thought better of displaying the evidence of his sado-masochistic activities.

But word was already out. That same year, the Olympic Games were held in Melbourne, and it might have been expected that the city's most famous musical son would play a part. But not a note of Grainger's music was heard. Australia, remember, is the country that invented the term 'wowser', having found 'prude' a bit too passive to cover all exigencies.

Grainger was certainly an appropriate composer for the Olympics (in Melbourne or anywhere else), not least because of his personal commitment to physical fitness. One feels he would have concocted music uniquely apt for the occasion, the spirit of the Games essentially in keeping with his ideals, which were democratic, anti-elitist and embracing of all the world's music.

These ideals make it difficult to gain an overall picture of Grainger's own musical works. Normally when one surveys a composer's body of work there are neatly catalogued opus numbers and a sense of chronology, but not with Grainger, whose pieces exist in multiple versions. Quite apart from the actual arrangements he himself made of pieces – for piano, piano duet, string quartet, chamber ensemble ('room-music') and orchestra – the composer's commitment to musical democracy led him to the concept of 'elastic scoring'. These scores do not allocate a musical line to a single instrument. Instead, various instrumental options are given to each line so that the possible permutations are nearly endless: just about any group of instruments may play any of these pieces.

The clearest exposition of Grainger's catalogue is by Barry Peter Ould in *The New Grainger Companion*, and it shows, for example, sixteen different versions of *Molly on the Shore*, the first dating from 1907, the last from 1949, including two with elastic scoring.

The catalogue, not surprisingly, is dominated by folksong arrangements, some of which, for instance *Country Gardens*, have long been popular with a wide audience. But just as Grainger himself came to loathe that piece, his folk-based pieces have tended to be sidelined by later composers and also some musicologists. They hold up Grainger's experimental work as a sign of his radicalism. It is not only that he composed music with irrational rhythms before Stravinsky, had his toe in the water of atonality before Schoenberg and discovered chance music before Cage: this experimentalism also led to the invention of machines for producing 'free music' with 'gliding tones' that slide around in the cracks between the notes of the Western 'well-tempered' scale (the one on your piano).

Grainger *did* do those things. He had an inventor's mind and a pioneer's spirit. But the trouble with celebrating this side of his creativity is that there's not much music to show for it. Grainger's insistence on being an 'all-round man' came with the recognition that he could not be a specialist ('any suggestion of specialisation is naturally insulting to an Australian'). That certain tasks were left incomplete, then, or not fully realised was inevitable, and many of Grainger's ideas remained little more than that.

What is important to understand, however, is the role that folk music played in both his 'all-roundedness' and his music. Collecting folksongs with Grainger in the west of England before World War I, H.G. Wells remarked that the composer was not only recording the music, but also the 'characteristic scraps of banter that passed between the old agriculturalists'. Grainger replied that the music and the way of life were the same thing. The anecdote is revealing. Grainger identified with the folk whose songs he preserved, and much of his work – the collecting, the experimenting, the linguistic crusade, even the racism – was part of what he called 'a Nordic revolt *against civilisation*' (my italics).

Central to this and to his 'all-rounded' art was folk music. It was in folksongs that he found irrational rhythms. He notated them exactly as the farmers and farm labourers sang them, adding beats or half beats in order to accommodate a word or a stress or indeed a breath. Some of Grainger's notated folksongs contain alternating bars of different lengths, and because his arrangements strove to be as faithful as possible to the source, they are preserved there too. Similarly, he wrote down as accurately as possible the elaborate, beat-delaying ornamentation typical of traditional singing and we also hear that reproduced in his arrangements – the tenor solo in the well-known choral version of *Brigg Fair* is wonderfully free and ornate.

The dissonance comes from folksong, too, or at any rate from Grainger's feelings about such songs. Just as he admired the 'tragic' chords of Britten's 'O Waly, Waly', he sought to mine the depths of feeling in the words and music of traditional songs, so many of which deal precisely in 'sickness, love, or loss / ... regret, starved hope, or heart-burnings'. The harmonies Grainger applied to his British and Scandinavian songs often seem to come from Wagner via Delius and there is sometimes a provisional quality to the results, as Grainger himself recognised when he made more than one version of *Irish Tune from County Derry* ('Danny Boy'), finding new chords to wring yet more 'tragedy' out of it. Of course, the very depth of feeling evident in Grainger's folksong settings has been a source of embarrassment to those musicians who find it sentimental (which it sometimes is) and the result of inauthentic harmonies (they are authentically Grainger!) in over-inflated arrangements.

Taken as a whole, Grainger's ideas about music were grand, but his music marks him out as a miniaturist. His longest continuous span of composition – the ballet score, *The Warriors* – lasts a little under twenty minutes. Still, this should not blind us to the very real originality of his best works: the free-roaming lyricism of the Hill-Songs; the creeping (and creepy) chromaticism of *The Power of Rome and the Christian Heart*; the magnificently odd, yet perfectly apt 'large room-music' scoring (for euphoniums, ukuleles, mandolins and guitars) of the 'sea chanty' setting *Shallow Brown*.

Grainger's estimation of his own importance was high and not always realistic. In the last years of his life, he exchanged a series of letters with the young Scottish composer Ronald Stevenson, now published as *Comrades in Art*. In a letter written in 1959, Grainger expounds on his influence on Stravinsky and Schoenberg:

> Neither of these superb geniuses developed their iconoclastic innovations until my innovations, incorporated in the Cyril Scott Piano Sonata Op.66 ... had been freely played & heard in Central Europe around 1908 – my 'unresolved discords' of 1908 leading to atonalism, my irregular rhythms of 1899 leading to irregular rhythms of [*The Rite of Spring*].

Setting aside the unlikely assumption that Schoenberg and Stravinsky were much indebted to Cyril Scott's piano sonata, it is interesting and poignant that, so early in his career, Grainger's innovations were resulting not in music by him, but by his friend and fellow Frankfurt student.

Another composer whose name has been linked to Grainger's, particularly in recent years, is the American Charles Ives. As composers, they share a reputation for being eccentric and well outside the twentieth-century mainstream.

Speaking of Ives's music, the composer and conductor Pierre Boulez once complained that so much of it was clumsy and amateurish, yet if you tried to correct this you lost the music's originality. Whether or not one agrees with the first part of Boulez's comment, he was surely on to something with the second, and it applies equally to Grainger. Unlike, say, Mahler, who was involved from day to day with orchestras and wrote scores of great practicality born of that contact, Ives did not even hear much of his music played. Perhaps as a result, his scores were not as practical as they might have been. Grainger, too, though much in demand as a soloist, was neglected by orchestras as a composer. Like Ives, then, he was less concerned with the smooth running of an orchestral work – with the professional side of composing – than with bold ideas. The originality of Grainger's music is bound up in its homespun oddness.

Should we care about his music? Of course we should: there is no one else like Grainger and his music is utterly distinctive. Was he a great composer? No (let's not be silly), but Australians should be proud of him, and we should play his music far more than we do.

Australian Financial Review, 2011

On Resisting Identity

An address to the Musicological Society of Australia

The words 'Australian identity' always make me feel uncomfortable. Individually, they are fine – though I would suggest that both words have become a bit semantically mobile of late – but together, I am afraid, they make me wince.

Let me say, at once, that I think the reason the phrase worries me is largely because I live in Australia. The expression 'Peruvian identity', for example, doesn't bother me at all. I have never been to South America. In my mind, it is an exotic place. Probably like any other tourist or potential tourist, I *expect* there to be such a thing as a 'Peruvian identity'. What is more, I would be disappointed if, as a visitor to Peru, I couldn't recognise its 'identity' rather quickly. That's why you travel, isn't it? That's why you become a tourist. But I cannot feel that way about the place I live.

Perhaps some of my attitude is explained by the fact that I grew up in England. I was a child in the 1960s and, apart from observing a momentary swelling of national pride over England's winning of the 1966 World Cup, was oblivious to any sort of patriotism. Now I realise that things might have changed in the years I have lived in Australia, but it has always seemed to me that the English are embarrassed by patriotism, and that when Dr Johnson said, in Boswell's hearing, that 'patriotism is the last refuge of the scoundrel', he spoke for the nation.

Patriotism is not quite the same thing as national identity, of course, but the two are certainly related. In both cases, it involves a nation – a *people* – being highly self-conscious. In time of war, this seems to me to be perfectly understandable, indeed inevitable. Even the English managed it during the Blitz. But why, in peacetime, would it matter a jot?

The other reason I baulk at the idea of an 'Australian identity' is that I am a composer. As a composer I spend my days trying to be unselfconscious – probably this is true of any artist. Self-conscious art tends to be egotistical: it is clever, manipulative and competitive, out to prove something, out to impress, out to second-guess its audience. Most of us fall pretty regularly into the trap of self-consciousness, and with luck we recognise what is happening and clamber out again as quickly as possible. But when a piece is going really well, when the music is just flowing and the composer is trying to keep up with it, that is when the ego vanishes. This is what we hope for, this is what we aim for, and this is why we do well to avoid aligning ourselves with any sort of self-conscious identity.

Now depending upon where you live, this sort of attitude can get you into trouble. Last week a Turkish court acquitted the writer Elif Şafak of charges that her novel *The Bastard of Istanbul* insulted Turkishness. Note that this was not a religious matter, not a charge of blasphemy; she was accused of offending Turkish national identity, Turkish values. The prosecution apparently stormed out of the courtroom leaving no one present in any doubt there would soon be another set of similar charges brought against another novelist. Or perhaps next time it will be a composer.

The first time I was ever aware of national self-consciousness was in the United States. This was 1981. My home was still the United Kingdom – I didn't arrive in Australia until two years later – and this was my first visit to the USA. In fact, to be precise, this was my first hour in the USA. I had arrived in New York and checked into a hotel on Lexington Avenue. I had been shown to my room, and I had done what one should always do in such circumstances: switch on the TV. I find local television an unfailingly reliable barometer for new destinations. The channel I selected was between programs

– American TV is nearly always between programs – and there was a trailer for a documentary to be shown the following evening. It was about ageing. The venerable actress Helen Hayes was the narrator, and she invited me to tune in to find out what happens to Americans when they get old.

I was immediately struck by this. Why had she not said 'find out what happens to people when they get old'? Why was it Americans? In this, my first hour in the country, I was, of course, terribly aware of being in the USA. To my astonishment and delight, a bellhop in a pillbox hat, straight from some Katharine Hepburn/Spencer Tracy film, had just shown me to my hotel room. The traffic blared noisily down on 23rd St, ten or fifteen floors beneath my window, while inside the room and immediately beneath my window the ancient radiator wheezed and whistled and hammered as, I now know, all Manhattan radiators do. So there I was, one hour into a kind of thrilling culture shock, all my nerve endings telling me that I was in America. But Helen Hayes had been there for eighty years. Why should she have thought it worth mentioning?

In 1994, Stephen Knight, after a quarter of a century in the English Department of the University of Sydney, published a book entitled *Freedom was Compulsory: Sins and signs in contemporary Australia*. He began by suggesting that you can tell a lot about a country from the word it most overuses. Americans, he said, overuse the word 'great'. No surprises there. Apparently in the United Kingdom the word is 'sorry', which is also not surprising but, you must admit, more interesting. Knight says the overuse of 'sorry' suggests the British are in a state of perpetual apology for their past behaviour.

What is the word Australians most overuse? According to Knight, it is 'Australian'. You don't have to think about this for long to realise that, even twelve years years later, he is correct. Our mass media are full of it. It isn't just in matters of national pride that it happens – Australia regaining the Ashes or Peter Carey winning the Booker prize – it turns up even when it is of no consequence. A crocodile attacks a middle-aged mother of two, holidaying in the Northern Territory, and it's 'Aussie mum taken by croc'. A TV current affairs show spruiks the latest baldness cure offering 'new hope for Australian men'.

You also come across this overuse of the national identifier in our musical life. Orchestras and concert organisations, radio stations, newspapers and magazines are all guilty of identifying my colleagues and me as 'Australian composers'. When you think about it, it is odd. 'Australian composer Nigel Butterley. Australian composer Carl Vine.' Why bring it up? The oddest thing about it is that we mention the nationality of our own composers when, very often, we don't mention the nationality of composers from other countries. When was the last time you heard or read of 'German composer Ludwig van Beethoven'?

Why do we do it? It could be that as a nation we are so proud of the music our composers write that, just as with our sporting heroes, we simply want to own them. I hope you won't think me cynical if I dismiss that as unlikely. Another possibility is that the tendency is inspired by a degree of cultural strut, which in turn is a defiant symptom of the cultural cringe: when we speak of 'Australian composer Graeme Koehne' what we are really saying – to each other as much as the rest of the world – is that We Have Composers Too, You Know!

All of that is a bit irritating and scarcely logical, but I wouldn't be raising it at all were it not for another aspect of the habit. This is to do with the perceived identity, not of the composer, but of the music itself. And this is rather more intriguing.

Most people know, or think they know, what they mean by 'Italian music', 'Russian music', 'French music', 'German music' or even 'English music'. Italian music is one long lyrical outpouring, and Russian music is rather wild and emotional. French music is full of colour and German music is serious minded and tightly structured. This is the same sort of cultural stereotyping that, in another context (for instance, claiming that all the French eat frogs' legs and smell of garlic, or all Germans are officious and humourless), we would consider cheap or boorish or insensitive, if not actually offensive. I think it may even be illegal in New South Wales. But the stereotyping of national music is not simply a matter of outworn prejudices.

What about English music? Well, surely now we are in the realm of long slow, march-like processionals, aren't we? Or *are* we, perhaps, expecting to hear block chords moving in parallel to the contour of something like a folksong? The answer is that it depends whether you are thinking of Elgar or Vaughan Williams. And this is a key point. Our idea of a nation's music usually comes down to which composer is on the top of the pile. One reason we think of Italian music as lyrical is that the most famous music from that country is nineteenth- and early twentieth-century opera. We are responding to the work of a group of composers, from Rossini, via Donizetti, Bellini and Verdi, to Puccini. Similarly, the idea that Russian music is passionate begins in the late nineteenth century (especially with Tchaikovsky and Musorgsky), while in the mid twentieth century, Prokofiev and Shostakovich did little to dispel the notion. And that is to say nothing of *The Rite of Spring*.

French music, for most people, is simply Debussy, and Debussy equals impressionism, notwithstanding the fact that the composer himself hated impressionist painting. If we add Ravel to the mix, a composer whom most music lovers will have heard was the greatest orchestrator in history, then we end up with a nation of instrumental colourists and orchestrators. Is it true? Well, it's true of Debussy and Ravel.

But the use of instrumental timbre allied to skill in orchestration is not an exclusively French trait. Wagner was a great orchestrator. His music is not only deftly scored, but full of instrumental innovation. The same is true of Mahler and Schoenberg. And Richard Strauss, like Ravel, was actually famous for his orchestration. By the same token the formal designs of a Debussy are every bit as impressive as those in works by Brahms or Bruckner. And yet the notion persists: French composers specialise in colour, Germans and Austrians in structure and form.

What about the Dutch? Suddenly it has got harder. I bring up the subject of Dutch music because I have read in more than one place that it has strongly influenced the compositions of 'Australian composer Michael Smetanin'. Smetanin has a predilection for rather combative music with a strong pulse – not all the time, but often enough. He shares this with his former teacher, Louis Andriessen, who happens to be Dutch. Since the rest of the world – doubtless to its shame – knows very little about Dutch music, the fairly recent emergence of a hugely distinctive composer such as Andriessen is, all on its own, sufficient in some quarters to lead people to believe that this is the sound of the Netherlands. At last we know!

But it is not the sound of the Netherlands; it is the sound of Louis Andriessen: bold, brassy and rhythmically relentless – and not always, because sometimes, as in his opera *Writing to Vermeer*, Andriessen's music is subtle, intricately scored and actually rather lyrical.

This tendency to reduce a nation's music to a few recognisable characteristics, belonging to one composer or a group of composers, is essentially tabloid. It trivialises music. And it happens here in Australia.

Consider Peter Sculthorpe. Historically, we can be rather accurate about the moment at which there began to be a broad consensus of opinion that Sculthorpe was composing 'Australian music'. *Sun Music I*, then entitled simply *Sun Music*, had its world premiere in the Royal Festival Hall in London on 30 September 1965. John Hopkins conducted the Sydney Symphony Orchestra as part of the Commonwealth Arts Festival and, as often happens today with new music, the event was poorly attended. There were, however, quite a few critics in the hall. The common feeling among them was that the shimmering surface of Sculthorpe's piece evoked something like a heat haze in the Australian outback. The anonymous critic of the *Times* mentioned the music's 'atmospheric sonority', David Cairns in the *Financial Times* called it 'powerfully evocative', while Neville Cardus, writing in the *Guardian*, came right out and predicted that Sculthorpe would 'lay the foundations of an original and characteristic Australian music'. Three days later it was announced that Sculthorpe had been signed to Faber, the first Australian composer on the publisher's books.

The idea of an 'Australian identity' in music was already in the air. It had been spoken of before – Percy Grainger, no less, had encouraged young composers, Sculthorpe included, to seek it in 'the islands' (he meant South-East Asia) – and it was generally regarded as something distinguished in part, at least, by a turning away from Europe. John Antill's *Corroboree* had obviously kicked things along nicely, and so had works by other composers (I am thinking especially of Margaret Sutherland). But suddenly in 1965, with *Sun Music I*, there was something to latch on to; something the cultural cringe could not deny because it had been sanctioned by London. Finally, this 'Australian music' really existed.

Now, insofar as an Australian identity in music means junking what we perceive to be European, I am all for it. I am speaking as a composer, remember, not a musicologist. Composers – *when we compose* – need to be intolerant. Outside composing, we are allowed fully catholic tastes, but to be any good as a composer you have to be single-minded and, I believe, you also have to be an outsider. So by all means let us trash European musical traditions – or at least let us imagine that is what we are doing – and while we're about it, let's trash everyone else's music, too: this is how new music is born, through intolerance and self-belief. It is not an especially pretty *modus operandi*, or even, you might think, especially moral, but it works, and it has worked for centuries. And that is precisely why lining up as a card-carrying creator of music with an 'Australian identity' is bad for a composer's health. Composers must resist joining clubs.

But what is this 'Australian identity'? Beyond the perception by a group of British music critics of a musical heat haze in *Sun Music I*, what are we actually talking about?

However I look at it – however I *listen* to it – I can't find much more than a set of clichés. This Australian style, we are told, has the musical equivalents of deserts – flat, wide and red – created by the use of musical space. There are slow, sometimes barely discernable tempos; the music is either very loud or very quiet, but without too many crescendos or diminuendos; there are lots of very high notes and lots of very low notes, often simultaneously. The music tends to be harmonically static with low pedal points that resemble a droning didgeridoo. There is no development – because that is European – and little authentic counterpoint, and the melodic lines tend to be based on pentatonic scales, which sound sort of Asian (Percy Grainger and his 'islands'). These lines also tumble down, starting high and ending low, like most Aboriginal chant or, for that matter, the songs of many other of the world's indigenous cultures, but not particularly like the melodies in European art music. This is pretty much what people have come to think of as the 'Australian identity' in music.

I have never been entirely sure to what extent Sculthorpe himself believes in this. As many of you will know, Peter is a very polite man, diplomatic even, and if he is being acclaimed as the Voice of Australia by a group of distinguished musicologists or the audience at an orchestral concert or a classroom full of school children or even a small coterie of 1960s British music critics, Peter will be the last person to inform them that they are fools. Anyway, after more than forty years of being told that his music is the quintessence of the Australian style, he has probably come to believe it, at least a bit: it would be hard not to. From time to time, he has said things that seem to reinforce the notion. He has spoken of melodic lines that move by small intervals – rather than big leaps – and often move slowly or, if quickly, then with a fair amount of repetition. Not only do these lines resemble a lot of Aboriginal chant, they also reflect the flatness and repetitiveness of the Australian landscape.

So is this, then, the sound of Australian music? No, of course it isn't. What is incontestable is that this is a good description of Peter

Sculthorpe's own work, and it is perhaps time that we began to appreciate that work for the singular and strikingly consistent individual achievement it is. What has occurred in Australia – not before time, you might say – is the same phenomenon that makes us think that French music is full of colour and German music obsessively formalistic. Sculthorpe's very distinctive music has captured the collective imagination. But this music is not the 'Australian identity'; it is Sculthorpe's identity. If we hear traces of it in the work of some other local composers – especially some of his former pupils – this is because its strong personality is catching. It's like picking up figures of speech from a charismatic friend.

Being influenced is a normal part of being an artist, a normal part of life. From childhood we copy things we like, and most of the time we do this unconsciously. There is nothing wrong with this, and neither is there anything wrong with composing slow, flat music, with no development, not much counterpoint and rather repetitious tunes employing narrow intervals. I would even go so far as to say that if musicologists and music critics wish to speculate about how 'Australian' all this is, then that too is a harmless enough pastime. Musicologists and critics have to do something to while away the hours, and it is always good, if a little surprising, to see them devoting their attentions to music composed in Australia. In fact I think composers might do more to encourage them in this activity, not so much by granting them interviews – musicology should not be about collecting quotes, and still less about conducting surveys – but by being better composers. As Richard Toop recently observed, musicologists will take a greater interest in Australian music when the music itself demands they do, and when the creators of that music learn to be a little less sensitive about what is written about them.

The idea of national identity in music is very likely outmoded in our often frighteningly international world. But even when it was common – in the late nineteenth century – national identity was never synonymous with artistic merit. A composer such as the Finn,

Jean Sibelius, certainly embraced a 'National Romantic' outlook in his early *Kullervo* symphony, in the four *Lemminkäinen* tone poems and, most famously, in *Finlandia*. But though it retains its popularity, *Finlandia*, at least, is not among the composer's very greatest works. Later in Sibelius's career, with Finland independent from Russia, and so with rather less need for the composer to wear his political heart on his sleeve, his music became less obviously 'about' anything. It still sounded very much like Sibelius, but it no longer identified itself as the musical expression of a nation. The composer, well aware that it was his earlier pieces – the ones with the patriotic titles – that people continued to love, found it harder and harder to compose, and eventually fell silent.

Whatever Margaret Thatcher might have said on the subject, we are all of us part of 'society', and we must all be affected by that. How could we not be? But it is also true that for music to be any good – I am talking about 'art music' – it must be created by individual men and women who, at the moment of composition, are intolerant of their society. What is potentially interesting about a piece of music, about any work of art, is its individuality, its uniqueness. These things are not easy to spot. It is easier to see shared characteristics, easier to write about similarities, and certainly easier to construct a theory around them. But similarities are only a small step away from being clichés, and clichés in art must always be rooted out.

As human beings we look for the connections between things. I suppose we find them reassuring. But art, which reassures by the very fact of its existence, must also provoke. If it is any good at all, it will do this by offering its audience something unique. That is its provocation. You are presented with something you did not know you wanted. And that is what Peter Sculthorpe has done, with music so distinctive that we have confused his voice with the voice of an entire nation. Art can do that. It can speak on behalf of what Jung called the 'collective unconscious', whether or not we want to believe that it actually *comes* from the 'collective unconscious'. Sculthorpe's music certainly seems to have succeeded in this, because so many people view it as uniquely Australian. That is quite a compliment to the composer. But we would pay him an even greater compliment if we recognised his music as the unique achievement of one human being, rather than partly our own achievement, and if we set out to pinpoint what makes his music different from that of other composers, and vice versa. And that is the musicologist's job.

We composers must lock our doors and take our phones off the hook. It is only by being single-minded that we stand any chance at all of capturing the imaginations of others.

University of New England
Armidale, NSW, September 2006

David Lumsdaine's Ground

Whenever the old conversation is had about what constitutes the authentic Australian sound in classical music – and I'm pleased to say it is had less and less – Peter Sculthorpe tops the list of composers. Anne Boyd's name usually crops up, too. It is hardly surprising. Sculthorpe's highly idiomatic style has long been identified (by himself and others) with the flat, expansive landscapes typical of much of this country, and so when we hear his music, that is what we think we see. Boyd's music, no less distinctive in its way, adds other sounds, some of them recognisably Asian in origin, but her harmony, like Sculthorpe's, moves slowly (when it moves at all), her melodies are long, flat and repetitious, and once again the landscape seems to shimmer before us.

What *is* surprising is that you seldom hear mention in this context of David Lumsdaine, the composer of a list of pieces that (if one knew no better) might look like a conscious pitch to the patriotic music lover. There is *Kelly Ground* and *Cambewarra*, both for solo piano; *Kangaroo Hunt* for piano and percussion; and the cantata, *Aria for Edward John Eyre*. There are the very different orchestral pieces, *Salvation Creek with Eagle* and *Shoalhaven*, and there's *Metamorphosis at Mullet Creek* for recorder. And it isn't only his titles that reflect Australia: since the early 1970s, Lumsdaine has made regular trips to favourite patches of bush, taking with him the latest recording equipment in order to document the songs, solo and *en masse*, of hundreds of Australian birds. Some of these recordings have been turned into compositions – soundscapes constructed, with minimal editing by Lumsdaine, to reflect the diurnal patterns of a particular place, its frogs, insects and weather, as well as the birds. Three of these – *Cambewarra Mountain*, *Mutawinji* and *Lake Emu* – have long been available on CD, and the temptation is to hear in their structures the same sensibilities that characterise Lumsdaine's concert music, especially the use of foreground, middle-ground and background. Indeed the idea of a 'ground' – in the musical sense of a continuum, a fixed element, sometimes repeating (though, with Lumsdaine, not often) – is very important to all his work.

That temptation to compare scores with soundscapes was too much for the composer's friend and colleague, Anthony Gilbert. *White Dawn*, a double-CD partly overseen by Gilbert, intersperses seven of Lumsdaine's later vocal and instrumental works with excerpts from five of his field recordings. It would be stretching things to say that the twelve items are of a piece, but nothing jars when the listener is taken from the tiny, bright toccata that concludes the *Six Postcard Pieces* for solo piano, straight to the thoughtful song of a pied butcherbird, and then to *A Tree Telling of Orpheus*, Lumsdaine's extended setting of words by Denise Levertov that themselves explore the points of contact and similarity between music and nature. 'Line is the driving force,' Gilbert writes of the Levertov piece, but he might as well be describing the butcherbird.

David Lumsdaine, who is eighty this year, left Sydney for England in 1953 and has lived there ever since. In fact for the first twenty years of his exile, he didn't even visit Australia. When he did begin to return, drawn by the new political climate as much as by a need to renew his experience of the continent, he commenced his field recordings, but it was another decade before he began turning them into composed soundscapes. Lumsdaine's biographer Michael Hooper has written that 'it is all too easy to emphasise [Lumsdaine's] expatriation', but when a composer has lived three-quarters of his life in another place, yet listened harder to the sounds of his homeland than any of his colleagues, one is forced to conclude there is a connection. And from the 1970s, Australian birds also became important elements in Lumsdaine's concert music. Gilbert insists that 'Lumsdaine does not *imitate* birdsong' (his italics), but if the orchestral clarinets of *Mandala 5* aren't trying to be Australian magpies, then I don't know what they are doing.

Another new CD of Lumsdaine's work contains just a single, hour-long composition, much discussed over the years, but never before publicly available. It is *Big Meeting*, one of the composer's earliest and finest soundscape compositions, and it has nothing to do with Australia and nothing (obvious) to do with birds. In 1971, Lumsdaine was teaching at Durham University in the north-east of England, one of the great coal-mining areas of the British Isles. That year marked the centenary of the Durham Miners' Gala (pronounced 'gay-la'), the midsummer coming together of pitmen from across the county, who would often walk considerable distances to join the celebration, marching into the city beneath their lodge banners, accompanied by brass bands. The miners would gather at the old racecourse for the 'big meeting' where they would hear addresses by union leaders and politicians and, from there, in an oddly English version of socialism, they would take their banners (some bearing images of Marx and Lenin) to be blessed at a service in Durham's great Norman cathedral.

That day in 1971, Lumsdaine and his students took tape-recorders out into the streets to gather the sounds – the speeches, the bands, the cathedral bells, the general hubbub that results from the sudden quadrupling of a city's population. Listening back to the recordings, Lumsdaine formed the idea for a soundscape and, over the next seven years, he shaped the piece. Making a stereo version of the original quadrophonic composition proved a more intractable problem. But now we have it and we can finally hear why the piece was talked about so much. It is an enormously powerful thing, made poignant by the knowledge that in the four decades since the original recordings were made, every coal mine in Country Durham has been shut.

In *Big Meeting*, the composer was forced to be more interventionist than in his later Australian soundscapes. He did not have nature ordering the sounds for him, so he edited and reordered material, building drama into the structure of the piece, and placing right at the centre the simple eloquence of a brass band playing the miners' hymn. Either side of this, human voices dominate, now rhetorical, now intimate, shouting, laughing, speaking singly or flocking together.

And then there are the silences. *Big Meeting* contains many pauses, some of them uncomfortably long. They are not moments of punctuation: on the contrary, the piece reverberates through the silences, the resonances linger in our memories, in our emotions. For *Big Meeting* is a profoundly emotional experience. In the penultimate section of the work, we seem to be standing at the side of a street as a marching band approaches – we hear the bass drum coming closer – and all round is a general babble of voices, some of them intermittently in earshot. Suddenly, very close, a child calls 'Dad? Dad?' And we hear the child tell its father something, and the father say 'All right'. But then Lumsdaine repeats the child's call: 'Dad?' And, very briefly, there's complete silence. Again: 'Dad?' Again, silence. There's an echo of the word, another full-throated 'Dad?' and abruptly a brass band is heard in ultra-slow playback, the cries of 'Dad?' proliferating in this new, dark, queasy sonority. It doesn't need spelling out. The whole dreadful history of mining disasters rises up in a moment.

But these silences are everywhere in Lumsdaine's music. There's the gradual and very beautiful falling away to nothing at the centre of his orchestral essay, *Hagoromo*, and the much more sudden silence just before the rapt coda of *Mandala 5*. You do not need to have listened to nature with a composer's awareness to have noticed the way that birds will sometimes stop singing one voice at a time, while on other occasions that will cease simultaneously as though cut off by a conductor. When Gilbert dimisses the idea of Lumsdaine as an imitator, he is right to emphasise that the composer's experience of nature has affected his work most profoundly at the structural level. The sound of Lumsdaine's Australia is as rich and multilayered as the sounds of the rainforest or bush. If Sculthorpe and Boyd offer us an idealised version of the country, Lumsdaine finds beauty in the complexity of its nature – and in the nature of that complexity.

In 1997 came Lumsdaine's longest silence of all. He announced, simply, that he had stopped composing. His last piece, *A Little Cantata*, dedicated to the memory of the soprano Tracey Chadwell, and setting three of his own poems, can be heard on *White Dawn*. At the centre of the piece are these words, addressed to Chadwell. They might be addressed to us:

> *I gave you some scores ...*
> *Some joyful minutes*
> *the music danced;*
> *timeless,*
> *in the ground of mind.*

The Monthly, 2011

Misunderstanding Malcolm Williamson

From his teenage years, the composer Malcolm Williamson was addicted to so many things, chief among them alcohol and sex, that he always seemed headed for self-destruction. In the event, however, it was the Queen of England who sealed his fate. In 1975, following the death of Arthur Bliss, she appointed Williamson Master of the Queen's Music, the first Australian to hold the 350-year-old post and for the foreseeable future, we may safely predict, the last. He was not a success. Worse, he was the very thing a member of the royal household is not supposed to be: loudly opinionated, controversial and always in the newspapers for the wrong reasons.

Malcolm Williamson was born in Sydney in 1931 and was a brilliant child. Until a series of strokes slowed him down in his final decade, he remained brilliant. He composed brilliantly, he played the piano and organ brilliantly, and he talked brilliantly; one might say he lived brilliantly. A musical chameleon, able to compose in any style and for any occasion – for great orchestras and famous conductors, for virtuoso instrumentalists, for amateurs, children and the mentally handicapped – his brilliance almost invariably shone through in his work, and yet this very facility seems to have blinded many colleagues and critics to the music's genuine worth.

Now that the British and Australian press has more or less forgotten about him and the composer himself is no longer around to assist them in sabotaging the reception of his music, what remains is the music itself – much of it available for the first time on CD – and a detailed, sensitive and beautifully written biography, *Malcolm Williamson: A mischievous muse*, by Anthony Meredith and Paul Harris.

Williamson's early musical promise led him, at the age of fifteen, to full-time studies at the Sydney Conservatorium. This was in 1947, the year Eugene Goossens became director. After hearing Williamson's songs sung by his fellow student, Joan Sutherland, Goossens agreed to take the boy personally for composition lessons. Williamson's abilities at the keyboard got him to the finals of the ABC concerto competition and, by eighteen, he and his mother Bessie were visiting London and making important contacts. One reason she insisted upon accompanying him was that young Malcolm had already developed a strong propensity for what we would now call binge drinking. And Bessie may have guessed that he was also enjoying a voraciously active gay sex life, which, in his case, went hand in glove with the drinking.

Three years later, Williamson was back in Britain for good, this time without Bessie. After first supporting himself (just) by working as a music publisher's proofreader, he soon began receiving commissions and performances. In short order the British press was routinely mentioning him in the same breath as Benjamin Britten. It was an apt comparison. Both were former prodigies, musical to their fingertips; both were happy composing to order and for a range of circumstances. Britten famously said that he believed composers should be 'useful – and to the living': this might just as well have been Williamson's own credo. But perhaps most significant was the matter of musical style. Williamson's natural facility produced a continuous stream of music in many styles, from the strictly serial to the strictly ballroom. But although, as a Catholic convert, he loved Messiaen's music, and (for a time, at least) he also admired Boulez's, he was not, temperamentally, a modernist. At heart, he remained a tonal composer.

'I am one of the few old-fashioned composers left who writes in keys or modes,' the 25-year-old Williamson wrote to Britten on the occasion of a commission from the latter for the opening of London's Queen Elizabeth Hall. ('And how wise you are,' Britten replied.) This attitude did not endear him to many of his more 'progressive' colleagues or to the more influential critics, but the commissions continued to roll in.

Alongside Williamson's growing reputation, the drinking also grew. Help and admonishments came from many sources. The elderly conductor Adrian Boult, who had taken an instant shine to the composer and now championed his music, sent notes counselling and encouraging him. The composer Elisabeth Lutyens, Williamson's great mentor and herself a heavy drinker, wrote: 'I've seen this dual activity – creating and boozing – kill so many. In the weakest (many who shall be nameless) the talent dies; in the strongest, like Dylan [Thomas], the body dies.'

To everyone's surprise, what saved Williamson, at least temporarily, was the love of a good woman. Dolores (Dolly) Daniel, a Jewish American, was perhaps more soul mate than lover, but they married in 1960, and for the next fifteen years Williamson remained off the bottle, reasonably faithful to his wife and seemingly enthusiastic about suburban domesticity. The Williamsons had three children (a fourth, twin to the youngest, died at birth), and, when he was around, Malcolm was an inspiring father, full of energy.

That energy, indeed, was the hallmark of Williamson's whole life. Even at his drunkest he had managed to be a productive composer. Sober, he was unstoppable. During the 1960s, with his intake of coffee and cigarettes expanding to replace the alcohol, he was at his most prolific. He wrote song cycles and choral works, chamber music, piano sonatas, a grand organ symphony, eight operas and fourteen orchestral pieces, among them an organ concerto for him to play at the Proms, with Boult conducting, and a violin concerto for Yehudi Menuhin. It was also in the 1960s that Williamson started composing his *cassations* – instant, ten-minute operas that might be rehearsed with amateurs, especially children, for a couple of hours, and then performed by them. The composer, bursting with energy, would typically preside over these occasions, conducting, directing and acting out everybody's parts. These pieces took him all over the world, endearing him to thousands of children. In the process, he saw increasingly little of his own.

He did, however, begin to return regularly to Australia, where his composer colleagues were not always welcoming; they were suspicious of the popularity of much of his music, and jealous, it would seem, of his considerable international success. To this day, no other Australian has been so widely commissioned and performed. It was on one such visit that a bureaucratic error led to the beginning of his work with the mentally handicapped. Expecting to work on one of his *cassations* with a group of physically handicapped children in Canberra, he found himself instead before some fifty children with Down's Syndrome and other mental conditions. Only momentarily fazed, Williamson got down to business and for the rest of his life would remain devoted to the cause of bringing music to the mentally handicapped. It was in Australia, also, that Williamson met the man with whom he would spend most of those remaining years. The organist Simon Campion returned to Britain with Williamson, and in 1975 the composer moved out of the family home.

The very next day, Dolly received the call from Buckingham Palace. In all respects the timing could not have been worse. Williamson was thrilled to accept, but he was now drinking again, with nowhere to live, no money and a stack of incomplete commissions. The post of Master of the Queen's Music came with an annual honorarium of one hundred pounds, so this only made matters worse. Williamson was expected to compose works for royal occasions out of a sense of duty, but the only way he could finance this activity was to take on yet more paying jobs. The second half of Meredith and Harris's biography makes sad reading, as Williamson begins to miss deadlines – including, very publicly, commissions for the Queen's Silver Jubilee – and the British press has a field day with the 'Australian born' Master of the Queen's Music.

Things go from bad to worse. Williamson sacks his international publisher, giving Campion the job of editing, printing and disseminating his music from a succession of cramped dwellings. Campion cannot satisfy his partner sexually, so Williamson continually has affairs, especially on overseas trips. And the drinking increases, making the composer a continuing target for the press: on any slow news day a phone call to Williamson invariably yields good copy. Andrew Lloyd Webber's music is everywhere, but then 'so is AIDS', he tells the *Sunday Times*, the difference between good music and Lloyd Webber's being 'the difference between Michelangelo and a cement-mixer'.

In spite of everything, the music continued to come, not as fluently as it had once done and never on time, but often enough with genuine quality. As late as 1995, his final Proms commission was the cantata, *A Year of Birds*, to words by his friend Iris Murdoch. Its premiere met with considerable acclaim.

And now it is only the quality of the music that matters. The re-release of the 1975 recording of the organ concerto – Williamson the soloist, the 86-year-old dedicatee Boult conducting the London Philharmonic – is a revelation. It is a vast, imposing work full of powerful dissonances, syncopated rhythms and boundless lyricism. The same CD contains the third piano concerto (the composer again the soloist), which is all dancing exuberance. Likewise, on brand new recordings of music for orchestra and for unaccompanied chorus, the mood shifts from the light Caribbean rhythms of the suite from the opera, *Our Man in Havana*, via the structurally cogent mysticism of the first symphony to the sublime *Requiem for a Tribe Brother*, composed in 1992 in memory of Vivian Walker, the son of Williamson's friend, Oodgeroo Noonuccal, and in 2003 sung at the composer's own funeral.

The neglect into which Williamson's music has fallen in Australia is regrettable. A great deal of his work still awaits its first Australian performance, including the sixth symphony, commissioned for the fiftieth anniversary of the ABC and involving, in its only radio broadcast, all of its orchestras. The ABC might have lost the orchestras in the intervening quarter of a century, but it is time there was a live performance, by a single orchestra, of what this British book describes as 'an Australian masterwork'.

As the composer and critic Bayan Northcott commented on Williamson's seventieth birthday, this music fits the twenty-first century rather better than it did the late twentieth century. Minus the blinkers of modernist correctness (which Australian music never wore terribly convincingly) and with no possible cause any longer for jealousy, it is time Williamson's own country gave his music its proper due.

If you type his name into an internet search engine, you will, before long, come across a reference to 'Sir Malcolm Williamson'. Even some of the ABC's music pages contain this fiction, one indication of how little Australia really knows about the composer. For while he longed for this honour, it never came to him. Malcolm Williamson was the first Master of the Queen's Music without a knighthood in more than a century.

Australian Financial Review, 2007

Richard Meale: A eulogy

In Richard Meale we have lost a bold and passionate musical imagination, a curious, penetrating, original intellect, a profoundly caring conscience and a mordant wit. Richard was a generous colleague, a shrewd judge of music – and of people – and an honest and considerate friend.

Music really mattered to Richard. It was important. Not some deluxe item, not a fashion accessory, not an entertainment (or not simply an entertainment). Music might be playful, it should certainly be alluring, but at heart it was intensely serious.

Richard's creative life was driven by several paradoxes. He was, without a doubt, the most cosmopolitan Australian composer of his generation. For a start, he was supremely well read: poetry, plays and novels, but also – and particularly – philosophy. His ears were open to all sorts of music; his mind was open to everything. And it was in his mind that he first began to travel, through European music and literature, through Asian art. His imagination took him round the world, even before the Ford Foundation Scholarship did. When he got to California, at UCLA, he studied Indian music, Balinese and Javanese gamelan and Japanese gagaku. He didn't just read about them or listen to them, he played them. And these experiences emerged, somewhat later, in his own music, not as quotations or borrowings or as the trappings of Orientalism, but fully absorbed. When you listen to the orchestral pieces *Clouds now and then* or *Images (Nagauta)*, you are hearing pure Meale. No quotations, no musical dress-up. And yet you sense a stillness, a timelessness that you feel can only have come from a genuine engagement with these other cultures.

It was the same with Spain. Richard drank in the language, the poetry, the painting and the music. But the works that sprang from this – *Las Alborados*, *Homage to Garcia Lorca*, *Very High Kings* and (let's not forget) the *Three Miró Pieces* – they are Richard, through and through. They are intense, passionate and intricate. They are also, it seems to me, Australian. So here's the first paradox. For when he actually went to Spain, Richard was surprised to discover that the light there reminded him of Australia, and that he wanted to come home. He would continue to steep himself in European culture, but he felt the need to be apart from it. He would love Lorca and Rimbaud, Bach and Bruckner, Monteverdi and Messiaen, but he would love them from afar.

In a way, I think it was the same with his friends. He loved his friends, but he came to feel the need to distance himself from us. This was behind his faintly quixotic move to Mullumbimby at the start of the 1990s. From then on most of his friendships, most of the time, were conducted on the telephone.

One of the last times I saw Richard – it was in 2007 – we ended up talking about God. It wasn't a long conversation: neither of us believed in Him. I said to Richard something stupid along the lines of it being essentially liberating that we didn't have a deity. We were responsible for our lives and our world, so we just had to try to be nice to one another. Richard gave me one of his more withering looks and growled, 'But I don't *wanna* be nice to people!'

Now this wasn't strictly true. In fact it's another paradox. Part of him craved company. When he lived in Julie Simonds's granny flat in the first part of this decade, Julie's children, Matt and Caitlin, would try to get out of taking Richard his mail. Because they knew they would never get away. There was no chance of just handing the letters in at the door; they'd have to stay for a chat and the chat would turn into a harmony lesson. The whole thing might easily take an hour. And yet they came to regard Richard as their grandfather, and when they were out together Richard took to introducing them as his grandchildren, enjoying the confusion this caused on the faces of his old friends.

At the end of his life Richard moved in with his niece Amanda, and he found, I think, a true kindred spirit, someone with whom he could be as quiet or as gregarious as he liked. Someone who simply understood him.

A good example of the gregarious Richard was the AYO National Music Camp at Monash University in 2005. The artistic director Richard Mills invited Richard to be the composition tutor. It was a brilliant idea, but on day one the signs weren't good. When Richard walked into the staff bar that first night, he seemed crestfallen and said he wasn't drinking any more. His doctor had told him he had to cut it out and it was the same with the cigarettes. To be social, though, he'd have a glass of red and just sort of sit on it all night. The plan lasted nearly three-quarters of an hour. He ended up having quite a few glasses of red, and before the night was out he was in the doorway lighting up his fags.

On the morning of day three, I bumped into Richard's composition students. They were looking bleary-eyed, and in one case actually ill. It turned out that the night before they'd gone for a drink with Richard. (The innocence of youth!) They'd finally got to bed around 5 a.m. Richard himself showed no ill-effects. He was having a ball.

The students came to love him during those two weeks; so did the instrumental tutors. It was touching to see how much respect they had for him and how happy they were in his company. By the end of the fortnight, Richard had committed himself to writing concertos for five of them. There was to be a harp concerto for Marshall McGuire, a clarinet concerto for Frank Celata – these of course were Richard's own instruments – as well as concertos for horn, cello and (I think) flute. I don't know whether the players truly believed these pieces would be composed, or whether Richard himself did. I doubt it. I think, perhaps, they were all engaged in a kind of communal euphoria brought on by Richard's presence and his good spirits.

There's no point, now, in regretting that these fantasies came to nothing, but I can't help thinking that horn concerto would have been something.

As the music camp proved, Richard was a very good teacher. But he wasn't a born teacher; he had learnt on the job. Those who first studied with him at the University of Adelaide in the early 1970s report that he could be doctrinaire and forbidding. Classes might be inspirational but occasionally also terrifying. Richard felt that everyone else should be as fascinated and informed as he was when it came to the music of Stockhausen, the poetry of Mallarmé and the philosophical writings of Wittgenstein. At the very least, they should *want* to be fascinated and informed. One suspects not many of his students measured up.

But here's another paradox. As Richard began to think more about writing his first opera, *Voss*, his musical style changed, tonality finding its way back into his work, first in *Viridian* then, more boldly, in the second string quartet. As his music mellowed, the composer began to experience doubt. For someone who had been as adamant about the modernist shibboleth as Richard, this was perhaps inevitable. One of the things he doubted was whether he should stand in front of his students anymore and tell them how to compose. He lacked certainty and felt, I suppose, that this was a weakness in a teacher. But it wasn't. It was a great strength. And a generation of students will testify to that.

When it was finally premiered on the opening night of the 1986 Adelaide Festival, *Voss*, with its inspiring libretto by David Malouf, was a turning point for Richard, for his music and for opera in this country. It was daring, rich, experimental and lyrical. Brought vividly to the stage in Jim Sharman's production, it told Patrick White's story with fidelity, while adding layers of meaning and resonance. It continues to resonate.

Before this year's 'Voss Journey' (the four-day symposium about the novel and the opera organised by the National Film and Sound

Archive and the National Library), I listened to the opera for the first time in years. I was moved and impressed all over again, but I was also amazed to discover that I seemed to know every note of the piece. I suspect that *Mer de glace*, Richard and David's second collaboration, might be an even better opera, but *Voss* has a demonstrated capacity to speak to a wide audience and to insinuate itself in our memories. What better place to start building an Australian operatic repertory?

Time changes our perceptions of art. Art keeps working on us even when we're not looking at it or listening to it or thinking about it. Today, when I hear Richard's great orchestral works of the 1960s, they don't seem especially atonal. And *Viridian*, which caused such a shock when first performed, doesn't seem so tonal. The stylistic fracture appears to have healed. Or maybe we've grown up. On the CD of Richard's music conducted by his friend and supporter Richard Mills, *Lumen* (from 1998) is followed by *Clouds now and then* from thirty years before. They are evidently the work of the same man, the man whom Wolfgang Fink calls 'one of the few Very High Composers of our time'.

It would be hard, truthfully, to overstate Richard Meale's importance to Australian music. But alas, it's proved all too easy to underestimate it. Our mass media prefer people whose ideas will fit neatly into the boxes they have already constructed. Richard's ideas were too big to fit. To make matters worse, he wasn't interested in giving interviews. In fact he hated all that: 'You always end up saying something stupid,' he told me. Unguarded, more like.

In a way, it's a shame he didn't give more interviews, because at his most cantankerous he'd have made fabulous copy. Sometimes, I suspect, he would drop a contentious remark into a conversation just to see what would happen. But I don't think he ever spoke meretriciously. When Richard said something outrageous, he meant it. He spoke his mind even when he spoke it too bluntly.

In the popular press, though, Richard held his peace. So they forgot about him. When a reporter rang me for a comment on the day he died, she wasn't even sure how to pronounce his name. 'Is it Meal,' she said, 'or Mealy?'

It's ironic. In the late 1960s and 70s, the newspapers were interested enough in Richard Meale and Peter Sculthorpe to create a rift between them. It wasn't a real rift, more a beat-up, but how extraordinary it seems from here that the press should have cared that much about concert music! Now half the time you can't even get your concert reviewed. It *was* a beat-up, but if newspapers are writing about a rift between you and someone else – a friend, a colleague … a competitor – well, it becomes hard not to get caught up in it. And Richard grew wary of Peter. At least on the surface.

But I'd like to finish by telling you a Richard Meale story. Anyone who met Richard has a story about him.

One day in 1993, Richard rang up. For many years he had served assiduously on the board of APRA – the performing rights association – and now it had fallen to him, at the forthcoming APRA awards night, to present an award to Peter Sculthorpe. It was the Ted Albert Memorial Award for a lifetime of achievement, and as Peter's colleague, contemporary and the only classical composer on the board, Richard was clearly the man for the job.

Well, he didn't want to do it. He told me he hadn't followed Peter's career, he didn't know his music and he couldn't imagine what he might have to say. Would I do it?

I said, 'No, Richard. You *must* do it. It would be a good thing for Australian music.' He wasn't buying this, of course. So eventually I agreed to write a speech for Richard to read.

As I wrote, I came to feel I was engaged in some great purpose. Working for the general good. I praised Peter's qualities and those of his music, and I praised them from what I took to be Richard's perspective. Single-handedly, it seemed to me, I was healing that rift, bringing our two most famous composers back together, uniting Australian music and musicians.

I sent the speech to Richard. And I printed out a second copy to take to the dinner in my jacket pocket. I just had a bad feeling that, come the big moment, Richard might have locked himself in the toilet. But no. There he was. On stage. Speech in hand.

And so he began to speak. And they were not my words. They were better than my words. They were his words. Personal words. Whatever he might have felt about Peter and about the rift, he couldn't help but stand there and speak the truth, honouring another composer's work and another composer's uniqueness.

I began by saying that Richard Meale was caring and generous, and that he was shrewd and honest. I think all those qualities shone out of his speech that night in 1993. They shine out of his music, too. And as long as his music is played, those qualities will continue to shine and to transmit themselves to anyone with the time, imagination and ears to hear.

And so now it's up to us to honour Richard Meale's work and Richard Meale's uniqueness. We do this, very simply, by playing his music. As well as we can. Again and again.

Spoken at Richard Meale's funeral, 27 November 2009

The Luck of Brett Dean

War and genocide, the plight of asylum seekers, AIDS, climate change, the pollution of our planet and the destructive power of Australian bushfires: the list reads like a particularly full and distressing episode of the nightly news. In fact, these are only some of the points of departure for the music of Brett Dean, one of the most successful composers of the early twenty-first century.

Since he is so regularly inspired by issues from which many people instinctively turn away, you might expect that Dean's music would be equally rebarbative, sonic representations of pollution or genocide hardly likely to endear themselves to the notoriously hidebound audiences at classical concerts. But this is not what Dean does. How could you find precise musical equivalents of such things? On the contrary, the composer responds to injustice or violence with music that is both very personal and – too rare in these postmodern times – emotionally direct. Perhaps this explains some of its success.

Brett Dean's music has been commissioned and performed by many of the best-known soloists, orchestras and ensembles in the world today, and his pieces are performed around the world with great regularity. To give some idea, in 2005 in London, the composer was the soloist in the premiere of his viola concerto with the BBC Symphony Orchestra; since then, the work has been performed about twenty-five times in eleven more countries with the composer as soloist on all but one occasion. Dean's violin concerto, *The Lost Art of Letter Writing*, first performed in 2007 by Frank Peter Zimmermann, is already in the repertoire of six other violinists. And in 2010, Opera Australia's production of Dean's first opera, *Bliss*, had seasons in Sydney and Melbourne before going to the Edinburgh Festival. A few days after that European premiere, a brand-new and completely different production of *Bliss* opened at the Hamburg State Opera. Meanwhile, there have been more than a hundred performances of *Carlo*, the piece that really launched Dean's international career as a composer in the late 1990s. Set beside the colossal international success of Beyoncé, Coldplay or Justin Bieber, this might seem small beer, but in classical terms Dean's success is remarkable, and not least for its apparent speed.

Born in 1961 into a musical family in Brisbane, Dean was the middle of three brothers, all of whom played musical instruments rather well. Young Brett, who began on violin before moving to the viola, did what talented instrumentalists do, playing in orchestras (both the Queensland and Australian Youth Orchestras) and enrolling at the local conservatorium. Then, in his early twenties, he did what talented Australian instrumentalists do: he left the country. Dean went to Germany to further his studies and, in 1985, found himself in the viola section of the Berlin Philharmonic under Herbert von Karajan. This was perhaps the most famous orchestra in the world and certainly the most famous conductor, and while Karajan himself lasted only a few more seasons, Dean stayed for fifteen.

It was during his time with the Philharmonic that he began seriously to compose his own music, fitting it in around the demands of helping raise a young family and holding down his day job. 'As composing occupied more and more of my mind,' he explains, 'my time in the orchestra was like going to school. At home we even referred to the Berlin Phil as "school" when I was heading off to work.'

'Going to school' is an irritant for the student who would rather be doing something else, but in Dean's case he was receiving an education that would equip him for the career that lay ahead. There can't be many better ways to learn about the workings of an orchestra than by sitting in the middle of the Berlin Philharmonic, week in, week out. Even after Karajan's departure, the orchestra was a conservative organisation with traditional musical tastes, but there is plenty to be learned from Beethoven, Brahms and Bruckner. And if Dean's pieces come partly in response to Australian news stories, the music itself is very clearly grounded in a European tradition that stretches back through the second Viennese school and the German Romantics, to the great Classical composers of the late eighteenth and early nineteenth centuries. Dean speaks of 'honouring the canon', and one detects this legacy in his grasp of musical 'architecture' (the composer's word) and, especially, the way in which the climaxes in his pieces arrive with such a sure sense of dramatic timing. All good composers feel their music, but for a performer–composer the physicality of sound is yet more visceral, and this aspect of Dean's experience communicates itself directly to the listener.

In November 2011, the Royal Stockholm Philharmonic Orchestra gave the first performance of *Fire Music* in a week-long festival of the composer's work in the Swedish capital. *Fire Music* is Dean's response to the Victorian bushfires that killed 173 people and injured many more in February 2009, and the score carries within it a strong sense of narrative, perhaps stronger than in any previous work, save *Bliss*. Dean's pieces might grow from imagery or emotions associated with some non-musical event, but as the process of composition unfolds, the music takes over. Certainly, if a string quartet played *Eclipse* to an 'innocent' audience, it seems most unlikely that the listeners would work out, from the music alone, that the piece was the composer's response to the Tampa incident. Music cannot address non-musical matters with that kind of precision. But in the case of *Fire Music*, Dean researched his subject much as Ian McEwan researches a novel. Before imagining the music, he wanted to know about the science of fires, as he explained to his publisher, David Allenby:

I corresponded with Dick Williams, a scientist from the CSIRO. The [musical] material which developed even included specific musical evocations of the event; for example, the extended electric guitar solo about halfway through the piece evolved as a musical interpretation of the momentous, dizzying heat that greeted Victorians on the morning of February 7th, 2009.

The opening of *Fire Music* is astonishingly powerful. Quiet and brooding, it rumbles darkly in a manner that might remind some listeners of that archetypal noise of distant seismic activity in so many of Peter Weir's films, most notably *Picnic at Hanging Rock*. On stage, a percussionist plays long, barely audible rolls on a bass drum, while another does the same on a tam-tam (a large gong). A third player, at a MIDI keyboard, adds samples gathered from thunder sheets (suspended sheets of metal that create the sound of thunder when gently agitated) and a deep groan recorded from a door in the Old Melbourne Gaol. In the auditorium, situated in galleries either side of the audience, two more percussionists also play thunder sheets. It is, in a word, the sound of foreboding, and it continues for more than a minute until a high bass clarinet contributes a gentle twiddle that gradually inspires answering figures from flutes out in the auditorium. The image of a spark catching and spreading across a wide space is irresistible, and slowly but inexorably the music roars into terrifying life.

Dean told Allenby that as he worked on the piece, the extra-musical images receded and the music dictated its own terms, leaving only 'the remnants of original "programmatic" ideas' as 'a point of reference'. In other words, all went according to plan and as usual the music took over. Still, one is tempted to conclude that, in this particular case, the compositional process itself mirrored the progress of a wild fire, the music flaring up and travelling at high speed, leaving in its wake mere 'remnants' of what was there before Dean ignited the thing.

In test cricket, which is a passion of Brett Dean's, we always hear how teams make their own luck and then capitalise on it.

When a side is batting well, bowlers offer up half-volleys and bats-men edge balls to the boundary, not the slips. Later, in the field, catches will stick, shies at the stumps will always hit middle, the opposing batsmen will make foolish errors and the umpires' decisions will all go your way. It's a matter of confidence: playing well brings good fortune.

Dean has had considerable fortune in his career, not all of it good, but in the end his artistic confidence has seen him through. On her appointment as music director of Opera Australia, Simone Young asked Dean to write *Bliss*, but her untimely departure in 2003 might well have seen the project scuppered. Luckily, her suc-cessor Richard Hickox embraced it, but just days after the first work-shop on the piece, he died of a heart-attack. This was in late 2008, when Dean, as artistic director of the Australian National Academy of Music, was embroiled in the fight to keep the institution open following the federal government's apparently whimsical decision to shut it. What Dean knew, but for the time being was obliged to keep secret, was that *The Lost Art of Letter Writing* had won the Grawemeyer Award, one of the world's richest composition prizes. The announcement about the prize came a few days before the government changed its mind. Then, in 2009, Opera Australia announced the appointment of Lyndon Terracini as its new artistic director. Terracini's first season had *Bliss* as its centre piece. All's well that ends well.

Perhaps the greatest piece of luck for Dean's career was entirely self-made, but luck it surely was, for when Dean joined the Berlin Philharmonic, he can scarcely have considered the potential ramifica-tions in his later composing career. In 1999 Dean left the Philhar-monic and the following year left Berlin, returning to live in Australia. This was partly for family reasons, but it was also the result of his decision to make a go of composing. He had had some early suc-cesses, both in Europe and Australia, but still there was a degree of risk involved, not least because at the start of the twenty-first century

Australian musical culture had reached a sort of nadir. Specifically, the nation's orchestras had no interest in programming challenging new music. The pieces they occasionally commissioned tended to be five minutes long and anodyne. The artistic vision of the orchestras was cooked up in their marketing departments.

But this is where Dean's luck came in, for which Australian orchestral publicist could pass up the opportunity to mention the Berlin Philharmonic? Dean began to get performances and, in the comparatively arid landscape of Australian music, his work bloomed. While initial interest in it might have been sparked by the Berlin connection, the quality of the music did the rest. What's more, the music was nearly always challenging and hardly ever five minutes long. Australian orchestral managements were still conservative, but a tide had begun to turn. Dean also did well by other musicians, working with festivals and national music camps, and first reinvigorating then saving ANAM. As a solo violist and chamber musician he was busier than ever, and now he added a third career as a conductor. And in all capacities he was generous about performing the music of his composer colleagues. Dean's luck, then, become everyone's. Australian musical life is less arid for his presence.

These days, with performances happening so regularly around the word and particularly in Europe, Dean and his wife, the artist Heather Betts, divide their time between Melbourne and Berlin. As Dean explains, there are advantages to both places.

'What makes Australia a good place to compose is its aesthetic freedom and lack of compositional dogma,' he says, 'especially compared to the parameters and expectations of, say, the German new music scene. What still makes Europe an attractive workplace for me, however, is the sheer abundance of artistic activity and the fertile environment that that critical mass creates. And of course with all that dogma comes a certain rigour which makes for a lively environment of discourse and debate which is sometimes missing from the Australian scene.'

If Dean should ever settle down it will be interesting to see what effect it has on his music. In some ways he is living his life backwards. We must remember that because he came to writing music late, everything he has done up till now has been the work of a 'young composer', albeit one who has recently turned fifty. Most young composers get by on nervous energy and forge their techniques as they go. Then, in mid life, they discover their real voices – they find a partner, perhaps they have families – and their music grows into something more solid. But as Dean emerges from his 'young composer' phase, his children have already grown up and left home. So the question is this: if, up till now, we have been hearing merely the fruits of youthful exuberance and brilliant hunches, whatever will Dean's maturity bring?

Australian Financial Review, 2012

Meeting Mary Finsterer

Mary Finsterer says she wants to write a Mass. As a composer – one of Australia's finest – she's entitled; composers have been making new musical settings of the Mass for the best part of 2000 years. But it is not such a common occurrence in the twenty-first century, and especially not among composers with Finsterer's impeccable modernist credentials.

Finsterer is that most interesting of figures – an artist in transition. Her first sketch for the Mass, a miniature for two saxophones performed this year in Berlin, bears the significant title *Until*, which the composer explains is directly related to her view of Catholicism.

'It is about anticipation … the Catholic tradition is all about that,' she tells me one early morning in a Bowral coffee shop where we've met, the composer delayed by last-minute baking duties – she likes her children to take fresh food to school. 'It's about what happens next. And the Mass is about meaning wrapped up in ritual.'

You could say the same of music. It was the poet Auden who pointed out that, existing in time, music is an art that 'goes on to become'. Besides, the very abstraction of musical language insists on experience (and musical experience is highly ritualistic) as the path to meaning, the meaning itself frequently veiled in its own mystery. It is not for nothing that religions have made consistent use of music. Music not only allows the singing of doctrine, but it also offers a sonic parallel of faith itself.

Mary Finsterer's journey to her Mass was more a matter of musical than spiritual exploration. And like many composers, she found her musical priorities shifting when she started writing an opera. Opera, with its words and pictures, colour and movement, and its dramatic rationale, challenges the abstraction of music. Pitches and rhythms may still have no intrinsic meaning, but they quickly borrow them from those other elements. If you write a sequence of chords and place them in the context of a seduction or a murder, then this is what the chords will come to signify and you do not have to be a semiotician to see it. Finsterer has long put her music to images – her husband is the photographer Dean Golja, and the two have collaborated more than once – but operatic narrative is something else.

There are also practical considerations in writing an opera. If you are setting words to music, and particularly if you are hoping your audience will be able to follow a plotline, you will need your text to be comprehensible. In the twentieth and twenty-first centuries, composers often created busy, intricate music – certainly Finsterer did – but in pursuit of verbal clarity the voice acts like a scythe in a thicket, clearing a path for itself. And then there's the singing itself. Singers in operas have to memorise their parts, so the notes a composer writes had better be memorable.

One of the most famous examples of a composer being changed by writing an opera was the Hungarian György Ligeti. The 1960s purveyor of multi-layered orchestral scores in which a myriad intricacies produce dense clouds of sound (most conspicuously in *2001: A Space Odyssey*), in the early 1980s Ligeti emerged changed from the slow business of composing his opera *Le grand macabre*. There was no going back. His next major work was a horn trio subtitled (of all things) 'hommage à Brahms'. Ligeti's trio didn't actually sound like Brahms, but the surfaces of his piece were now translucent, the compositional mechanisms laid bare, and the music told its story with great clarity. The piece also packed an emotional punch that was very hard to deny.

Mary Finsterer's music was also once full of information and gesture. It is possible to listen to *Nextwave Fanfare* (written for the Melbourne Symphony Orchestra) or the final stages of her pugnacious little violin concerto *Cōnstāns* (for John Rodgers and the Australian Art Orchestra) in terms of their often implacable totality, but you can also switch focus and zoom in on individual elements in the teeming detail beneath the surface. The composer and writer Michael Hannan, reviewing *Catch* – a stylish two-CD compilation of Finsterer's music up to 2002, which contains both these works – recognised the dichotomy, but he went further, commenting on the 'jamming' in the music and remarking that the pieces had 'some kind of bizarre groove element working in them'. Composers don't always hold critics in high regard, but Finsterer remembers this review with gratitude.

'I felt he "got" the music,' she explains, 'looking past the more immediate layers to find that the pieces were rooted in what I call "urban folk music".'

It is a good description, and one might add that Finsterer's 'urban folk music' has always been rather fast and very noisy. One of the things that has happened in her work of late is that she has allowed herself more time for events to unfold – her music no longer seems in a hurry. It is also noticeably quieter.

These things often happen to artists in mid career. They have life experiences, successes and setbacks; they have children (Finsterer has two); they move to the country (she lives in the NSW Southern Highlands); they get older (she turns fifty in 2012). Finsterer is well aware of how her changing circumstances have affected her music, particularly the way in which her children have disrupted her work patterns – remember, most composers work at home – but, she points out, they have also helped her.

'I had to lose a certain preciousness about what I needed in terms of the right conditions to compose,' she explains, 'the right environment, the right amount of time. My kids have helped me to be more creative in my approach. I love how they have brought this to my life. They are very kind to me when I can't focus on them. Actually – I would say they are very patient with me!'

All of this might account for a certain maturity in her musical outlook, but the main catalyst, one suspects, was that opera. Commissioned by the Song Company and now finished after five years' work, *Biographica* has at its core an A.S. Byatt–like conceit in which a modern writer attempts the biography of the sixteenth-century Italian polymath Gerolamo Cardano and finds he has something in common with his subject.

Finsterer describes Cardano as 'a typical Renaissance man'. 'He published 125 books, with 112 more manuscripts unpublished at his death, and wrote on all manner of topics, including science, mathematics, biology, philology, astrology, numerology, architecture, astronomy, music, alchemy and gambling.' Especially gambling. Cardano's weaknesses in this area do not make him an attractive character, but they endear him to the biographer, deep in debt and drawn to Cardano's main vice as a possible solution.

To prepare herself for the opera, Finsterer began researching the music of the Renaissance and soon found her own music drawing on the sounds of the sixteenth century. The composer had long made use of systems – series of notes, chords, rhythmic figures, all of different lengths and moving at different speeds, looped and overlapping. In *Biographica*, this technique remains more or less intact, but the nature of the musical materials is altered. The chords and bass lines are now more likely to be tonally related, so the repetitions come to resemble the ground basses of Renaissance music.

'I knew perfectly well that the research I had undertaken would take me in a different direction,' Finsterer admits. 'That's not easy … it's not really the done thing to change style. But my desire to venture down the path of exploration became more important to me than the criticisms I might have to endure.'

In fact, rather than criticism, Finsterer's new music has attracted plaudits. In 2009, her orchestral work *In Praise of Darkness* – a richly luminous procession through a Borgesian labyrinth, so far heard only in Europe – won Australia's richest composition award, the Paul Lowin Orchestra Prize.

But there's more to Finsterer's new direction than research. *Biographica*, with a libretto by Timothy Daly, is a comic opera, and in discussing it Finsterer refers to Mozart, pointing out that the style of *The Marriage of Figaro* is not that of *The Magic Flute*. In other words, Finsterer no longer feels constrained to write in a particular manner. The opera requires one sort of music, Shirley Barrett's film *South Solitary* needed another. And now there's the Mass. At this point it is just a notion, but *Until* – that saxophone duo, which is presently all that exists of the project – is already living up to its anticipatory title. With the addition of percussion, it has morphed into a trio.

A little while ago in Australia, we invented the expression 'emerging artist', a phrase rather like 'developing nation'. It's a bureaucrat label devised, I think, by the Australia Council for the Arts to signify promising young artists whom no one much has heard of (and who might therefore receive smaller grants and think themselves lucky). But as Finsterer's good friend the composer David Worrall once pointed out, the expression is a form of tautology, for 'any artist who is not emerging is dead'.

Without a doubt, Mary Finsterer is emerging.

The Monthly, 2011

Messiaen and Carter: Two centenaries

Most twentieth-century music for the concert hall and the opera house was written by composers who might be described as 'rugged individualists'. Along the way there were trends and fashions, schools and cliques, mainstreams and dead ends, but the more distance we gain from that century of unprecedented musical change, the more it all seems to be the work of individual men and a few women whose music owed little to their forebears and who founded no dynasties. Even the three Viennese composers who actually announced themselves as a school – Schoenberg, Berg and Webern – mostly shared basic beliefs, their individual musical personalities and attitudes remaining quite distinct. One can no more imagine Webern composing Schoenberg's piano concerto than Schoenberg writing Berg's *Lulu*.

Two of the most significant individualists of the later twentieth century – and two of the most rugged – were Olivier Messiaen and Elliott Carter. Messiaen was born 100 years ago, at Avignon in the south of France on 10 December 1908; Carter was born in New York City the following day. Messiaen died in 1992; Carter, remarkably, is still alive and attending his own centenary concerts. More remarkable yet, he is still composing and some of this year's concerts have contained world premieres of his music.

Messiaen and Carter represent twin musical poles in a number of areas. Fittingly, given their respective birthplaces, Messiaen was inspired by landscape and nature, particularly birdsong, and Carter by ideas, both literary and philosophical. Perhaps because of this, Messiaen's music has always tended to appeal to an audience beyond

contemporary music circles, while Carter's has seemed more intim-
idating, maybe more intellectual. And significantly, in a secular
century, Messiaen was a believer – not in some feel-good, New Age
vagueness, but in scary, mystical, heaven-and-hell Catholicism;
Carter remains a humanist sceptic, holding dear the principles of
the eighteenth-century Enlightenment. Early in their lives, one
doubts that either man would have imagined how stark this divide
would have come to seem – and how current – by the time of their
centenaries. But then neither was thinking much about the future,
for both composers were busy being prodigies of sorts.

Of the two, Messiaen was by far the more obvious 'marvellous
boy'. Even before he was born, his mother, the poet Cécile Sauvage,
was convinced that a great artistic career awaited her son (she was
also convinced of his gender) and she dedicated a series of poems to
him *in utero* entitled 'L'âme en bourgeon' ('The Burgeoning Soul').
Once out in the world, young Olivier was given every opportunity
to shine. Proud and pushy, Mr and Mrs Messiaen gave their eight-
year-old Christmas presents of opera scores, which the boy appears
to have relished. Soon enough he was composing his own music
and, rather miraculously, his early pieces sound quite a lot like the
Messiaen the world would come to know. There seems to have been
no searching for a personal voice: the nineteen-year-old, who in
1928 wrote the serenely slow organ piece entitled *Le banquet céleste*
(The Heavenly Feast), is evidently the same composer who would
go on to produce *Quatuor pour la fin du temps*, *Catalogue d'oiseaux*
(Bird Catalogue, 1956–58) and *Des canyons aux étoiles* (From the
Canyons to the Stars, 1974).

Across the Atlantic, Elliott Carter was interested in everything.
Though never a musical prodigy in the accepted sense, he was precocious enough in most regards. Immediately after World War I he
joined his father on business trips to Europe and began learning languages. He read all the books he could lay his hands on, and attended
concerts in the company of his parents. His liking was always for the

modern. Today his bookshelves hold first editions of Proust and Joyce – not because he is a collector of first editions, but because he bought and read these books when they were first published – and he seems to recall having been at every important American musical premiere, including Stravinsky's *The Rite of Spring* in 1924, which really excited his interest in composing music. (He also remembers, at the US premiere of Berg's *Wozzeck*, in Philadelphia in 1931, sitting behind George Gershwin.)

Carter's parents encouraged his cultural development, but they were not in favour of his pursuing a career in music. It was another composer, Charles Ives, who helped to develop the boy's enthusiasms in this area. Ives wrote him a letter of recommendation ('Carter strikes me as rather an exceptional boy') and he was accepted by Harvard, studying English to please his parents, but taking every music subject he could squeeze in along the way. Finally, in the 1930s, by which time Messiaen was already in full-flight as a composer, Mr and Mrs Carter bowed to their son's wishes, and the young man went to Paris to learn from the great pedagogue, Nadia Boulanger. Boulanger's pupils studied a lot of Bach and she tended to turn out composers of a neoclassical persuasion, especially in the 1930s when this style was in its ascendancy, exemplified by the music of her hero, Stravinsky. Carter didn't disappoint his teacher and the works he composed following his studies with her were broadly neoclassical.

But in New Deal America, Carter's friend and colleague (and fellow Boulanger pupil) Aaron Copland was forming the view that a simpler, more direct, more populist, more overtly American style of music was wanted, something that might prove the musical equivalent of Roosevelt's attempts to jump-start national confidence and pride in the post-Depression years. Carter was taken with his friend's attitude, but his heart was not in the music. The score of his ballet, *Pocahontas* (1939), while more interesting than is often supposed to be the case, could never match Copland's *Billy the Kid* and *Appalachian*

Spring in the popularity stakes. Carter persevered with this style of music throughout the 1940s, but with ever lessening enthusiasm. On his fortieth birthday, he drew the double bar line at the end of his Sonata for Cello and Piano, the work that displayed the first real indications of his later mature style. He was, in effect, about to begin all over again.

Almost the same day, Messiaen finished the final revisions to his great *Turangalîla–Symphonie* and the following year he travelled to the United States to hear the world premiere conducted by Leonard Bernstein. *Turangalîla* is a sprawling, eighty-minute, ten-movement symphony-cum-piano concerto, full of colourful, sensuous orchestral sonorities, joyously leaping melodic lines and intricate rhythmic structures, often superimposed several at a time. It is hard to think of a more extroverted or flamboyant piece of music from the last hundred years and in performance it can seem fulsome in its high spirits. Bernstein was the ideal conductor for it, and it made Messiaen's name much more widely known.

But this flamboyance was immediately followed up with something close to asceticism. The purely musical ramifications of the composer's rhythmic experimentation in *Turangalîla* came in a work for solo piano entitled *Quarte études de rhythme* (*Four Studies in Rhythm*, 1949). For the second of these pieces, the title of which translates unsatisfactorily as 'Modes (or scales) of values and intensities', Messiaen drew up a chart that gave each note on the keyboard its own length (value), articulation and dynamic (intensity). These remain fixed for the duration of the piece, so that every time we hear middle C it is played as a heavily accented *fortissimo* lasting five crotchets (or quarter notes). Every other pitch, likewise, has its pre-ordained length and loudness. The process of composition sounds highly contrived and artificial, but the composer's own performance of the resulting piece was sprightly and dance-like. Within a short time, however, Messiaen's piece opened the door to 'integral serialism', the *lingua franca* of scorched-earth modernism in which every parameter of a piece of music was plotted in advance and every sound might be traced back to a set of charts. Messiaen's pupils, including the young Pierre Boulez and Karlheinz Stockhausen, took the ball and ran with it, at least for a while.

Elliott Carter was dealing in asceticism too, the search for his own style leading him to retreat to the Sonoran desert in Arizona. Away from New York City, Carter finally struck gold and after a year of uninterrupted work he produced his first string quartet, forty minutes of utterly original music that would set him on the musical path he would follow for more than half a century. Like Messiaen's music of the period, the most striking aspect of Carter's quartet was its rhythmic vitality and innovation. The difference between them was that Messiaen's rhythmic structures tend to be layered on top of each other, forming massive polyrhythms, while Carter's music is more concerned with flexibility. It is partly a matter of what is usually called metrical modulation. This is not quite as complex as it sounds. If you have a pulse which is subdivided into (say) four, then you have two metric planes: the basic pulse of big beats and another, on the surface, with small beats running along at four times the rate. You can alter the surface rate by subdividing the big beats differently – for example, you can subdivide it into threes (in which case the surface will seem to slow down) or fives (in which case it will speed up) – but you can also keep the surface notes moving along at their original rate of four small beats to every big beat, and then move the big beats so they appear every three or five small beats. Now you've changed the basic tempo while leaving the surface movement exactly the same.

Well okay, maybe it *is* complex. But the effect was nicely summed up by the English composer and conductor (and great champion of Carter's work) Oliver Knussen, when he described Carter's music as hitched up to a multi-speed gear box. The result is a musical world of continual change and that is what Carter has pioneered. In his five string quartets – central to his work – he has gone further.

Referring to Mozart's operas, those emblems of the Enlightenment, Carter has spoken of the way the eighteenth-century composer often had several characters sing simultaneously and yet retain their dramatic individuality. That has been Carter's aim in his quartets. The new-found rhythmic flexibility allows the four members of his quartets to play at different speeds and with different basic materials. In effect, they perform musical roles, coexisting as much as interacting. It is complex and radical, and it is what makes Carter distinctive.

While Carter's *métier* has been chamber music, Messiaen's was not. Apart from *Quatuor pour la fin du temps*, there is hardly any other chamber music in his output. At the heart of Messiaen's musical personality was the organ, and every Sunday that he was at home in Paris, he could be found at the console of the great Cavaillé-Coll organ at the church of Sainte-Trinité. Not only did he compose a substantial body of work for the instrument, but he also extemporised as church organists will. In many ways, those Sundays at La Trinité were his laboratory, the organ his workbench. It was here, in the presence of his god, that the composer experimented.

Carter's string quartets and Messiaen's organ music have been the best indicators of their composers' musical success. The five Carter quartets continue to demand exceptional virtuosity from their performers. But they have always had performers, and new ones are coming along all the time. At first it was a few dedicated groups such as the Juilliard Quartet that championed the pieces. They were the first group to play the composer's String Quartet No 3 in 1973, a piece that took the complexities of his previous pieces even further, not least in requiring the greatest possible spatial separation of the four players to emphasise their individual roles. But in recent years, younger groups have discovered a real rapport with the music. The Pacifica Quartet, for instance, has been known to play all five quartets in a single evening. Carter's quartets are now regarded, along with those of Bartók and Shostakovich, as the great string quartets of the twentieth century.

Messiaen's achievement is still greater. When it comes to organ music, there is Bach and there is Messiaen, and then there is everyone else. For a twentieth-century composer, and a modernist to boot, this is an achievement without parallel. And when one considers that Messiaen's body of organ music has established itself with perhaps the most conservative group of musicians on earth – church organists – the achievement is all the more impressive.

Carter and Messiaen's musical paths seem never to have crossed. If you look in books about the composers, you will not find many references to Messiaen in the Carter books or to Carter in the Messiaen books. They were, after all, very different composers. And yet there are points of similarity. Both men managed to draw on the music of earlier composers (Debussy and Stravinsky in Messiaen's case, Schoenberg and Stravinsky in Carter's), synthesise those influences and produce something totally original. Both men taught students who went on to sound nothing like them – the mark of a good teacher. And in old age, both men produced their first operas, though they could scarcely have been more different. Messiaen's *Saint François d'Assise* is an evening-long meditation on one of his favourite saints. Hardly dramatic at all, it includes no quartets, trios or even duets, only solo voices and choruses. Carter's opera, mischievously entitled *What Next?*, is in a single forty-minute act and was inspired by a movie – Jacques Tati's *Trafic*. It begins with a car crash from which the six victims emerge all singing at once.

Elliott Carter's late productivity is unparalleled. Other composers have worked into old age and we remember them for it: Verdi wrote his last opera, *Falstaff*, at the age of seventy-nine (Carter composed his first at eighty-nine); Vaughan Williams produced five symphonies after he turned seventy, the last at eighty-four. Michael Tippett worked on into his eighties, as did Stravinsky. But there is no precedent for a major composer still active in the year of his centenary. It is not simply that Carter is still writing music, but that he is writing more of it than in his supposed prime. In the decades from 1951 and

1971 (Carter's early forties to early sixties), he composed ten pieces, including four major orchestral works and the first three string quartets. In the single decade to 2008, he has completed fifty works. And he seems unstoppable. When the American pianist Ursula Oppens recorded a disc in February 2008 entitled *Elliott Carter at 100: The complete piano music*, she really should have known better. By the time it was released in October, Carter had composed two new pieces not included on Oppens's 'complete' CD.

If the sheer quantity of music composed by Carter in his nineties has been extraordinary, the nature and quality of the music are no less so. Stravinsky, in old age, came to specialise in miniatures – shards of musical granite lasting anywhere from one to five minutes, generally written in response to the death of an admired friend or colleague. Carter, too, has written his share of miniatures, but he has also continued to work on a large scale. For example, there are recent concertos for cello, horn and flute; two new piano concertos, a chamber concerto and the so-called *Boston Concerto*, really a second concerto for orchestra. There are also other orchestral pieces, chamber pieces and musical settings of modern Italian poets, William Carlos Williams, Wallace Stevens and a selection from the *Pisan Cantos* of Ezra Pound. There is even a persistent rumour that Carter is planning a new opera.

As to the quality, there is certainly evidence of what we might take for a 'late style'. Like Beethoven and Bartók before him, some of Carter's later works display a lyrical proclivity and simpler forms and textures. Some, but not all. Carter has spoken of the years spent generating thousands of pages of sketches for one piece as a kind of preparation for the music he is now composing. He is no longer searching for his music; he has found it and can produce it, if not exactly on-demand, then at least without the years of work that went into the early string quartets and the great Concerto for Orchestra (1969). But lest we conclude he has become a little too comfortable as he approaches the three-figure milestone, some of Carter's recent pieces are as abrasive and confronting as anything he had previously produced. The piano concerto, *Dialogues*, for instance, positively rages against the dying of the light.

Perhaps the most impressive thing of all about the composer in extreme old age is that he is still experimenting. Earlier this year at the Tanglewood Festival of Contemporary Music, a student string orchestra premiered *Sound Fields* to an audience of dropping jaws. Just when you think you know the work of a 99-year-old composer, and you know that, whatever else it might be, it will be rhythmically complex and volatile, continually changing, he produces a piece in which a sequence of chords passes slowly and regularly before us in a precession of minims – half notes – that never changes from the start of the piece to the finish. What next, indeed!

Australian Financial Review, 2008

In December 2011, Elliott Carter's 103rd birthday was celebrated with the New York premieres of song cycles to words by e.e. cummings and T.S. Eliot, both of which he attended. As this book goes to print, he is writing a new orchestral piece.

Luciano Berio Remembers the Future

Have you noticed how modern music used to go 'plink-plonk' but now it goes 'dugga-dugga-dugga'? This question was put to me by the American composer Matthias Kriesberg in the late 1980s, when the nature of contemporary concert music seemed to have changed every bit as significantly as it had altered in the years after World War II.

In the 1940s, young composers in Europe such as Pierre Boulez and Luigi Nono – and a little later Karlheinz Stockhausen – had spoken of a musical 'zero hour' in which the decadent past would be destroyed and a new musical language invented from the ground up. Developing the ideas of Arnold Schoenberg and Anton Webern, many of the post-war musical avant-garde wished to subject all aspects of music – not just pitch, but rhythm, dynamics, timbre and everything else – to the accountability of a numerical series. Pieces would be assembled pitch by pitch (those plinks and plonks) according to the dictates of a pre-composed chart. This was an important moment in history. The idea was to rid music of anything derivative, tearing up the past. There could be no going back, and that also meant avoiding repetition within an individual piece of music.

Obviously this couldn't last, and it didn't. After just a few pieces, integral serialism itself began to sound hugely derivative. Also, from the beginning there were composers, such as the Italian Luciano Berio, whose musical interests were simply too wide to accommodate such a narrow view. Finally, of course, there were other composers, especially in the United States, whose upbringing rendered the European obsession with eradicating history quite redundant. In 1988, Matthias Kriesberg – whose music of the time still contained remnants of the earlier 'plink-plonk' style of music – felt that the broad change in direction that started in the mid 1960s and began to make itself felt in the 1970s had come about very largely as a result of the growing popularity of the so-called minimalist composers in the United States, specifically Terry Riley, Steve Reich, Philip Glass, and then, in the 1970s, John Adams.

Kriesberg had a point. Early minimalist music had been every bit as extreme and austere as integral serialism. The minimalists presented 'common tones in simple time' (to appropriate the title of Adams's orchestral piece of 1979). In contrast to serial music, these tones sometimes added up to major or minor chords, and for the minimalists there was a lot of repetition, all of it hitched to a basic repetitive rhythmic structure: discontinuous plink-plonks replaced by 'dugga-dugga-dugga'. But it was equally hermetic.

Again, it couldn't last. In the nearly two decades since Kriesberg and I had our conversation, Reich, Glass and Adams have become more popular and more influential, even as their own musical worlds have expanded to include a rather richer harmonic palette than was originally the case. You couldn't call them minimalists now. Their rhythms have grown more complex, too, though they remain underpinned by a readily perceivable pulse. It is perfectly true that these Americans have effected great change in our musical lives, but they didn't do it on their own. Luciano Berio spent much of his own career inside the United States. It was a welcoming land for his extrovert intellect and it nurtured his ideas and his music. In turn, he also affected music in the United States and everywhere else.

Berio is the composer I always recommend when people ask me where they should begin with contemporary classical music. His pieces are seldom easy listening, but they generally explain themselves sufficiently on first hearing that even an inexperienced listener can grasp something and feel that contact has been made. Berio's music is full of colour and dramatic gesture. A melodic impulse is never far from the music's surface, and, yes, often enough, there is a strong pulse driving the music along: quite a few of Berio's pieces themselves go 'dugga-dugga-dugga'. For example, *Sequenza VI* for solo viola does this and little else for a quarter of an hour, as the player risks RSI in pursuit of the composer's vision. It is virtuoso writing in the nineteenth-century sense, in the Paganini sense, and it speaks directly, even aggressively, to its audience.

There was never an ivory tower that could contain Luciano Berio. Apart from anything else, he was far too fond of the good life to remain locked away in creative confinement for long. This showed in his work, as much in the music he *didn't* write as in the long list of works he actually completed. In 1995, when the British–Australian tenor Gerald English was approaching his seventieth birthday, he contacted all the living composers he had worked with over his long career, asking if they might find their way to provide him with a new song (he celebrated the birthday in question with a concert consisting entirely of world premieres). Berio replied to the invitation with typical ebullience, many good wishes for a happy birthday, and an apology. While he would have loved to contribute a song, he told English, he found himself already stretched. He was, he confessed, now seven years behind with his commissions.

This was the same year the composer outraged the late John Drummond. Drummond in his final year as artistic director of the London Proms had commissioned a new orchestral work from Berio to premiere during the two-month summer festival. Berio attempted to palm him off with a piece that had not only been performed somewhere else, but for which he had already been paid once. When Drummond found out, he refused the piece, and gave the incident a prominent mention in his memoirs.

This is not intended to denigrate Berio's memory. On the contrary, it is evidence that the composer was possessed of some very human foibles. That seems to me, on balance, a good thing in an artist. Berio was a flesh and blood composer, always slightly apart from his rather more ascetic colleagues in the European avant-garde. If Boulez,

Nono and Stockhausen were all – at least in the 1950s and 60s – to some extent musical idealists, setting out to change the very fabric of music, Berio was more an artisan. And the idea of tearing up history was anathema to him. He could never be a party to that. (Neither could Boulez, as it turned out, but that is another story.)

History was important to Berio. He loved old music, and not just classical music, which he would frequently reclaim, quote, parody, complete or rearrange in his own works. Folksong, too, was a vital part of Berio's musical make-up, and its gestures and sounds (and sometimes actual tunes) found their way into his pieces. Far from wishing to forget the past, he was concerned with 'remembering the future', as he entitled his Charles Eliot Norton lectures at Harvard University in 1993–94, now published under the same title. The phrase came from the last words his friend Italo Calvino wrote for the character of Prospero at the end of Berio's opera *Un re in ascolto*. Actually the phrase – *ricordo al futuro* – translates more literally as 'a memory for the future' or perhaps 'a recollection of the future', but either way the sense is clear enough. For Berio, the future must contain and remake the past.

From early childhood, the composer's experience of music was always ecumenical. Born in Oneglia, Berio received his first music lessons from his father and grandfather. Both were themselves composers, not of symphonies but of popular songs. On Sunday mornings Berio's father played the organ in the local church, but on Saturday nights he played piano at the movie theatre. There was little sense of hierarchy in Berio's musical upbringing, of one type of music being inherently better than another. And we should remember, too, that the young composer grew up in a country where everyone went to the opera. Music in Italy was, and is, a highly social art, and other people were central to Berio's art as a composer. These people were his audiences and his performers. They were also his students, for Berio was an inspiring teacher. And many of those students were in fact Americans, especially in the 1960s when the composer taught at the Tanglewood and Aspen Summer Schools, at Mills College in Oakland, California (where his class included the young Steve Reich), at the Juilliard School in New York, and finally as Charles Eliot Norton Professor of Poetry at Harvard in 1993 and '94.

The fact that he should end up as a poetry professor is a quirk of academic fate: it's simply what they call the giver of the Norton lectures. But it suited Berio, who collaborated extensively with writers of all sorts: poets, novelists, philosophers and dramatists. Indeed nearly all of Berio's pieces are dramatic in some way, even when they are purely instrumental. That hard-working violist in *Sequenza VI* is struggling to cope with the notes on the page and the struggle (visible and audible) is part of the music and part of the theatre. Violas are not usually given this sort of work-out. Their tones are more muted than those of violins or cellos and composers tend to treat them accordingly. So in composing his solo piece, Berio was deliberately casting this instrument against type.

Berio began the series of solo pieces he called *Sequenzas* in 1958, with *Sequenza I* for flute. There would be thirteen more of them, for harp, voice, piano, trombone, viola, oboe, violin, clarinet, trumpet, guitar, bassoon, accordion and finally, in 2002, *Sequenza XIV* for cello. On paper this makes Berio look like a latter-day Hindemith, the German composer who wrote sonatas for just about every instrument invented, favouring, in particular, the poor relations. And perhaps there was an element of this with Berio and his *Sequenzas* – the composer as artisan, again – but there was much more to these pieces than the plugging of holes in the repertoire. For a start, there is that theatrical element. Mostly, this is abstract – *viz* the viola player frantically sawing away – but sometimes it is quite overt. Two works of the mid 1960s demonstrate this. *Sequenza III* for female voice and *Sequenza V* for trombone each have a protagonist who must, like the violist, struggle to a degree, but the circumstances surrounding these struggles are somehow recognisable.

Sequenza III was composed for Berio's first wife and principal muse, the American soprano Cathy Berberian. In the piece she comes on stage muttering to herself like a bag lady in a bus station. Yet the singer is not playing a role, unless it is the role of a singer. The piece itself might best be thought of as her attempt to express herself – her attempt, indeed, to sing. The actual words she speaks and sings are by Markus Kutter and are themselves about singing: 'Give me / a few words / for a woman / to sing ...'

As the piece continues, we feel increasingly that the singer is playing her voice as she would an instrument, just like the performers in the other *Sequenzas*. Indeed, exploring the relationship between performer and instrument is partly what each of these pieces is about.

In *Sequenza V*, composed for the American trombonist Stuart Dempster, the performer and his instrument seem slowly to trade places. The performer sings into his instrument as he plays, heavily articulating the trombone's characteristic *wa*, which becomes the primary sound module of the piece. Berio also notates certain positions for the player to adopt, the end result being a rather stilted mime act. Much of the piece was inspired by the Belgian clown Grock (Adriano Wettach), who was a neighbour of the Berio family back in Oneglia. In his stage act, which was largely musical, Grock would suddenly pause, stare fixedly at the audience and ask the question 'Why?' The same thing happens in Berio's pieces as the trombone's repeated *wa* is transformed abruptly into the clown's question.

Sequenza V is as overtly theatrical as these solo pieces ever get, yet there is a purely musical theatricality that runs through the entire series, and this, in turn, relates to the technique of performance. At that level, these works are all *études* – not *études* in the sense of rigorous studies for instrumental practice, but concert *études*, designed to display the virtuoso performer's hard-won technique to the public. Even in the nineteenth century this was as much a theatrical display as a musical one (we're back again with Paganini), and like most nineteenth-century *études*, Berio's *Sequenzas* each concentrate on one or two techniques, pushing them to the limit (the fast-muttering soprano, the *wa-wa*-ing trombonist, the violist's bow going 'dugga-dugga').

The final significant aspect of the *Sequenzas* is that they all serve as explorations, *in extremis*, of monody – of a line of notes spinning itself ever longer, going in search of melody, of song. Paul Klee's remark about his drawing technique being a matter of taking a line for a walk comes to mind. But Berio was seldom, if ever, so spontaneous in his composition, even if the results of his work – and most of the *Sequenzas* are examples of this – can seem improvisatory. Berio might have been a child of Italian popular culture, but he was a student of the avant-garde. If his tastes were undoubtedly broader than Boulez's, his commitment to intellectual accountability was no less rigorous. He planned his music down to the last detail.

For Berio, however, detail arose from the substance of the music. It did not generate the substance, as it often did for Boulez; and neither was detail a mere byproduct of the music, as in the work of John Cage and the chance composers. Berio spoke eloquently on just this point in his Norton lectures:

> In either situation – that of the generalized series or that of indeterminacy and chance – it is always *detail* that falls by the wayside: the very detail that, more than any other factor, accounts for the completeness, the meaningfulness, and the dignity of a musical work. In the first case the fetishism of the detail, saturated with information, often makes performance and listening almost impractical; in the second case indifference with regard to detail transforms the work itself into one abnormally bloated detail whose result in terms of sound may here and there be rather involving on account of the association it evokes (clouds, wind, seas, summer fields).

It is Berio's use of the word 'dignity' that jumps out from this paragraph. It is a word nearly always used in the context of a human being, rather than a work of art. It reinforces the personal nature of Berio's music, the fact that it was designed – tailored, one might say – to specific performers, and nowhere more so than in the *Sequenzas*. It comes back once more to song, singing being the most fundamental musical act, the one in which everyone, to some extent, participates.

Monody – *proto*-song – dominates even Berio's chamber and orchestral works. The single line often enough generates the rest of the music. *O King* was composed in 1968 in memory of the assassinated civil rights campaigner Martin Luther King Jr. It exists in two versions. One is an independent piece for soprano and five instruments; the other – for eight voices and orchestra – is the second movement of *Sinfonia*. The latter is better known, but the former easier to explain. For the five minutes of its duration, a slow melodic line is loudly punched out by the piano. The other instruments – including the wordless soprano voice – quietly pick up and sustain these pitches, even as the piano moves on to hammer out new notes. The piano's monody is like a jet plane seen from the ground, apparently moving very slowly, yet leaving in its wake a sonic vapour trail. In this way, Berio's melodic line forges its own harmony.

O King also contains a further instance of vocal/instrumental transformation. At the beginning of the score, the soprano is instructed to sing like an instrument, the instruments (with the exception of the piano) to play like voices. The soprano may have no words, but the vowels to which she sings her notes are what are left behind when the consonants are removed from the line 'O Martin Luther King'. On the last page of the score, she finally sings the words themselves, while the instrumentalists, speaking softly, appropriate her vowels.

The business of transformation is a recurrent theme in Berio's music. Songs – by Mahler, Falla, Kurt Weill – are transformed in new performing editions; repertoire pieces are completed – Puccini's *Turandot* in an entirely traditional manner, Schubert's tenth symphony in such a way that the missing passages are replaced by stretches of a kind of neutral filler (Berio called this piece *Rendering*);

transformed folk music enters the concert hall and, in turn, transforms it. But Berio's own pieces were also ripe for transformation. Several of his solo *Sequenzas* accrued ensembles of other instruments and became mini concertos. Berio called some of these pieces *Chemins* – routes or pathways – the monody now threading its way through a dense undergrowth of other music. *Sequenza VII* for oboe, composed in 1969, became, six years later, *Chemins IV*: the same oboe part, but with a group of eleven string players amplifying and commentating on the solo piece. In *Chemins II* (1967), the 'dugga-dugga'-ing viola of *Sequenza VI* is amplified by a mixed ensemble of nine instruments to the extent that its music is obliterated at least twice. Berio didn't stop there: he composed *Chemins III* (1968), which took the solo viola and the nine instruments of *Chemins II* and added a full orchestra to the mix. Then in 1970 he produced *Chemins IIb*. This was the same piece again, but this time with the solo viola having disappeared, its music taken over by an enlarged woodwind section. Finally in 1972, came *Chemins IIc*, which was effectively *Chemins IIb* but with a new soloist – a bass clarinet – playing an almost totally new solo part.

This process of transforming old pieces into new pieces, and then transforming them again, is partly a matter of seeing all the possibilities on offer. Berio's contemporary and compatriot, Franco Donatoni, never one to let musical ideas go to waste if they had further potential in them, used to tell his students that, like peasants, they should always use 'the whole pig'. Berio had a different analogy. He spoke of onions: one organism, many layers. At the heart of most of his multi-layered onions was a single line of music, often enough a *Sequenza*.

Berio's *Sequenzas*, spanning forty-four years of his creative life, really do form the spine of his work. When he gave those Norton lectures, each of the six began and ended with a performance of one of the *Sequenzas*. There was no specific mention of the pieces in the lectures themselves. There didn't have to be. Berio's music speaks for itself.

Australian Financial Review, 2006

Keith Jarrett and
His Archetypal Standards

Towards the end of a track on his trio recording, *Yesterdays*, pianist Keith Jarrett plays a melodic phrase that sounds as though it has escaped from the Oasis song, 'Wonderwall'. It brings the listener up short, because of course Jarrett is not that kind of jazz musician. Younger players such as Brad Mehldau might tap pop music from Paul Simon to Radiohead to 'Wonderwall' itself in search of potential new standards, but Jarrett remains a traditionalist. His idea of a standard is little different to Bud Powell's or Bill Evans's. It's either a classic bebop tune by the likes of Charlie Parker, Thelonious Monk or Powell himself, or it's from the Broadway/Tin Pan Alley pantheon of composers such as Richard Rodgers, Harold Arlen and Jerome Kern. Certainly nothing much after the 1950s. On *Yesterdays*, it is actually Kern's 'Smoke Gets in Your Eyes' (from 1933) that yields the presumably unwitting fragment of 'Wonderwall'.

The concept of the standard has long been a matter of contention in jazz circles. Most concepts in jazz are more or less contentious – jazz musicians and, particularly, jazz fans are an opinionated lot – but the standard is something of a special case, because it goes to the heart of the matter. Jazz is an improvised music and some say it should pour out of its performers: spontaneous, free and unhampered by a dependency on the harmonic template of a song composed eighty years ago by George Gershwin. Others would argue that if the music is merely spontaneous and free there is no special reason to label it jazz. It is only the templates – harmonic, melodic, stylistic, instrumental – that situate the music within that particular genre.

And anyway, knowing your standards is to jazz musicians what drawing is to visual artists. It's a training; it keeps them honest. You see why this is contentious. And since no one in this discussion is actually right or wrong, the contention will always continue and much time will be wasted.

In one sense, however, standards really are like drawing. If you ask a group of very different artists to draw the same vase of flowers, you will quickly discover their various aesthetic preferences, their technical differences and similarities, even the contrasting ways in which they see a bunch of peonies in water. It's the same with jazz musicians. The rich variety of jazz available today can seem baffling in its stylistic range. The neophyte can listen to half a dozen different players and quickly get lost in the range of styles and approaches. But ask those same six players to give you their versions of 'Polka Dots and Moonbeams' and you gain perspective, you hear exactly where they're coming from. And because players tend to have their favourite standards, tunes to which they return over their whole career, it is also possible to gain a historical perspective, to hear a player changing across ten, twenty or thirty years or, perhaps, within the space of a few days.

It is now twenty-six years since Jarrett first invited bassist Gary Peacock and drummer Jack DeJohnette to record standards with him and in that time twenty trio albums have been released on ECM, including a few that contain free improvisations. Over the years quite a few tunes have returned like old friends. A short list of Jarrett favourites might include 'Autumn Leaves', 'When I Fall in Love', 'If I Were a Bell', 'My Funny Valentine', 'Things Ain't What They Used to Be', 'You Took Advantage of Me', 'Scrapple from the Apple', 'Smoke Gets in Your Eyes' and 'Stella by Starlight', the last four of which, in fact, turn up on *Yesterdays*.

Most of Jarrett's albums are recorded in concert. All the tracks on *Yesterdays* come from a Tokyo concert in April 2001 (the final track was actually recorded at the sound check), and it's worth noting that four of Jarrett's last five trio albums have come from concerts in that same year. We might infer that the trio was on something of a roll. Certainly here it's on very good form indeed, alternately exploring the lyricism of Carl Fischer's 'You've Changed' (with a lovely, loping, melodic bass solo from Peacock), 'Smoke Gets in Your Eyes' and the album's title track, and energetically displaying its bebop credentials on tunes by Parker, Dizzy Gillespie and Horace Silver. One of the particular delights of the recording is the way in which Jarrett and his colleagues demonstrate the line that runs from bebop back to ragtime. On Gillespie and Parker's 'Shaw 'Nuff', for example, Jarrett's left hand goes in for some athletic stride playing, while Rodgers and Hart's 'You Took Advantage of Me' begins as pure ragtime, moving gradually into a fast bop workout – a manic real-time analysis of the tune's melodic and harmonic nuts and bolts – before slipping back into ragtime. (The trio performed a similar feat with the same tune, though at a slower tempo, on their previous release, *My Foolish Heart: Live at Montreux*, also recorded in 2001 but three months after the Tokyo session on *Yesterdays*.)

'You Took Advantage of Me' was composed in 1928 for a Busby Berkeley show, *Present Arms*, and it has its roots in ragtime. Jarrett's approach, then, is historically apt. But in mixing up the syncopations of ragtime and bop, Jarrett is also demonstrating a belief in the oneness of jazz, and this philosophy seems to lie at the very heart of his playing, even when he is unaware of it or wants to repudiate it. It is certainly at the heart of his solo playing.

When Jarrett is not working with his standards trio, he plays solo improvisations. Indeed he is probably more famous for these than for his work with the trio, simply because what he does here has a sensational quality. Alone on stage with nothing in mind, Jarrett coaxes and coerces sounds from his piano that will send him off on a unique journey of musical exploration. On the face of it, this is the polar opposite of playing standards and Jarrett himself is most insistent that not only does he not know where he is headed at the start of the evening, but also at the end he doesn't know where he has been. He enters something approaching a trance-like state in which his characteristic high-pitched vocalisations are as involuntary as his writhing on the piano stool and occasional levitations over the keyboard. When he listens back to a recording of the event, he is as interested to hear what he has created as his audience was on the night.

In the documentary film *Keith Jarrett: The art of improvisation* (2005), the pianist stresses that the music he plays in these concerts comes from him alone: Jarrett's mind in Jarrett's body is sending impulses to Jarrett's fingers: there is no will involved, there are no conscious choices being made. The pianist will have no truck with the idea that all music is about other music: these improvisations, he maintains, give the lie to that piece of mythology.

Well, yes and no. André Malraux once pointed out that no one becomes a painter by looking at landscapes. You become a painter by looking at paintings. It is no different with music. Other music lies behind it. Doubtless Jarrett's state of mind and physical fitness on the day contribute to his improvisations, as does the nature of the piano at which he is sitting, the design and acoustics of the hall, and – most important of all – the more or less palpable intensity of the listening from the audience. (Jarrett is famously sensitive to the last.) All these things are significant, and yet however good Jarrett is feeling on the night and however hard the audience is willing him on, one note must still be placed after another. It is not as though Jarrett's fingers are producing music the like of which has never before existed. On the contrary, the metres and rhythms, textures and harmonies, chordal voicings and melodic contours that emerge from one of these improvisations can almost always be traced back to earlier music. If the memory is able to function while we sleep, dredging up images and sounds in the form of dreams, it can certainly contribute to a piano improvisation, no matter how much the player might be 'in the moment'.

Jarrett's solo improvisations also draw on what we might think of as 'standards'. These are forms, styles and archetypes that are as much a part of this pianist's make-up as a knowledge of the chord changes in old Victor Young tunes. Jarrett might not be conscious that he is mining the rich seams of American musical history, but that, in part, is surely what he is doing. At a performance at the Vienna State Opera in July 1991 – on a CD called simply *Keith Jarrett: Vienna Concert* – the opening chords conjure the luminous, white-note harmonies of Aaron Copland, who himself drew on older templates such as New England hymnody and Appalachian (Celtic) folksong. This type of music often turns up in Jarrett's improvisations, some-times forming the 'still centre' of his 'turning world', sometimes, as in Vienna, providing the launching pad for an astonishing display of spontaneous musical invention that leads to faster, busier, louder, more complex, more rhythmically driven music, before subsiding into a lengthy and still more hymn-like coda.

Jarrett's improvisations are a subtle compendium of American style. Jazz from ragtime to bebop to cool at some level underpin most of his playing. Blues harmonies are regular visitors. Even the mini-malism of Steve Reich and Philip Glass rears its head when Jarrett seizes on a particular riff and locks it into a holding pattern. Other, less obviously American templates also turn up some nights. On the *Vienna Concert* CD, for example, the second improvisation begins with a scale that might be Japanese and later leads to harmonies redolent of Arvo Pärt, a composer whose music Jarrett (in classical mode) has played and recorded. His long involvement with Bach's music is also surely relevant when it comes to his ability to improvise intricate counterpoint.

In Tokyo's Metropolitan Festival Hall in October 2002 – on a DVD entitled *Keith Jarrett: Tokyo Solo* – the performance kicks off with a passage of atonal counterpoint that sounds rather like a ran-domised reimagining of one of the more complex passages of Schoen-berg's piano concerto. (We shouldn't forget that even this is an

American piece, composed in 1942 in Hollywood.) This passage is another staggeringly impressive piece of invention from the pianist, all the more so for coming out of the blue. He walks on stage, sits down and out come thousands of notes, each one perfectly placed and apparently judged – if spontaneous judgement isn't too much of a paradox – to produce a thrillingly nervy, edge-of-the-seat effect. But once again the music eventually comes to rest in a sort of Coplandesque reverie. There are usually moments of balm in a Jarrett performance and they often feature block chords moving stepwise as in a hymn, emphasising a gentle modality and often enough giving rise to a melodic line that seems to belong to the ages. And of course it does. That is the point. He may not know it and may wish to deny it, but Jarrett can hardly avoid tradition.

Like Tennyson's Ulysses – and like the rest of us – Keith Jarrett is a part of all that he has met. He might enter a state of unknowing at the beginning of a night of improvised music, but everything he has learnt and experienced lies deep in his memory, ready to colour his spontaneous outpourings and to help make sense of them. Just as conventional standards provide context and perspective in jazz, so these archetypal 'standards' bring perspective to these improvisations. For the art of improvisation – like the art of its far slower and more painstaking counterpart, composition – is also the art of memory, however subconscious.

Inside Story, 2009

Cole Porter: Words and music

It doesn't seem right that Cole Porter should have died only in 1964. After all, that's the same year as the Beatles' *A Hard Day's Night*. Surely Porter's talents belong to another era entirely. He's as 1920s as a cocktail shaker. When we listen to his witty, poignant songs, we're taken back in time. Porter's sophistication becomes our sophistication: isn't that how it works?

I began thinking about this after watching *De-Lovely*, the Porter biopic with Kevin Kline as the songwriter. What struck me most forcefully was how Porter's songs are so unlike other people's. You would hardly be likely to confuse a Porter song with one by Irving Berlin or George and Ira Gershwin or Rodgers and Hart, let alone Rodgers and Hammerstein.

In spite of – possibly because of – the presence in the film of Alanis Morissette (singing 'Let's Do It'), Sheryl Crow ('Begin the Beguine'), Robbie Williams ('It's De-Lovely') and a parade of others in search of a soundtrack Emmy, the best musical performances in the film come from Kevin Kline himself. Kline has no more of a singing voice than Cole Porter did. Like Porter before him, he has precise diction, an actor's timing and he brings out all the sophistication we expect from these songs. And yet to say that Porter's songs are sophisticated is ultimately a bit too glib. Lorenz Hart's lyrics weren't sophisticated? George Gershwin's music wasn't? Porter's brand of sophistication was unique. It is in his music as much as his words, but significantly it is most evident where his words and music collide and combine.

'Is it an earthquake or simply a shock?' he asks in 'At Long Last Love'. 'Is it the real turtle soup or merely the mock?' That's a fabulous line for its rhythm and rhyme, as well as for the drooping cadence of 'merely the mock'. And there's self-deprecation in the song, too. ('Will it be Bach I shall hear or just a Cole Porter song?') Now that's sophisticated.

'At Long Last Love' is a list song. The making of lists and the pairing of unlikely counterparts are as old as folk music, but Porter polished the technique. He uses it to great effect in 'You're the Top': 'You're a Botticelli, / You're Keats, you're Shelley, / You're Ovaltine' and 'You're a Waldorf salad / ... / You're a Berlin ballad' (more of that self-deprecation).

But Porter's songs are not only witty, they are often also risqué. 'Let's Do It', another list song, is ostensibly about falling in love, when it is actually purely about sex. Noël Coward, who wrote a brilliant 1950s version of this very 1920s song, made that much plain ('Monkeys whenever you look do it'), but some of the seldom heard verses of Porter's original are scarcely less precise ('Old sloths who hang down from twigs do it, / Though the effort is great. / Sweet guinea pigs do it, / Buy a couple and wait').

While the lyrics might be witty and memorable, Cole Porter's songs are by no means uniformly cheerful. As a melodist and harmonist, Porter was an authentic melancholic. 'What Is This Thing Called Love?' has a deliberately dreary tune that creeps around taking small steps – often semi-tones – and if not actually in a minor key, certainly seems to want to be. The same might be said of three of Porter's best-known songs, 'Night and Day', 'In the Still of the Night' and 'I Get a Kick Out of You'. These are all love songs, yet their music sinks slowly downwards (the harmony if not the melody) in a profoundly dejected manner. And the melodies tend to be difficult, chromatic and wide-ranging. The tune of 'Night and Day', indeed, covers nearly two octaves and the singer must be strong at both the top and the bottom of the range because the melody lingers at the extremes.

'So in Love' ('Strange, dear, but true, dear'), which at least sets out in a minor key, is one of Porter's most beautiful love ballads.

The music is unutterably sad, especially on top of one of Porter's typical 'beguine' rhythms. This is how band-leader Buddy Bregman arranged the song for *Ella Fitzgerald Sings the Cole Porter Songbook*, and somehow the forward propulsion of the syncopated rhythm only lends the music a degree of desperation, as though the singer isn't quite in control of the situation. Once you factor in the words, you realise that this last interpretation is singularly apt, for far from being genuinely sad or desperate, the song is about resignation. The singer is resigned to being hopelessly in love and therefore out of control. Sung by Kevin Kline, 'So in Love' is the show-stopper of the film.

Some of Porter's songs are genuinely unhappy. 'Love for Sale', which also begins in a minor key, is an example. It might not be the first song on the subject of prostitution, but I can think of no other that is sung so unapologetically from the tart's point of view. To all intents and purposes, this is a 'come on', a musical act of solicitation ('Appetising young love for sale. / If you want to buy my wares, / Follow me and climb the stairs').

Sometimes it seems as though Porter was trying to prove something with his dark melodies. For example, 'I Love Paris' displays a frankly rebellious side to the songwriter. The book of *Can-Can* was by Abe Burrows and at one point he asked Porter for a new number. His instructions (whatever you do, not another song about Paris) were presumably interpreted by the composer as the throwing down of a gauntlet. Porter took himself off for the weekend and returned with a song commencing in an especially moody melodic minor, the first four lines of which begin with the words 'I love Paris' ('... in the springtime / ... in the fall / ... in the winter when it drizzles / ... in the summer when it sizzles'). The song then modulates abruptly to the major – and it always feels like the sun coming out – and then the next four lines mention Paris three more times. You can almost imagine Porter's thinking here. So he doesn't want another song about Paris? Well I'll give him a song about Paris he can't refuse.

The music to 'I Love Paris' actually alters the meaning of the words. Reading them on the page, they are not undistinguished (the 'drizzles'/'sizzles' rhyme alone would make the song memorable), but the mournful minor really does undermine the apparently joyous repetitions of that opening phrase. The change to the major key ('I love Paris every moment') clarifies the meaning, because it directs our attention ('Why, oh why, do I love Paris?') to the punchline ('Because my love is near') which reveals that the song was not about Paris after all.

Probably because he was his own lyricist (like Berlin and Stephen Sondheim), Porter often married his words and music more tightly than the songwriting teams. Porter's music comments on his words and vice versa. But it is not quite enough to say this, because often there is meaning in a Cole Porter song that is neither in the words nor the music: a new meaning emerges from the performance itself, and it doesn't require the presence of an Alanis Morissette to bring it about: a change of tempo will do it.

Take 'It's All Right with Me' (another song from *Can-Can*). Generally it's given a breezy, up-tempo treatment, but imagine it sung quite slowly. Suddenly, it becomes rather dark. 'It's the wrong time and the wrong place, / Though your face is charming, it's the wrong face ...' This is a song about sex with a stranger. 'There's someone I'm trying so hard to forget, / Don't you want to forget someone too?' And later: 'They're not her lips, but they're such tempting lips, / That if some night you're free, / Dear, it's all right ... with me.'

With Cole Porter, there is no substitute for getting the words across. Fail to communicate them and you simply diminish the material. But rearrange the music, however subtly, and the words magically reveal new layers of meaning. You might never have noticed these meanings before, but you can be sure Porter intended them. And that's sophisticated.

Sydney Morning Herald, 2004

Hoagy Carmichael, the First Singer-Songwriter

In some ways it is easier to say what Hoagy Carmichael wasn't than to say what he was. He wasn't, like Irving Berlin or George Gershwin or Jerome Kern or Richard Rodgers, a composer of songs for the musical theatre. He wasn't, like Duke Ellington, a jazz composer. He was no virtuoso of the keyboard and he didn't have much of a voice.

But there's a series of paradoxes here. For a start, the songs of Hoagy Carmichael are among the most famous American songs of the twentieth century. Many of them are shot through with a jazz sensibility and melodic inflections that could only have been composed by someone steeped in jazz and the blues. And when you call those songs to mind, as like as not, it's Hoagy playing the piano and Hoagy singing. Hoagy Carmichael was the prototype of that modern commonplace, the singer-songwriter. Before him, composers composed and sometimes played the piano, singers sang and occasionally accompanied themselves, but the idea that one human being might regularly do all three – however homespun the piano technique, however idiosyncratic the voice – was to all intents and purposes unknown, at any rate since the time of the troubadours.

With Hoagy you got the complete package. He might have sung, as he himself admitted, 'the way a shaggy dog looks', but no one made a better job of delivering his songs. In some of them there's a hint of Norman Rockwell's sentimental mythologising of America – Carmichael's 'Little Old Lady', indeed, might have stepped out of a Rockwell painting – but usually the portraiture (for that is surely what these songs are about) goes a little deeper. There is a wistful quality to the outwardly nostalgic 'Rockin' Chair' and 'Moon Country', and it is created as much in the music (and the shaggy-dog voice) as the words. These songs are only 90 per cent sentimental. They are 10 per cent something else – something darker.

As Richard M. Sudhalter underlines in his classy biography *Stardust Melody: The life and music of Hoagy Carmichael*, it is curious how few genuine love songs Carmichael wrote. There are songs about love, certainly, there's even a song about a love song ('Star Dust', no less), but there are remarkably few conventional first-person-to-second-person declarations. Perhaps the best of Hoagy's love songs, indeed, is the ironic 'I Get Along Without You Very Well'.

The other important facet of Hoagy Carmichael's songwriting is the absence of anything like a really typical song or style of song, either in terms of words or music. Hoagy wrote his own words to some of his songs ('I Get Along Without You' is the prime example), but mostly he worked with other lyricists, and in this he had no regular partner. There is no George and Ira Carmichael, no Hoagy and Hammerstein. Instead there are songs with words by Johnny Mercer ('Skylark', 'Lazy Bones'), Mitchell Parish ('Star Dust'), Frank Loesser ('Two Sleepy People'), Ned Washington ('The Nearness of You') and Stuart Gorrell ('Georgia on My Mind'). I am delighted to report, however, that in my favourite Carmichael song, 'Baltimore Oriole' (words by Paul Francis Webster), my favourite line turns out to be by Hoagy himself:

Forgivin' is easy,
It's a woman-like now-and-then-could-happen thing.

Perhaps it was the shifting nature of the collaborations, but the music he supplied in his work with these different lyricists also varies greatly. Blue notes are everywhere, though with the exception of 'Hong Kong Blues' it is hard to think of a full-blown example of the genre, but other than that the melodies of his songs seem to fit themselves to the lyrics. This is an illusion of sorts, because the tunes came first, and in the case of 'Star Dust', one of the greatest melodies of the twentieth century, the words came quite a long time afterwards. But fit they do, Mitchell Parish's lyric wondering and wandering as Hoagy's marvellously elliptical tune sets off in search of a cadence, which it only finds at the very end. ('Star Dust' is one of the *longest* tunes you will ever hear.)

Part of the biographer's task is to sift the details of the songwriter's own self-mythologising. Carmichael produced two volumes of auto-biography, *The Stardust Road* (1946) and *Sometimes I Wonder* (1965). While not exactly fabricated, they were part of a carefully constructed public image. Folksy yet sharply literate – Holden Caulfield with a dash of Truman Capote – Carmichael's prose seems an extension of his songwriting and singing. And the songs can also give a false impression.

On the basis of 'Georgia', 'Memphis in June', 'Washboard Blues' and 'Riverboat Shuffle', and remembering that lazy, bluesy voice telling of the 'Baltimore Oriole' heading to the Tangipahoa river 'down in Louisiana', it would be fair to assume that Hoagy was a Southerner. But he wasn't. Like Cole Porter, he came from Indiana where his law studies at Bloomington were regularly interrupted by a passion for modern music. The passion was encouraged by friend-ships with a fellow student, the composer and would-be bohemian William Ernest 'Monk' Moenkhaus, and with the jazz legend Leon 'Bix' Beiderbecke. Both these men died in their twenties and it would not be melodramatic to suggest that Hoagy never really got over the losses. *The Stardust Road* begins and ends with Bix's death and Carmichael named his first son Hoagy Bix.

Richard M. Sudhalter calls Monk and Bix Carmichael's 'muses' and you can hear the influence of Bix's horn in many of Hoagy's vocal lines, including his first really striking song 'Washboard Blues' recorded in 1927 by the Paul Whiteman orchestra with Bix on cornet.

Understudying the nervous Carmichael at that session was the young Bing Crosby, and it could reasonably be argued that the great Crosby picked up a thing or two from Hoagy, particularly regarding matters of phrasing. As Sudhalter points out, there is no doubt that the invention of the microphone was the making of both singers' intimate styles. And intimacy is surely the keyword for Carmichael's work, not only as a singer but also as a songwriter. There is something rather 'ordinary' about his body of songs. The situations they describe seem familiar, even if one has never personally floated up a Lazy River or tasted Cousin Amanda's rhubarb pie. The voice that tells of these situations is familiar, too.

It's small wonder then that Carmichael, if not America's greatest songwriter, had become, by the time of his death in 1981, one of its favourites. A late blossoming acting career, including a stint as Jonesy the cook in the NBC series *Laramie*, made him a familiar face in American homes, while his best-known songs had been sung by everyone from Louis Armstrong to Crystal Gayle. Still, the ubiquity of 'Star Dust' and 'Georgia on My Mind' shouldn't blind us to their quality.

Sydney Morning Herald, 2002

Bob Dylan's Missing Voice

One should always be wary of a book that examines song lyrics in isolation from their music, especially when the examination runs to 500 pages. That the author of this book is Christopher Ricks, formerly Professor of English at Cambridge and now at Boston, might incline one to give it the benefit of the doubt. So might the fact that the songs under consideration are by Bob Dylan.

Dylan is probably the best-read and most literary popular song writer of the last fifty years, and one suspects that this is his main attraction to a scholar like Ricks whose previous books include monographs on Milton, Keats, Tennyson and Eliot. When he analyses a lyric, Ricks always reaches first for analogues from the Western literary canon, so Milton, Keats, Tennyson and Eliot also feature rather heavily in *Dylan's Visions of Sin*.

These references are not as far-fetched as you might think. T.S. Eliot, in particular, is an important poet for Dylan. Not only do we find Eliot 'fighting in the captain's tower' with Ezra Pound on 'Desolation Row', but a close reading of 'Maybe Someday' from *Knocked Out Loaded* reveals a surprising number of correspondences with the diction if not the subject matter of Eliot's poem 'The Journey of the Magi'. Ricks points all of this out, together with examples, at the very beginning of his monumental book, as though seeking to convince us that his academic enterprise is wholly valid.

And of course it is. Only an anti-intellectual or a snob would suggest that popular culture is an inappropriate area for academic inquiry or that a rock lyric cannot be analysed as convincingly as Milton. But to leave out Dylan's music to the extent that Ricks does is dangerous. You end up believing that Keats and Eliot are more significant reference points in Dylan's work than, say, Dock Boggs or Woody Guthrie, and before long, like the author, you're drawing parallels between Dylan and Philip Larkin, which I think probably *is* far-fetched.

The whole business of building this book around the seven deadly sins and their supposed opposites, the four virtues and what Ricks calls the three 'Heavenly Graces' (that's faith, hope and charity), strikes me as a very literary conceit. And the author bolsters his theories with reference to rather too many minor songs. The examples discussed in the chapter on charity, for instance, are 'Watered-Down Love', 'If Not For You' and 'Eternal Circle'. For sloth, Ricks gives us 'All the Tired Horses', 'Time Passes Slowly', 'Clothes Line Saga', 'Lay Down Your Weary Tune' and 'Mr Tambourine Man'. With the obvious exception of the last, these are scarcely important Dylan tracks. One wonders, indeed, whether 'Mr Tambourine Man' is on the list just to make it look more respectable. Certainly, if you listen to the *music* of that song, with its 'skipping reels of rhyme', there is nothing slothful about it at all. In one of his rare references to music, Ricks himself is forced to admit this point. And anyway, this is a lyric about *not* being sleepy. Whether you take the Tambourine Man to be a purveyor of inspiration or amphetamines, the singer of the song avowedly doesn't want to go to bed.

The other problem with the sin/virtues/graces theme is its insistence upon Dylan's Christianity. Not only does Ricks return again and again to songs from the overtly Christian albums of 1979–82 (albums that most of Dylan's fans just barely tolerate), but he also finds evidence everywhere of Christian imagery and values. And much of that evidence is tangled up in those literary analogues.

There are brilliant exegeses in Ricks's book and some startling insights. The author delivers a virtuoso analysis of 'The Lonesome Death of Hattie Carroll' (in the chapter on justice), and I loved the comparison between 'Lay, Lady, Lay' and John Donne's elegy 'To His

Mistress Going to Bed'. But the fact remains that there are people who cannot quote a single line of Dylan yet would instantly recognise his voice. That is because the sound of Dylan's songs is as important as the way they read on the page; indeed, the two can't be separated. To ignore this, as Ricks almost completely does, is to write half a book, however enthralling that half might be.

Sydney Morning Herald, 2005

Finishing the Hat:
Sondheim on songwriting

Stephen Sondheim's songs are too clever for their own good. They lack warmth and emotion. They try too hard to impress. There's a cynical, show-off quality about them and they can't be hummed. Those are the standard criticisms of Sondheim's words and music. The composer himself has heard them often enough and much of the time he would agree. Sondheim has no more persistent critic than Sondheim.

In particular, the older Sondheim is tough on the work of his younger self. In *West Side Story* alone he finds lines in 'America' that 'melt in the mouth as gracelessly as peanut butter and are impossible to comprehend'. He squirms as he admits that 'Somewhere' places the most unimportant word of its opening line ('a') on the most important note. And he confesses that he blushes to this day at a simple Puerto Rican girl being forced to sing 'It's alarming / How charming / I feel'. These are lines that belong to 'a character from a Noël Coward operetta' and are included only 'because the lyricist wants to show off his rhyming skills'.

Sondheim also frets over a mis-stressed word at the climax of 'Everybody Says Don't' in *Anyone Can Whistle*. The line 'I insist on miracles, if you do them!' stresses 'if' when it should stress 'you'. It bugs him still, but then, to Sondheim, mis-stressing is one of the cardinal sins of the songwriter. In his book, *Finishing the Hat*, he shows us example after example of this and other sins from the greatest songwriters of the twentieth century.

The book's subtitle is 'Collected lyrics (1954–1981), with attendant Comments, Principles, Heresies, Grudges, Whines and Anecdotes', which means that it is also an autobiography, a brilliant collection of critical aperçus and a songwriting masterclass.

The stories certainly flow and the author tells them brilliantly. Jerome Robbins, directing *West Side Story*, objects to the orchestration of 'Somewhere', so Leonard Bernstein, who disliked confrontation and disliked Robbins, vanishes from the rehearsal, leaving the antagonistic director to re-orchestrate the song himself (Sondheim finds Bernstein in a bar). Hermione Gingold insists on auditioning for the role of Madame Armfeldt in *A Little Night Music*, in spite of the fact that Sondheim and the producer Harold Prince believe her to be quite wrong for the role, and she knows that they think this. Having sung for them, not too badly, she points out that she is the same age as the character and that, like the character, she wears a wig. Whereupon, she whips it off to reveal a bald head and promptly wins the part.

You could buy this book for its lyrics and its anecdotes and not feel short-changed. Sometimes the stories and lyrics coincide, especially when Sondheim is writing for a particular actor/singer. In *Gypsy*, 'Everything's Coming Up Roses' was tailored to Ethel Merman's brashness. 'The Ladies Who Lunch', Joanne's song in *Company*, 'was not only written for Elaine Stritch, it was based on her' (Stritch, already drunk, had once entered a bar with the writer George Furth in the early hours of the morning and said to the bartender, 'Just give me a bottle of vodka and a floor plan'.) 'Send in the Clowns', a last-minute addition to *A Little Night Music*, was shaped by Glynis Johns's inability to sustain a note: 'Isn't it rich? / Are we a pair?' are short lines followed by big breaths.

That's the thing about Sondheim's stories, they generally lead back to the masterclass, and that is the real meat of *Finishing the Hat*.

Sondheim begins by laying down the principles he considers essential for a lyric writer. There are three of them: 'Content Dictates Form', 'Less Is More' and 'God Is in the Detail'. These are 'all in the service of Clarity without which nothing else matters'. In a sense, the rest of the book is a series of case studies that demonstrate the importance of these principles and what happens when they're not followed.

A song lyric, Sondheim points out, is not a poem. The lyric needs music, the poem already has it. It follows, then, that a lyric does not want to be too 'poetic'. Plain, simple words are best – the right words, the kind of words the character singing the song might actually say – and they must make sense. It sounds obvious, but Sondheim lists hundreds of examples where songwriters have got it wrong.

He doesn't pull his punches, but he lands them with great elegance. There are the too-clever rhymes of Cole Porter and Coward, the latter writing 'lyrics I cordially but intensely dislike', not least for their tendency to draw attention themselves (which is presumably why Sondheim's own lyric for 'I Feel Pretty' reminds him of Coward). The trouble with many such lyricists is that they are drawn, for the sake of the rhyme, into using the wrong words, or the wrong stress or twisting the syntax. He gives plentiful examples of this last habit, including Alan Jay Lerner's 'syntactical train wreck' from *My Fair Lady*: 'I'd be equally as willing / For a dentist to be drilling / Than to ever let a woman in my life' – this written for a character who has earlier demanded to know, 'Why can't the English learn to speak?' And even if, for the most part, Lerner's lyrics were 'smooth and tasteful', these were 'virtues particularly inappropriate to *Paint Your Wagon*' and so once again the lyrics are at odds with the characters. It is all a matter of context (where content should dictate form) and therefore truthfulness. A lyric we can believe, that's the thing.

Another lyricist who tries too hard is Ira Gershwin. Sondheim quotes the verse from 'How Long Has This Been Going On?'

> *'Neath the stars,*
> *At bazaars,*
> *Often I've had to caress men.*

Five or ten
Dollars, then
I'd collect from all those yes-men.

Sondheim complains: 'In his insatiable need to rhyme, Gershwin surrenders sense (How often are charity bazaars conducted outdoors at night? Do women sell caresses – I thought they sold kisses – and why are the singer's customers "yes-men"?); stress ("Often *I've* had to caress men"); and syntax (by "Five or ten / Dollars, then / I'd collect …" he means "Then I'd collect five or ten dollars").'

One of Sondheim's early mentors – almost a surrogate father – was Oscar Hammerstein II, but even he is not spared criticism. What does 'a lark who is learning to pray' sound like, and how might that differ from the sound of one that has already learnt to pray?

But it is Richard Rodgers's first lyricist, the brilliant Lorenz Hart, for whom Sondheim reserves his most carefully considered criticism. Brilliant he might have been, but he was lazy without a doubt. Sondheim lists numerous sins committed by Hart, ranging from the sacrificing of meaning for rhyme ('Your looks are laughable / Unphotographable' – of course he means unphotogenic), to tortured syntax ('An angel I married / To heaven she's carried / This fellow with a kiss'), to a cornucopia of mis-stressed words and syllables ('Seven to midnight I *hear* drums' and 'Psychoana*lysts* are all the whirl'). Mis-stressing is such a bugbear for Sondheim that one pictures him choking on his breakfast recently as he read a review of this book in the *New York Times* from the same pen responsible for the lines 'Because a vision soft*ly* cree*ping* / Left its seeds while I *was* slee*ping*'.

Sondheim quotes another (unnamed) writer of pop songs: 'I'm not a great believer in perfect rhymes. I'm just a believer in feelings that come across. If the craft gets in the way of the feelings, then I'll take the feelings every day.'

'I've never come across a near rhyme that works better than a perfect one would,' Sondheim remarks, '… craft is supposed to *serve* the feeling'. If it doesn't, the craft is either deficient or the writer is being lazy. Like Lorenz Hart.

Sondheim likes journeyman lyricists such as Irving Berlin and Dorothy Fields and he believes in hard work. He has stockpiled his favourite thick pencils and yellow legal pads for fear that one day he might be unable to buy them and now he has a lifetime's supply. And if he claims to prefer working lying down so he can fall asleep, this is partly a recognition that songs don't come easily or quickly.

The song that gives this book its title comes from *Sunday in the Park with George*, a show dating from 1984. In a single, glancing reference to it, Sondheim insists that it is 'the only song I've written which is an immediate expression of a personal internal experience'. I suspect it is more than that.

'George' is the French post-impressionist painter, Georges Seurat, and in the first half of *Sunday in the Park* he is painting his great study of Parisian society, *A Sunday Afternoon on the Island of La Grande Jatte*. Indeed it might be truer to say that he is living it. 'Finishing the Hat' is George's song and it expresses – simply, clearly and in everyday words and images that rhyme and scan and stress the right syllables – how it is to feel driven. Yes, to some extent it glorifies the creative act, but apart from in its final line there is no elation, no satisfaction, no gloating. It is a song about work: not about '*Finishing* the hat' at all but 'How you *have* to finish the hat' (my stress!) and how everything and everyone else must wait. And so it is also about the selfishness of the artist, even as the artist is engaged in the generous act of making 'a hat / Where there never was a hat'.

Like George, Sondheim knows that selfishness is unpardonable and rarely goes unpunished, but he also knows that, without it, art – music, lyrics – would be a series of unfinished hats.

That's the point of the song, and really it is the underlying subject of this book.

Inside Story, 2010

Randy Newman's Songbook

Randy Newman's songs are character studies. His voice is cracked and craggy, acting as much as singing, and it is the voice you notice first, though it wasn't always. Before Newman was a singer-songwriter he was merely a songwriter, and others, such as Judy Collins, Alan Price and Harry Nilson, had his hits for him. But no one, not even Nina Simone singing 'Baltimore', gets the vocal character of the songs right like Newman himself. The more pared-back the treatment, the more the voice takes centre stage, the larger those characters loom. There are, so far, two volumes of *The Randy Newman Songbook* (a third volume is promised), just Newman's voice and Newman's piano performing a retrospective of his best work, and the songs have never seemed more powerful.

Newman's often extreme characters range from the posturing rock stars of 'My Life is Good' and 'Lonely at the Top' to the pathetic wastrel declaring his love for his wife in 'Marie': 'I'm drunk right now baby / But I've got to be / Or I never could tell you / What you mean to me.' These are complex songs, and they contain surprises. For example, the racist redneck who sings 'Rednecks' ('we don't know our ass from a hole in the ground / ... / And we're keepin' the niggers down') is nevertheless capable of social and political acuity when he notes that 'the North has set the nigger free' – free, that is, 'to be put in a cage / In Harlem, New York City / And ... on the South Side of Chicago'. When Newman speaks for God (in 'God's Song') he's not so much vengeful as amused: 'You all must be crazy to put your faith in Me / That's why I love mankind / You really need Me.' One of the benefits of printed lyrics is that you stumble across exquisite details such as that upper-case M.

Occasionally the diction of the songs is close to poetry. 'The milk truck hauls the sun up' (the first line of 'Living Without You') is perhaps even a shade too poetic, but the next line brings reality with a thud as 'the paper hits the door'. That's more typical, Newman finding his poetry in concrete images ('Six feet of water in the streets of Evangeline') and stark juxtapositions ('Beat-up little seagull / On a marble stair') that speak clearly and simply for themselves. But they still require music to make their full effect, and Newman is adept at leaving room for it. His songwriting begins, he says, with the music, and it is as complex and surprising as the lyrics.

It is illustrative, too, especially on the *Songbook* albums. Take 'God's Song' and those silences that pepper the slow piano boogie. Which is scarier? God's sneering ('How we laugh up here in Heaven at the prayers you offer Me') or God's silence? I know what Ingmar Bergman would say. Or take 'You Can Leave Your Hat On' in which the singer watches a woman strip, then stand on a chair with 'all the lights' on. Dark and wry, it is one of Newman's most famous songs – famous, that is, for having been sung without a trace of irony by Joe Cocker on the soundtrack of *9½ Weeks* and with only a modicum of it by Tom Jones on the soundtrack of *The Full Monty*. Newman first recorded the song in 1972 for his album *Sail Away*, the loneliness of the singer's voice emphasising the vulnerability of the watcher, but to hear him sing it with just piano is to have your attention drawn inexorably to his right hand, pumping away energetically. The words, music and piano technique coming together, as it were.

The more you listen to the *Songbook* albums, the more you sense that Newman composes against a background of all American musical history. Revivalist hymnody and ragtime, boogie-woogie and the blues, Stephen C. Foster and Ray Charles: you can hear them all. In 'Dixie Flyer', the gentle Joplinesque ragtime that accompanies the first verse about the singer's birth turns subtly in the direction of boogie-woogie, a few authentic Professor Longhair roulades thrown in, just as soon as the train of the title heads off to New Orleans. The chords that underpin songs such as 'I Think It's Going to Rain Today' and 'Cowboy' are poignant in their unpredictability – especially bare and unadorned on the piano – but also in their evocations of the prairie music of Aaron Copland. Copland, indeed, lurks in the harmony of many of Newman's most touching songs.

Newman's templates are fascinating to consider and come from a lifetime in professional music-making; occasionally they also reflect his knowledge of the classical canon. The introduction to 'In Germany Before the War', which returns before the final verse, brings echoes of Brahms, specifically the *Poco allegretto* movement of the third symphony. But, for a while, I was bothered by the imperial march on 'The Great Nations of Europe'. It wasn't really Elgarian, so what was it? The answer, of course, is that it is Hollywood's version of an imperial march, and there are various contenders, not least John Williams's big *Star Wars* march, although if we must pinpoint the model then I lean towards the national anthem of Freedonia in the Marx Brothers' *Duck Soup*.

Newman, we must always remember, is part of Hollywood's most famous musical dynasty. Uncle Alfred composed the music for *The Hunchback of Notre Dame*, *The Grapes of Wrath* and *Wuthering Heights*. Uncle Lionel scored Elvis Presley's first film, *Love Me Tender*, *Doctor Dolittle* and countless TV series. There was also Uncle Emil who wrote the scores to a lot of movies you've never heard of, but was music director on plenty that you have. Alfred's sons are David (*The Nutty Professor*) and Thomas (*The Player*, *American Beauty* and *The Road to Perdition*). Although Randy's father Irving, the Gummo of the Newman brothers, was a doctor, that didn't stop his son making a spectacularly successful entrance to the family business with *Ragtime*, going on to win Oscars for *Monsters, Inc.* and *Toy Story 3*.

The film experience shows in the arrangements of the songs on his original albums. These are nearly always appropriate, often spectacular and sometimes outrageous. On *Harps and Angels* (2008), the inflated Kurt Weill style of 'A Piece of the Pie' (harmonies as well as orchestration) and the oriental-kitsch of 'Korean Parents' are brilliantly observed and hilarious. The film experience is also possibly behind Newman's discipline as a songwriter. With a new album due, he typically rents an office in downtown Los Angeles, puts a piano in it, and goes to work until the songs are written.

But there is one further trace of the film composer's art, and that is in knowing when the music must take over – when, indeed, words are no longer of use. Possibly Newman's darkest song is 'In Germany Before the War', a moment in the life of a child-killer, apparently based on Peter Kürten, the so-called Vampire of Düsseldorf in the 1920s (not 1934, as Newman's song has it). Brahms aside, the basic template here is that of a traditional ballad, the song oscillating, as ballads will, between third-person past-tense reportage and first-person present-tense. The harmony, too, swings back and forth between major and minor chords in the deliberately child-like piano accompaniment. But then comes the final verse, and the first-person suddenly takes over: 'We lie beneath the autumn sky / My little golden girl and I / And she lies very still.'

That's the killer singing. His words run out, his voice stops mid-verse, mid-line, but the piano accompaniment continues, its major and minor chords now superimposed to the end of the song. The eerie effect is perfectly judged and the music says everything that needs saying.

Australian Financial Review, 2004/2012

What to Listen for in Music

An address to the Association of Music Directors
in Independent Schools (Victoria)

Where does music happen? Where is it made? Obviously it is brought about by an act of will, but whose will: the composer's, the performer's or the listener's?

Without the composer, you might think, there are no notes to play, so surely the buck stops there: no composer, no music. In a way that is true, but without the performer, there is nothing to hear. The notes on the page, so many dots on a paper landscape, are hardly music on their own. They are a recipe for music – follow the instructions in the score of Beethoven's Op 109, and you will end up with a three-movement Piano Sonata in E major lasting approximately twenty minutes. The score, however *Urtext*, is not the thing itself.

But, as John Cage understood, music that is not listened to is not music at all. It is like that tree falling in the forest. In order for Cage's *4'33"* to work in the concert hall (in which a piano player comes on stage and doesn't play) we have to be listening. While we wait for four minutes and thirty-three seconds in the hope that something might occur, something, in fact, *is* occurring. The ambient and, perhaps, not-so-ambient noises in the room are conspiring to provide the music. Cage recognised that the moment immediately prior to a performance, the moment when the pianist's fingers are poised ready to strike, is one of extreme concentration for player and listener alike, and *4'33"* is an extension of that moment. The expectant focus of the audience registers the tiniest sounds and does so more acutely than it would register the music, because if that awful ambient void were filled with piano playing, we might all relax.

For Cage, attention to ambient noise was all that was necessary to have a musical experience, the listener's imagination arranging – ordering – the noises so that they fitted the composer's definition of music as 'organised sound'. And the opposite is also true. If a performance of Beethoven's Op 109 is ignored – perhaps it is playing on the radio as we clean the house or drive through heavy traffic, perhaps we simply get caught up in our own thoughts and pay the music no heed – does it remain music? It might be just an irritating noise. More of that later.

We can trace this discussion back to a time long before John Cage. And the only useful conclusion is that music exists in a triangular relationship between the composer, performer and listener, always assuming they are not the same person. What interests me is not the philosophical question so much as the business of listening and how it affects and controls all levels of music. I'm thinking of the listening composer and the listening performer as well as the listening listener.

I want to stress listening, because I have a hunch that in our classrooms we have tipped the balance a little too far towards *activity*. A while ago, someone had the idea that all school students should become composers. And it is not necessarily a bad idea. Certainly I remember school music classes in which scores were handed out and followed while a gramophone record of the 'Unfinished Symphony' played. To be honest, I recall these sessions with a degree of affection, but I'm fairly sure a lot of my classmates were bored. Certainly there was no attempt to relate the listening to anything practical. We sang songs, too, including Britten's *Friday Afternoons*, and by the time I was fifteen or sixteen I was composing my own music, but nobody else was. And I certainly didn't compose at the bidding of my music teacher.

In art lessons, students paint or draw or make models; in creative writing classes, they write. This isn't to say that art students shouldn't soak up all the art of the past they can, and plainly writing students will be better writers if they have also read widely, but from pre-school on these arts are about activity. The same goes for drama and dance. Until recently, music tended to be about performance – about joining in on a glockenspiel, about singing, about learning the recorder and, perhaps later, about learning something more expen-sive. And then at high school, it was also about what used to be called 'Music Appreciation' – the term so redolent of the Workers' Education Association – and that meant sitting and listening. Still, whether you were singing 'The Wheels on the Bus' in kindergarten or listening to Schubert in high school, the point was that music already existed: it was something you re-created or listened to. That's changed. Now – in high school, at least – we're all composers.

But what music does a sixteen-year-old compose? How original is it likely to be? And is originality the point?

When it comes to judging a new composition – even by a sixteen-year-old composer – originality should always be the point. And, paradoxically, originality is linked to an ability to listen, to listen hard, to listen critically and, yes, appreciatively. Because real listening involves the imagination. It, too, is an activity. To listen imagina-tively is to participate in the music, to join in, to make the music in your head.

*

The composer Karlheinz Stockhausen once told Jonathan Cott in an interview that he believed orchestras would benefit from devoting some of their time to improvising.

His proposal was that the players would head off to a mountain-top retreat where they would clear their minds of Brahms and Tchaikovsky the better to hear the sounds around them. From this deep listening, the players would improvise new sounds, as it were intuitively. The benefits to the orchestra and its audiences back at ground level would be immense. All that time spent listening to each other would even improve their Brahms and Tchaikovsky.

Now, I'm sure he was right, just as I'm sure his theory will never be tested. And I don't suppose even Stockhausen really expected the world's orchestras to start climbing mountains in order to improvise, because he knew as well as anyone that the very prospect of improvisation provokes a terrified response from the average orchestral player. Stockhausen even made a joke about it in *Trans*, an orchestral work for performance in the theatre. Among many bizarre interruptions to the piece, at one point a stage manager wanders on with a music stand and lamp – the orchestra is sitting in semi darkness. The music stand is set down in front of one of the cello players. The lamp is switched on and the cellist begins to play the music on the stand, launching into a big virtuoso solo, but then suddenly stopping when the light goes out. The light is switched on again and the playing continues; it goes off and the playing stops. You get the idea. Stockhausen's point is that orchestral musicians can only play when they can see the music.

While it might be a joke, it is also a heartfelt complaint because around the time Stockhausen composed *Trans*, he was also working more and more with the members of his hand-picked ensemble in the area of intuitive music. I'd like to say a little about this, because in some ways it marks my own start as a composer and I think it provides a useful exemplar for listening-based spontaneous composition in the classroom – or anywhere else, for that matter.

In 1968 – to be specific, between 7 and 13 May 1968, just as the so-called *événements*, the general strike and student riots, were getting underway in Paris – Stockhausen was on hunger-strike at his home in Kürten, West Germany. In point of fact, Stockhausen's protest was only political in so far as the personal is political. Stockhausen had stopped eating in an attempt to persuade his estranged wife to return to him. But during this week of hunger and little sleep, the composer was radically productive. He composed a sequence of fifteen pieces – collectively known as *Aus den Sieben Tagen* (From the Seven Days) – all of which consisted, on paper, not of notes but of words laid out like poems. One of these is called 'Gold Dust', and it makes some extreme demands:

> *Live completely alone for four days*
> *without food*
> *in complete silence, without much movement*
> *Sleep as little as necessary*
> *Think as little as possible*

That is only the beginning of it. In this desensitised state and with no discussion, the players must now begin to play. Stockhausen dictates that they produce only single sounds and do so without thinking.

I mention 'Gold Dust' for several reasons. For one thing, I've taken part in performances of the piece, though I'm afraid we cheated in our preparations. We did eat, we did sleep and we did talk. But really it's the final instructions that strike me as significant: 'play single sounds / WITHOUT THINKING which you are playing / Close your eyes / Just listen'. That is Stockhausen's upper-case, by the way.

It's very hard to play without thinking. Each time you go to play, you tend to stop yourself in case you're acting consciously. You really do have to try very hard to clear your mind and I expect the recommended starvation allied to sleeplessness and sensory deprivation helps. But the other three final instructions help too. 'Play single sounds / … / Close your eyes / Just listen'. I'll come back to them.

Over the next couple of years, Stockhausen created a second book of intuitive music, *Für kommende Zeiten* – 'For Times to Come' – and he worked on both sets of pieces with his own ensemble, recording them for Deutsche Grammophon, his exclusive label at the time.

As you listen, you're struck by how much like Stockhausen's music it sounds. These players who are not even thinking, let alone reading, are still managing to produce *echt*-Stockhausen. It seems like a hell of a trick, and in photographs of these performances, with Stockhausen sitting behind a mixing desk or cross-legged on the floor among his players, you can imagine that telepathic connections have been established, the performers sucking the music right out of the composer's head and into their instruments. Stockhausen himself spoke of musical ESP.

Well, perhaps. But it surely helped that these players were all very familiar with the composer's notated works.

In 1972, Stockhausen created a piece of intuitive music for a larger ensemble: *Ylem*, for nineteen players or singers. 'Ylem' is a word coined by scientists in the 1940s to refer to the primordial substance from which all life comes. Subatomic particles, I suppose. Stockhausen writes in his program note about the universe exploding and reforming every eighty billion years, and within this piece's rather more limited timeframe, that is exactly what his *Ylem* seeks to portray. So it's ambitious, you might say. Yet arguably the most ambitious thing about it was the composer's taking this intuitive music out of the inner sanctum of his regular collaborators, because *Ylem* was composed for the London Sinfonietta. The first performances took place during an extended collaboration between the composer and orchestra involving a concert tour and recordings of six pieces, including the new one. In place of the brief, poem-like instructions of the earlier intuitive pieces, *Ylem* came with five full pages of small print, which I'll try to paraphrase.

The piece features mobile and immobile instruments, four of the latter being either electronic or amplified acoustic instruments capable of creating sliding tones. *Ylem* begins with everyone on stage, gathered, as far as possible, around the lidless piano, their instruments directed at its strings. There's a moment's silence, and then a big bang on a tam-tam jerks all the performers into action playing either an A or an E flat in the middle of their ranges, repeating the notes fast and loud. This opening tritone is the only precise indication of pitch until the end of the piece.

What happens next is that the players of portable instruments leave the stage and move out into the auditorium until they surround the audience. As they go, they begin to modify their playing, introducing first other pitches, then other parts of their registers and other dynamics, and varying the lengths of their notes. But they always play single notes and in between them they begin to make pauses. When they reach their new positions, the players shut their eyes, the better to listen to each other.

As the piece thus starts to open out, the electric/amplified instruments act as links between the other players. Their job is to listen for pitches out in the auditorium – out in 'space', if you like – then to latch on to one pitch and start sliding until they close in on another, effectively joining the two together. Joining the dots, indeed.

By the middle of the piece – around the eleven-minute mark – the pauses have grown longer and there are moments of silence, punctuated by extremely loud, extremely quiet, extremely long and extremely short sounds, all played at the extremes of the instruments' ranges. Then the piece goes into reverse, the ranges of pitch and dynamics narrow, the notes coming thicker and faster in more uniform lengths, until everyone is back on stage playing the opening tritone. There's a second tam-tam bash, the whole piece jerks up a tone and off we go again, except that this time everyone leaves the stage (the players of non-portable instruments, having picked up toy instruments) and they keep going, still playing their instruments, until they have left the auditorium and even the building. In one performance that I directed, a couple of the players, finding themselves out on the street, caught a bus to another part of town.

On tour with Stockhausen back in the early 1970s, the London Sinfonietta made an appearance on television. It was a live, weekly, prime-time Saturday-night arts program on the BBC, which seems extraordinary now. As an impressionable schoolboy I watched the performance of *Ylem* and then an interview with the composer. I recall people rang in with questions. Someone – a young composer – rang to ask if he could dedicate his next piece to Stockhausen and Stockhausen told him he should dedicate it to God. I was not a young composer, but by the end of the program I had decided to become one. I'd never heard anything like this music and I wanted to be part of it.

Ylem remains a most unusual piece – unique, I suppose – and one that I keep coming back to. I've done the piece quite a few times in England and Australia, with students and with professionals. The last time was with members of the Australian Chamber Orchestra in a midnight concert at the Huntington Festival. At the end of that performance the players left the winery building and went out into the night across the vineyards with half the audience following them. Since you're supposed to play until you're out of earshot, this had the makings of a never-ending performance.

But beyond the piece itself – the shape of the music, the moving around and all the stuff about the universe – the principles of Stockhausen's *Ylem* have proved to be extremely useful working with students of all ages. Improvising within these sorts of constraints – playing only single sounds, short or long, separated by silences, also short or long – strips away learning, repertoire, preconceived ideas, instrumental technique, even imagination, until finally all that's left is listening. And on this foundation, imagination and technique – if not the other things – are swiftly rebuilt in new ways that sometimes startle the student and, indeed, lead right back to even deeper listening.

I like to work with a group of about ten or twelve players or singers. With fewer, there's an embarrassment factor that can take too long to overcome; with more than a dozen it can be hard to get enough discipline into the group – including musical discipline. But with the right number a lot can be achieved in a very short time, even a single session.

I usually start by giving the players no information at all. I just tell them to improvise. Once, in a high-school classroom in Yorkshire, I'd just begun when the teacher interrupted me.

'We know all about this, don't we, class?' she said proudly, winking conspiratorially at her hapless students. 'It's what *we* call "free expression".'

Well it's what I call a pointless waste of time. No one knows what they're doing and they all play continuously, often relying on scales or bits of their instrument's repertoire. This is the gist of that joke against the cello player in *Trans*. But if you only allow 'free expression' to continue for a couple of minutes, you won't have wasted very much time and it won't be pointless. Now, you will have a yardstick for what follows. It often comes as a revelation to students – especially those who have endured sessions of 'free expression' – that improvising is something you can practise and get better at, and that discipline plays a role.

So we play. It sounds horrible, and so we stop and talk. Because no one knew what they were doing, they don't have much to say, but they generally recognise that it sounded horrible. Next, I'll give them one piece of information. It might be to do with listening, with trying to establish contact with another player (as in *Ylem*, I spread the players out as much as possible). Then, I'll get them to close their eyes. Immediately, they listen harder. Then we move on to playing only single sounds. Two notes without a gap between them constitute a phrase and are therefore wrong. But as in the central part of *Ylem*, a sound might go on for a long time, and it might bend or change timbre or dynamic.

Each piece of information, you'll notice, is not about giving, but about taking away, and with each removal listening becomes correspondingly more important. Finally, I encourage them not to play for the sake of playing. Indeed, I tell them, it's all right not to play at all. Usually they can't resist playing something.

I once had a short residency in Cornwall working with the local education department and, over the course of a week, going from school to school. I worked with age groups ranging from seven to eighteen. Sometimes I played them some of my music and we talked about it, and in every session we improvised music together. I learnt a lot. I learnt, for instance, that the younger the child, the more open to new sounds. Seven-year-olds had no problem listening to the pieces I played them, and came back with instant reactions in the form of detailed scenarios, none of which was remotely in my mind as I had composed the music, but all showing an unfailingly imaginative response to what they had heard. Some of the high school students took a little more persuading, and by the time I got to what we used to call sixth-formers, there was a slightly combative atmosphere. One of them actually said, 'This isn't music', an echo, I suppose, of his parents' views. Or maybe his teacher's.

And yet the great triumph of that week was with a group of older students at a girl's school on Bodmin Moor. There were maybe a dozen girls, spread out around a classroom. Our improvisations followed the pattern I've described and after some mild resistance, they took the thing very seriously. The listening was palpable. By the end of the session, they were playing – and listening – with real intensity. One of the little miracles of any improvisation that's going well is that it ends of its own accord. The players all seem to know when it would be crass to play another note and a wonderful thick silence hangs in the air. On this occasion, it was a distant motorbike that brought the playing to an end. The musical tension in the room had been so acute that when this foreign sound joined the mix of sounds intermittently produced by the girls' instruments, it was immediately embraced, becoming part of the music. And then, as the motorbike gradually disappeared down a winding Cornish lane, fading to nothing, it took the music with it. For a while no one spoke. It was magical, and everyone in the room felt it. I'd like to think some of the girls remember the moment as vividly as I do.

It has been a long time since I conducted one of these sessions either in a school or a university. It's partly that I don't seem to have much to do with schools and universities anymore, and when I am invited along it's usually to talk about my own music or give a lecture on some topic to do with music history or aesthetics. But there's another reason, and this is to do with style in contemporary music.

The first time I put on a performance of *Ylem* was as an undergraduate in 1978. The piece was only six years old. The first time I ran an improvisation group was around the same time. My visit to that school on Bodmin Moor was only a few years later. Things were different back then. When we spoke of 'modern music', we generally meant pieces that sounded a bit like Stockhausen. Rhythms were irregular, tonality was avoided, so was repetition. There weren't many tunes, either. Stockhausen's temporary move to intuitive music was bold in that he was abandoning notation, but the sound of these pieces wasn't so very different to the sound of his notated pieces.

But with modernism put in its place, composers young and old, student and professional, realised there was plenty of mileage in regular rhythms, tonal harmonies, repetition and melody. Of course you still had to do something new, but if you wanted you could do it in C major. Indeed, to continue to be a modernist was about as bad as writing tonally had been back in the 1960s and 70s. It seemed to me, then, that improvising, as it were 'in the style of Stockhausen', was maybe not what was wanted anymore. Worse, it might look, to some, as though I was fighting a rearguard action on behalf of modernism. Though what would be the point of that, I don't know.

But recently times have changed again. For one thing, Stockhausen is dead and his obituaries were surprisingly generous. I had expected a certain amount of postmodernist gloating, but it seemed that by December 2007, we had all grown up. The obituaries lamented the passing of one of the most original musical imaginations of the twentieth (or any other) century, and many of them wondered aloud when we would again encounter such single-minded musical ambition. It's a good question. Since then, a lot of Stockhausen's music has been performed all round the world, including quite a lot in Australia. In short, it seems there are fewer party lines in composition, fewer right and wrong ways to think about music. Yes you can use C major, but you can also take leaves from Stockhausen's book. Or maybe you can find a way of doing both. After all, in *Stimmung*, Stockhausen had begun with a chord of B flat and seventy-five minutes later was still sitting on it.

Of course the great danger with musical pluralism is that anything goes. We front up to our computers and, with the latest composing software, we take a template – a twelve-bar blues, a simple song structure, a sonata, a fugue (does anyone still write fugues?), a twelve-tone piece (God help us) – and we fill up this template with notes … But this is not how composers compose. At least, not the good ones.

So this is where listening – and Stockhausen – come in. Improvising along the lines I've described does not tell you how to compose, and it certainly doesn't tell you what style to compose in, but it does help you discover how to think and feel like a composer, and especially how to listen like one.

You are essentially playing with the building blocks of all music. The subatomic particles of sound and time. The harder you listen to these, the more they tend to form up into shapes, large and small. But listening is the key. Because most composers imagine with their ears.

All Clocks Are Clouds is an excellent Barrie Gavin documentary about György Ligeti in which the composer revealed how he worked with a stopwatch. It's that age-old problem, often the trickiest problem of all: how long to allow a particular musical idea to continue. Too long or too short, and it doesn't have the right effect. In a word, it's about timing. So what better way to solve it than with a stopwatch? What's important is to get away from the manuscript paper – and for that matter the piano – and really listen to the sounds in your head. Ligeti would walk around his studio doing this, stopwatch in hand, and when a section ended, he'd click the stopwatch and make a note that that particular passage lasted two minutes and twenty seconds, or one minute forty-five, or whatever it was. He found that, for timing, listening always beat calculation, and I have followed his advice ever since. I live in the country and occasionally I will take my stopwatch for walks so I can listen to what I'm working on and time it as I go.

Timing in music is of the essence. It's not just a matter of how long something should continue; it's also about when to start things. There's a lovely clip of Chet Baker playing at Ronnie Scott's club in London in 1986. It's just Chet with piano, bass and drums, and at one point, when he's not playing, the camera watches him from a distance, listening to the other three. Slowly, Chet raises the trumpet to his lips and the camera edges closer. He closes his eyes, inhales ... and then he puts the trumpet down again, without having played anything. It's like *4'33"* with a rhythm section. The clip should be mandatory viewing for every improviser and every composer. The question it raises is simply this: is your next note really necessary?

Now I do realise that this is a dangerous question to pose to all but the most talented student. It's a while since I taught composition, but my recollection is of trying to get more notes out of my students, not fewer. In most student compositions, none of the notes is really necessary. The piece isn't being composed out of an artistic imperative, but because the student has been handed an assignment.

But a lot of the time that's what it's like being a professional composer, too. The phone rings and there's someone asking you to write a piece for solo piano or string quartet or some combination of instruments that has never before occurred to you and that you're not especially drawn to. If I have the time, I nearly always say yes. Stravinsky said that a good composer takes the commission on offer and turns it into the piece that was already bubbling away in the imagination. There's a lot to be said for that approach. But equally, being confronted with a commission for piano or string quartet – or tuba quartet – can force you into an imaginative corner. It's not unlike being in an improvisation and told you may only play single notes. Most commissions are restricting, and a tuba quartet – where there isn't even an existing repertoire – strips away so many possibilities that it throws you back on your ears. That's where a composer should be. Listening to the sounds in his or her imagination – in this case, the sound of four tubas – and letting the musical ideas arise from those sounds.

But very likely most students aren't equipped with that kind of imagination. So how do they develop one? And what do they do in the meantime? Where do a student's ideas come from? There's an unfortunate and misleading cliché out there among the general public, fed by the mass media, by Hollywood, and, it must be admitted, by the things that composers themselves say when they're in a tight spot with a journalist. It's this. Music comes from our experience of life, from looking at a beautiful sunset or a snow-covered forest, from swiftly flowing rivers and swelling oceans, from falling in love, from falling out of love, from contemplating the victims of Hiroshima or the death of a cosmonaut or from taking a short ride in a fast machine.

Those things might well be the inspiration for the title of a piece of music, or perhaps even its shape, but you've still got to find the notes. Inspiration and musical substance are different things. Perhaps it's because we experience feelings when we listen to music that we assume that in order to compose it, the composer simply had to marshal his or her feelings. But as Boulez has said, music doesn't express feelings – it expresses music.

So we teach our students about composing – indeed we inspire them to compose – by letting them hear great music, ideally also by letting them sing and play great music. Music appreciation! And we talk about it – having to formulate an opinion about music also helps us to listen. How do pieces of music work? What makes one sort of music easier to listen to than another? And what can we listen out for?

In 1939, the American composer Aaron Copland wrote a book called *What to Listen for in Music*. For a while it was rather famous. Now it's a kind of classic and, like most classics, it is more often mentioned than read. In fact I only read it myself very recently. It's interesting for all manner of reasons, not the least of which is that it's the work of a composer in mid-career. Seventy years on, we know another seventy years of music. And we also know that Copland, who wrote the book right at the time of his famous Americana period – between *Billy the Kid* and *Lincoln Portrait* – and who seems in the text ambivalent, if not antagonistic to twelve-tone music, would himself be a twelve-tone composer within a couple of decades. But the importance of *What to Listen for in Music* lies in its title, and especially the two words 'listen for'. The phrase is active, suggesting a three-way collaboration between composer, player and audience; suggesting effort, in fact, on the part of the listener; suggesting that we have to construct the music in our minds.

Some of Copland's language in *What to Listen for in Music* is a bit fusty, and so are some of his ideas, but it is worth the read, partly because it takes you inside the listening brain of a composer. Copland says that there are four component parts to music – rhythm, melody, harmony and timbre – and he includes chapters on texture and form. We can simplify this. Sound and time: Stockhausen's subatomic particles. They encompass everything else and they're basic to music. In fact you don't need melody to have music and you don't need harmony. It's hard to avoid rhythm in its broadest sense, because any sounds moving in time are going to give you rhythm, and they will leave behind form even if it wasn't intended.

I would like to stress, once again, the importance of returning regularly to those subatomic particles, to sounds in time. It is not that I see this as a starting point for composition – though it could be – or even a starting point for listening. No, it is that it does us good as listeners and composers, as students and teachers, to strip away our musical preconceptions. It sharpens our listening, because that is all we are left with. And just as Stockhausen's improvising orchestras would return to Brahms and Tchaikovsky as though discovering this music for the first time, so do we.

Since I have been talking about listening, I'd like us to end by listening to some music: the first movement of Beethoven's Sonata in E major, Op 109. I mentioned the piece at the start of this talk, and I didn't pick it at random. A few years ago, I was invited by ABC local radio in Adelaide to be a regular weekly guest on its breakfast show, talking about a different composer each week. It meant being enthusiastic about Berlioz and Brahms at 6.30 a.m., but I had a book to sell. So each week I would propose a composer and then suggest a piece of music that we could play and talk about, and it had to be short enough – three or four minutes – to sit easily on local radio.

I didn't want to play grabs, but complete pieces or movements, so choosing the music was sometimes a bit of a poser. But when it came to Beethoven, I had a very good idea. The Sonata Op 109, in case you don't know it, has an unusual structure: two very short movements followed by a much longer set of variations. The first movement, in particular, demonstrates many of the characteristics of Classicism and indeed early Romanticism. It is lyrical, and yet rhetorical: *arioso* and *recitativo*. The music sets off at a graceful canter, stops to interrogate itself, then starts again, then stops again. It has humour (I think) and something like pathos. In other words, it is full of contrast. So it seemed perfect. And, very importantly, it lasted three and a half minutes.

The day before the broadcast, I got a phone call from the presenter. 'We can't play this,' he said. 'It's awful. Everyone will hate it.'

'Awful?' I said. 'It's Beethoven. It's beautiful.'

'But it doesn't go anywhere,' he said. 'It's confusing and you can't follow it.'

'But the way that initial outpouring of melody suddenly comes to a shuddering stop; that discontinuity: that's what I want to talk about.'

'But that's exactly the problem with it,' he said. 'It doesn't keep going. We have to choose something else.'

There was no point in arguing. It was his show for one thing. In the end I think we went with *Für Elise*.

At first I was dismayed by this episode, but when I thought about it, I could see his point of view. The program normally played pop music, and pop songs generally have a beat that remains the same from start to finish. Also there's lots of repetition. And in the pieces of music I had offered in previous weeks, I had, without thinking about it, more or less matched this tendency. We'd heard the Intermezzo from Sibelius's *Karelia Suite*, and we'd heard the central chorale tune, 'Zion Hears the Watchmen Singing', from Bach's cantata *Sleepers Wake*, with that marvellous long violin line, running beneath it in perpetual counterpoint. By comparison, I suppose, the Beethoven was quite different. In interrupting itself after just a few bars, the music demanded the listener's attention in a way that didn't sit easily on breakfast radio. If you're in traffic or running late or trying to find a child's sock, you could easily resent having your attention demanded. And thus, the first movement of Beethoven's Sonata Op 109 becomes an irritating noise. The presenter knew his program and his audience well enough to avoid this.

True listening is collaborative. We bring not only our attention and our concentration, but also our imagination. We collaborate with the minds of the composer and the performer. In a way, what we listen for in music is where we fit in.

Healesville, Victoria, March 2011

Acknowledgements

The lines from 'Little Gidding' are from *Four Quartets* © Estate of T.S. Eliot and reprinted by permission of Faber and Faber Ltd. Excerpt from 'For the Union Dead' from *Collected Poems* by Robert Lowell. Copyright © 2003 by Harriet Lowell and Sheridan Lowell. Reprinted by permission of Farrar, Straus and Giroux, LLC. The extract from 'Anthem for St Cecilia's Day' © 1941 by W.H. Auden (renewed) is used by permission of Curtis Brown Ltd. William Soutar's poem 'The auld aik' is reprinted by kind permission of the trustees of the National Library of Scotland.

I would like to thank a number of editors who first commissioned articles, then improved them, particularly Hugh Lamberton and later Robert Bolton at the *Australian Financial Review*, Angela Bennie at the *Sydney Morning Herald*, Ian Irvine at the *Independent on Sunday*, Ben Naparstek of the *Monthly*, and Peter Browne at *Inside Story* (inside.org.au). The radio series *Music and Fashion* was commissioned by ABC Radio National, researched by Anni Heino, and produced by Penny Lomax and Jenny Parsonage. My colleague Tim Ritchie supplied a list of current dance-music categories in 2005 when the series was written, and then a new (and far longer) list for this book. In the series, I spoke to Sarah Woodcock, Kristina Olsen, Jessica Nicholas, Carol Williams, Jeff Crabtree, Paul Kildea, Gail Edwards, Robyn Archer, Bruce Elder, Anna Picard and my much-missed colleague and friend, the late Geoffrey Tozer. Many of their remarks and ideas have been incorporated into this present text.

I must thank Black Inc., especially Chris Feik for wanting the book in the first place and liking it when he read it, and Kate Goldsworthy for her sensitive and eagle-eyed editing job. My thanks also go to my wife Anni and daughter Elsie for tolerating my repeated disappearances to the back room. Finally, my thanks to David McCooey for suggesting the title of this book, and Neil Finn for thinking of it first.

Bibliography

Balough, Teresa (ed.), *Comrades in Art: The correspondence of Ronald Stevenson and Percy Grainger, 1957–61, with interviews, essays and other writings on Grainger by Ronald Stevenson* (2010)

Bax, Arnold, *Farewell My Youth* (1943)

Berio, Luciano, *Remembering the Future (Charles Eliot Norton Lectures)* (2006)

Burton, Humphrey and Maureen Murray, *William Walton, The Romantic Loner: A centenary portrait album* (2002)

Cairns, David, *Mozart and His Operas* (2006)

Copland, Aaron, *What to Listen for in Music* (1939)

Fenby, Eric, *Delius as I Knew Him* (1936)

Furtwängler, Wilhelm (ed. Michael Tanner, trans. Shaun Whiteside), *Notebooks 1924–1954* (1989)

Giroux, Robert (ed.), *One Art: The selected letters of Elizabeth Bishop* (1994)

Hamilton, Saskia (ed.), *The Letters of Robert Lowell* (2005)

Hayes, Malcolm (ed.), *Selected Letters of William Walton* (2002)

Heffer, Simon, *Vaughan Williams* (2000)

Holst, Imogen, *Gustav Holst: A biography* (1938)

Knight, Stephen, *Freedom Was Compulsory: Sins and signs in contemporary Australia* (1994)

Lockwood, Lewis and the Julliard String Quartet, *Inside Beethoven's Quartets: History, performance, interpretation* (2008)

Mellers, Wilfrid, *Beethoven and the Voice of God* (1983)

Mellers, Wilfrid, *Celestial Music?: Some masterpieces of European Religious Music* (2002)

Mellers, Wilfrid, *Singing in the Wilderness: Music and ecology in the twentieth century* (2001)

Mellers, Wilfrid, *Vaughan Williams and the Vision of Albion* (1989)

Meredith, Anthony and Paul Harris, *Malcolm Williamson: A mischievous muse* (2007)

Mitchell, Donald, Philip Reed and Mervyn Cooke (eds.), *Letters from a Life: Selected letters of Benjamin Britten, volume III, 1946–51* (2004)

Ricks, Christopher, *Dylan's Visions of Sin* (2003)

Sachs, Harvey (ed.), *The Letters of Arturo Toscanini* (2002)

Schuttenhelm, Thomas (ed.), *Selected Letters of Michael Tippett* (2005)

Searle, Humphrey, *The Music of Liszt* (1954)

Sondheim, Stephen, *Finishing the Hat: The collected lyrics of Stephen Sondheim (volume 1) with attendant comments, principles, heresies, grudges, whines and anecdotes* (2010)

Sudhalter, Richard M., *Stardust Melody: The life and work of Hoagy Carmichael* (2002)

Taruskin, Richard, *The Oxford History of Western Music* (2005)

Thwaites, Penelope (ed.), *The New Percy Grainger Companion* (2010)

INDEX